# Broken Music

# Broken Music

*Sting*

A MEMOIR

THE DIAL PRESS

BROKEN MUSIC
A Dial Press Book / November 2003

Published by
The Dial Press
A Division of Random House, Inc.
New York, New York

*Book design by Virginia Norey*

The Dial Press is a registered trademark of
Random House, Inc., and the colophon is a trademark
of Random House, Inc.

Library of Congress Cataloging-in-Publication Data is on
file with the publisher.

ISBN: 0-385-33678-0

Manufactured in the United States of America
Published simultaneously in Canada

RRC    10 9 8 7 6 5 4 3 2 1

# Broken
# Music

# 1

It is a winter's night in Rio de Janeiro, 1987. It is raining and the boulevard in front of the Copacabana Hotel is deserted. The road is slick and shining in the light of the streetlamps. My wife, Trudie, and I are sheltering beneath an umbrella, while high above our heads two seagulls wheel recklessly in the wind; and the sea is a roaring threat in the darkness. A small car pulls up to the curbside. There are two figures silhouetted in the front seat, and an opened rear door beckons us inside.

A series of discreet phone calls have secured us an invitation to a religious ceremony in a church somewhere in the jungles that surround the great city. Our drivers, a man and a woman, tell us only that the church is located about an hour and a half from the Copacabana, that we will be looked after, and we shouldn't worry. The church, while nominally Christian, is the home of a syncretic religious group that uses as its core sacrament an ancient medicine derived from plant materials known as ayahuasca, and it is said to induce extraordinary and profound visions.

It is now raining heavily as we head south, and a massive

lightning storm strobes above the mountains that surround the city, followed by the deep rolling percussion of distant thunder. Trudie and I sink back into our seats, excited and a little apprehensive, wondering what the night holds in store. The driver is intent upon the road in front of us. I am seated directly behind him; he has a large head atop wide athletic shoulders and, when he turns toward us, an intelligent and aquiline face, framed in wire-rimmed spectacles and untidy brown hair. His companion, an attractive young woman with long dark curls and a wide Brazilian smile, turns to us reassuringly and asks if we are comfortable. We both begin to nod mechanically, clearly nervous but not wanting to admit it to each other or to our hosts.

We leave the wide boulevards of the city, and as the luxury hotels of the Copacabana give way to the chaos of the hillside favelas that glitter like Christmas trees in the darkness, the streetlights grow scarcer and scarcer. Soon the road becomes a dirt track and the car slows down to a walking pace as our driver negotiates axle-breaking potholes and sullen, immovable dogs. The rain has stopped, but the jungle drips in the heavy air, the noise of the cicadas all but drowning out the cheap cantina music on the little car radio. Eventually we pull into a clearing where many cars are parked chaotically around a large building with a tiled roof. The structure, while simple and utilitarian, is not one I would normally associate with the word "church" (it has no doors or windows), and the event has more the air of a town meeting than a religious gathering.

Men and women of all ages, including teenagers and small children, and the ubiquitous dogs mingle in the car park and inside the church, which is lit by naked electric bulbs strung from the ceiling. Everyone is wearing either a blue or green shirt, on which several have sewn gold stars. These are clearly uniforms. Our two drivers take off their coats to reveal that they too are wearing blue shirts. Suddenly I feel vulnerable and conspicuous. We didn't expect uniforms. Uniforms make me feel uneasy, and for me are somehow linked to ideas of control and conformity, to something belying freedom, something cultish. A lurid newspaper headline flashes into my head: SINGER AND WIFE ABDUCTED IN JUNGLE BY RELIGIOUS CULT. Would I have felt more comfortable if everyone had looked like a stoner freak? Probably not, but the uniforms definitely throw me.

As we step into the light of the large hall, we are welcomed with warm, open smiles and introduced by our two drivers to what appears to be a cross section of Brazilian society. Many of them speak English, and after some brief courtesies I ask a few of them what they do for a living, explaining that my wife is an actor and I'm a singer. "Yes, we know," says one woman. "You are very famous, but my husband and I are schoolteachers."

They all seem like everyday working people, and many are professionals as well: doctors, lawyers, firemen, an accountant and his jolly wife, social workers, civil servants, computer programmers, teachers; not one stoner freak among them. I don't really know what I was expecting, but this large and hospitable group reassures me.

"Is this your first time to drink the vegetal?" asks a doctor.

We haven't heard the fabled medicine referred to in that way before, but assume that they mean ayahuasca, which I suppose is its indigenous Indian name.

"Yes, it's our first time."

There are a few knowing smiles. "You'll be fine," says one of the schoolteachers.

We attempt to smile back, again suppressing whatever apprehensions we may be having.

There are now about two hundred people in the room, which is filled with lounge chairs of woven plastic over metal frames arranged in a circle around a central table. Above the table is a wooden arch painted blue with *LUZ, PAZ, AMOR* written in bright yellow letters. "Light, peace, love," I manage to decipher in my rudimentary Portuguese. Our two drivers, who seem to be our guardians for the evening, reappear and usher us to our seats near the front. They assure us they will help out should we get into difficulties.

"Difficulties?" I query, unable to mask my concern.

There is a slight uneasiness in the man's voice as he replies, "You may experience some physical as well as emotional discomfort. But please try and relax, and if you have any questions, I will try and answer them for you."

Around the table are five or six empty dining chairs. Silence filters through the room as half a dozen men enter the church from a side door and make their way to the central table. There is a distinct gravitas in their stately procession, and from the bearing of their shoulders I surmise they are figures of some authority. Perhaps the drama of the occasion is already distorting my perception, but they all seem to have the drawn, ascetic look of monks or wise elders. These are the *mestres* who will preside over the ceremony.

The central chair is occupied, we are told, by a visiting *mestre* from the northern city of Manaus. It is he who will lead the ritual. He is a man in early middle age with deep-set, thoughtful eyes, which peer out from a faintly ironic but not unkind face, as if he is viewing the world outside from a long dark tunnel. He seems to me like a man with an amusing secret to impart, a story to tell, or a piece of arcane wisdom. I am intrigued. I also feel a little happier in noticing how easily his face breaks into an engaging smile when he greets someone he knows. His obvious warmth is comforting.

In the middle of the table is a large glass container full of brown, sludgy liquid. I assume that this is the legendary sacrament I have read so much about, ayahuasca.

The *mestre* indicates that we should join the orderly queue that is forming in the aisle and snaking to the back of the room. We seem to be the only novices present and are guided politely to the front of the queue, then handed white plastic coffee cups. The *mestre* fills these reverently from the glass container, which has a metal spigot at its base.

Despite the reverence of the ceremony, the sacramental liquid looks like something you would drain from the sump outlet of an old engine; a furtive twitch of the nostrils confirms my apprehension that it smells as bad as it looks. "Are we really going to swallow this muck?" I think to myself. "We must be crazy."

Still apprehensive about the difficulties we may encounter, I try to forget that we could be carousing right now in the comfort of the hotel bar on the Copacabana, quaffing sweet caipirinhas and swaying to the gentle rhythm of the samba. But it is too late to turn back now. My wife and I look at each other like tragic lovers on a cliff top. The room begins to reverberate with a chanted prayer in Portuguese. Unable to join in, I mutter, "God help us," under my breath, only half ironically. Then everyone drinks.

"Well, bottoms up," says Trudie, with her usual gallows humor. "Here goes."

I manage to swallow the entire brew in one shuddering gulp, and yes, it tastes foul, and I'm relieved that most people in the room seem to think so too. I know this from the grimaces and the hurried sucking of lemons and mints that have been distributed to suppress the noxious taste it leaves in the mouth. I manfully decline a proffered mint for no reason other than obstinate pride in taking it straight, while the ever practical Trudie wisely accepts the kindness. One of the attendant *mestres* places a record onto an old-fashioned turntable; it is simple Brazilian folk music, light and pleasantly banal. The congregation begin to make themselves comfortable in their seats, and Trudie and I try to follow suit, dozing to the pleasant cadences of guitars strummed in major keys and the easy rhythm of a tambura. We sit down and wait, neither of us having any clear idea of what will happen next. I too begin to drift off, keeping a discreet eye on the room, while breathing softly and deliberately, trying to calm my nerves.

I wonder if William S. Burroughs and Allen Ginsberg suffered the same apprehension when they had this experience. The novelist and the beat poet had gone in search of ayahuasca in the late fifties, the medicine having an almost legendary status as the sine qua non of the ethnogenic realm. Known also as yaje, the vine of the soul, and dead man's root, among many other names, its origins and usage are perhaps thousands of years old and inextricably linked with the development of the ancient religious philosophies and rituals of the Amazon basin. From my reading I had gleaned that ayahuasca is brewed from two indigenous plants, a liana known as *Banisteriopsis caapi* and a shrub of the coffee genus, *Psychotria viridis*. The active molecule in the medicine is almost identical to the neurotransmitter serotonin, and its chemical interaction with the human brain is just as complex and mysterious. I had been reassured by my research that the practice is legally protected by the Brazilian constitution and that its ingestion is said to be non-addictive and its effects profound.

I am in the country at this time because I'm about to begin a Brazilian tour, and in a few days I will be playing the biggest concert of my life. Two hundred thousand people will be packed into the Maracana Stadium in Rio. The event will mark the pinnacle of my solo career in South America, but it will also be something of a wake. My father has died only a few days before, and his death comes only months after my mother has passed away. For complex reasons I have attended neither funeral, nor will I seek any consolation from the church. But just as the recently bereaved can be drawn to the solace of religion, psychoanalysis, self-reflection, and even séances, despite my agnosticism, I too am in need of some kind of reassuring experience or ritual that will help me to accept that perhaps there is something beyond the tragedy of death, some greater meaning than I can conjure for myself.

I was finding it difficult to mourn my parents. Their deaths had upset me greatly, but I felt that I was somehow blocking normal emotional responses, that I wasn't dealing with their loss in a psychologically healthy manner. I hadn't cried, not even a tear, but had merely felt cold, isolated, and confused. I had no easy faith within which to seek solace.

What I'd read about ayahuasca and its transcendent visionary qualities intrigued me greatly, and in my current frame of

mind I thought if I experienced the miraculous potion in a serious ritual setting, then I might come to some deeper understanding about what had happened to my parents as well as
myself.

I'd only ever had a passing, superficial interest in recreational drugs, but taking ayahuasca had been described to me
as a deeply serious and life-changing experience, and one that I
now considered myself ready for. If I was to find myself in any
danger from this experience, psychological or otherwise, then I
would have to regard myself as having been adult enough to
take the risk, in much the same way as I would climb a mountain, or get on a motorcycle. In speaking to experienced
ayahuasceros it had been impressed upon me that ayahuasca is
not a drug but a medicine. "A drug," one had told me, "gives
you an instant reward, some kind of gratification, whether it's a
cigarette, alcohol, cocaine, or dope, but later you pay with a
headache, a hangover the next day, or worse, dependency and
addiction. Smoke enough cigarettes and you will die. Traditionally medicine doesn't give you an instant reward. You may
be gratified eventually but you will have to pay first. Ayahuasca
is such a medicine."

I had no idea what he could have meant, but I was about to
find out.

Maybe twenty minutes pass. The music continues. The
chair of the officiating *mestre* is never unoccupied; if he leaves
the room, one of the attendants takes his place until his return.
There is a soothing formality about all of this, a sense of order
and ritual.

The first indication that the potion is taking effect is the
emergence of a high-pitched frequency inside my head like a
dog whistle, followed by an increasing numbness in the lips

and a distinct drop in my body temperature. I begin to shiver, gently at first but with increasing intensity, starting at my feet and moving up my legs in wave after wave, until my whole body is shaking violently. It is difficult to tell whether the shivering is a psychological reaction due to fear or simply that I'm cold. I am conscious enough to know not to panic and to attempt to steady my breathing, but nausea wells in my throat and then proceeds to grip my stomach with increasing intensity until it feels like a writhing serpent inside of me trying to escape. It is all I can do to prevent myself from projectile vomiting. I grip the arms of the chair and breathe as deeply as I can.

Something powerful and relentless is coursing through my entire body, through every blood vessel and artery, down the length of my legs to my toes, and along the sinews of my arms. My fingers are shot with an alien energy. The foul taste that remains in my mouth seems like a physical analogue of fear itself, and I realize I'm in the grip of some kind of chemical entity that is at this moment vastly more powerful than I am. While the storm rages inside me, the thunder outside begins again, another ominous and rolling threat from the heavens. I turn to Trudie, who looks to be sleeping, but there are rapid eye movements below her lids, and her brows are knitted together in intense concentration. I whisper, "God, please keep us safe." And this time there is no irony at all.

The entire room seems to be gripped in this same visceral struggle. Some writhe in their seats, others have clearly capitulated, openmouthed and corpselike, while others seem calm and transfixed as if by beatific visions. Then, as a bizarre counterpoint to the call of the thunder, the retching begins.

I had been warned of this, but nothing can quite prepare you for the piteous sound of this woeful, violent music, the music of abject, physical misery. I am barely able to control my own intestinal tract as I watch others leave their seats to scramble unceremoniously for the door. Some make it, some do not. There are buckets of sawdust on hand to cover the offending pools of bile.

*Please, let this pass, I don't want to throw up, I don't want to be embarrassed here, let this pass.*

The *mestres* sit impassive and stoic in the center of the room, as if this is the normal run of events. They too have partaken of the brew, and in large doses, but do not seem to be succumbing to the growing nausea and discomfort in the room.

Outside the nearest window, one tortured soul seems to be exorcising a relentless train of hideous demons from the bowels of his personal hell. I try stopping up my ears with my fingers and breathing deeply; I really can't take much more of this. I am no longer shivering, but the anaconda inside me is furious to leave my body. Beads of sweat begin to form on my face and chest, and my eyes roll back in my head. Did I really elect to do this? I must have been out of my mind. I have never felt this bad in my entire life, nor do I remember having been so afraid. Another peal of thunder compounds the agony, but just when I imagine I am drained of all will to withstand this onslaught, I hear the singing. I hear the beautiful, unearthly voice of the *mestre* from Manaus, unaccompanied and floating on the moist air, filling the room with the sweet fragrance of melody. I close my eyes, the better to drink in the gentle balm of the song, and I find myself in a vast cathedral of light.

The song has become light and color, the fantastical architecture of Dante and Blake, and I am suspended from a roof of souls, a sky-arching dome of seraphic hosts. The visions are transmuting into miraculous spiraling, geometric structures, towers, tunnels, vortices, chambers. The clarity of the visions and the electricity of the colors are so alien to the experience of waking life as to be of a different order of reality entirely. And yet to open one's eyes is to return to the room as it was. But these are not hallucinations. There is no distortion of visible reality; the colors and the visions are a separate reality projected onto the back of the eyelids. Closing your eyes transports you to this other world, as real as any other, where sound becomes light and light becomes color and color turns into geometry and geometry triggers memory and stories and emotions not only from your own life, but astoundingly from what seems to be the lives of others. I am either dreaming awake or I am dead.

I am in a bomber over a fire-stormed city at night; I am in a longboat under a sail in a gray sea. I am in a battle, and the thunder outside has become the roar of ordnance. I am deep underground in a filthy trench and there is someone at my side in the corner of my vision, almost like a shadow. I shall call him "the companion." There are others too, the artillery barrage shaking the ground everywhere around us. The others are little more than youths in ill-fitted battle dress and steel helmets flecked with mud, fearful and shivering in the damp tunnel. I too am afraid and shake my head in an attempt to alter the vision.

Suddenly I am in the town of my childhood in the north of England. I am a small boy, gazing at lists of hundreds of names carved into stone, watched over by two soldier-sentinels cast in weathered bronze, their heads lowered solemnly over the stocks of upturned rifles. My child's hand is touching a cold metallic foot.

The thunder and the barrage continue and here I am, back again underground with the companion, watching as those with him line up in an anxious file beneath the lip of the trench. Someone is coughing uncontrollably. I have a sense that when the guns stop it is the companion, just out of my line of vision, who will give the order to clamber over the parapet into danger. I can taste the fear again in my mouth, as acrid and bitter as the brown liquid I have ingested. The ordnance suddenly falls silent. Every face is turned toward the companion, but I still can't see him.

A faraway whistle blows, although it may be the call of a tropical night bird deep in the jungle, and then another, closer and closer all the way down the line. The *mestre* is still singing, beautifully, but with an occasional atonality, a quarter tone that is darkly disturbing and otherworldly. I sense that the companion has become still and rigid like one of the bronze statues, a whistle buried deep in his hand.

"Blow the fuckin' whistle, Sergeant!" spits a furious and anonymous voice, and I hear more angry shouts along the line.

"Come on, Sergeant, for fuck's sake," they shout, seeming desperate to kill or be killed, and I'm struck by the thought that some of them are too afraid to be thought cowards, too afraid to step out of the lineage of brutality and cruelty that is as old as history.

"Will you blow that fuckin' whistle?"

But no one moves as the guns begin to rattle aboveground, and I know they are spraying death across the wire. We hear screams of anger and agony. The companion gives no order and no one moves from the relative safety of the trench. The *mestre* holds a long suspended note, hanging like a flare in the sky, as a terrifying battle rages around us.

I too am angry and confused: what the hell does this have to do with me? I feel as if I'm in some kind of virtual theater, an experiment in reality, or a waking nightmare, but one that I don't seem able to shake off. It is clear that the figures around me are in mortal danger. Their terror is palpable and hideously claustrophobic. Yet at the same time I have the unwelcome impression that I am the cause of this, and am being asked to navigate the realm of my own deepest fears. I sense too that I will not be harmed, but that I am undergoing some kind of test.

My head is spinning with questions, but I am so astounded by the clarity of these visions that I am unable to speak and unable to exit this other reality that is not my own. But there are levels of thought below these visions that observe and comment on them, and farther levels beneath those, commenting in turn to infinity. And where normal objective thought can give comfort, allowing the mind to step outside of an imagined or real danger, here the strategy only compounds the fear that there is no bedrock to reality, that so-called objective reality is only a construct, and this realization I suppose is akin to madness.

In this new context, I'm forced to question the foundations of my rarified and privileged existence, my life in the world of friends, colleagues, and family. Isn't what we refer to as reality merely a consensus, an agreement between us that certain things are real and others aren't? I may be at this interface now, shivering in a jungle church with two hundred others but also quaking with fear in a dark and sodden trench. This is how I imagine that those close to death must feel. Confused, disoriented, and afraid.

Our species, like every other, has annihilation written into its DNA, the difference being that we know it. How are we supposed to learn to die without fear, to die with courage, dignity, and acceptance? And why must we live in such paralyzing terror of what is preordained? How prepared were my parents to face their deaths? For that matter, how prepared am I? Well, the honest answer is, not at all. I think that is why I'm here in this awful trench, because I have something to learn.

I have never had a genuine religious experience. I say this with some regret. I have paid lip service to the idea, certainly, but a devastating, ego-destroying, ontological epiphany I simply have not had. More devout souls than I may have visited this realm through prayer, meditation, fasting, or from undergoing a near-death experience. Religious literature is full of such visionary claims, and while I've no reason to doubt their veracity, I would venture to say that such experiences are rare. For every St. Teresa, Ezekiel, or William Blake, there are millions like me with no direct experience of the transcendent, of the eternal, of the fathomless mystery at the root of all religious thought. But the ayahuasca has brought me close to something, something fearful and profound and deadly serious.

I've never been able to fully accept the idea of reincarnation—I've met too many people who thought they were Cleopatra or Charles the First in some previous life for me ever to take seriously the extension of the ego beyond death. I do believe, though, that a battle, for example, is a massive psychic event that could leave powerful aftershocks in what Carl Jung would call "the collective unconscious." On July 1, 1916, at the opening of the Battle of the Somme, there were fifty thousand casualties before midday—and that was just the British. But why should an event like this have significance for me? Why this particular scenario? Perhaps I'd taken to heart too many Wilfred Owen poems at school, or was being punished for my morbid fascination with the local war memorial as a child. I don't know the answer to these questions, and they keep tumbling into my mind. In a kaleidoscope of color, fractal geometry, and strangeness, the visions continue.

I am now an invisible witness in a military court. The companion is standing between two soldiers as he is cross-examined in precise legal jargon that I may have read at some time or heard in a movie but have no conscious knowledge of. He displays no emotion as the sentence is read. I turn my head and we are in a cold gray field emerging in the light of early morning. There is a firing squad arranged in a ragged line in front of us. They look reticent, some of them angry to be out in this cold field shuffling awkwardly like nervous horses, their breath visible in the chill morning air, but when I look closely they have the same faces as the boys in the trench. The rifles are raised to their shoulders as orders to take aim are barked across the empty fields, and I shudder with the certainty that these boys will kill the man who had saved them. The moment is frozen like a tableau, and I am its witness.

The *mestre's* song is rising to a mournful, keening coda. My eyes are full and I begin to weep, silently at first, and then uncontrollably, with racking sobs. My eyes are streaming bitter salt while all the colors behind them are bleeding to red.

Time passes. I am in my mother's womb, and the song of the *mestre* has become the voice of my father. Why would I be surprised that such overwhelming sadness, such betrayal, such eerie tragedy should conjure up the memory of my remote and tormented father, and of my mother, my beautiful, sad mother?

He was a dashing soldier fresh out of the army and she was a teenage bride, a dazzling beauty who became an emotional shipwreck, and a victim of breast cancer at fifty-three, while he would succumb a few months later at fifty-seven. I was the bright red apple in her green eye, just as I was a thorn in his side, and we have unfinished business. That is why we are together in this strange echoing hall that is my memory. I am, as I have always been, surrounded by ghosts.

✦

MY MOTHER WAS SLIM and attractive with long fair hair and startling green eyes. She had good legs, wore short skirts and stiletto heels with pointed toes, and I remember with some pride as well as embarrassment that men whistled at her in the street and then pretended that they hadn't when she turned her glacial stare in their direction. She was proud and difficult to please. She had left school at fifteen and began her working life as a hairdresser, and had developed a convincing hauteur and a heightened sense of her own specialness. People whispered about my mother as she walked by, but she felt she was not like them, nor did she want to be. Her name was Audrey, and when my father met her she'd stepped out with only a few beaux before him. He was her first love.

The earliest memory I have of my mother coincides with my earliest musical memory: sitting at her feet as she played the piano and watching the soles of her shoes on the pedals, rising and falling with their strange rhythmic counterpoint against the swing of the tango music that she was so fond of playing. I was fascinated by how she could translate the marks on the manuscript sheets into coherent music. This skill coupled with her innate style created an intoxicating glamour around her.

I remember too my mother playing the piano in my grandparents' front room, while my father, who had a fine tenor, sang a plaintive version of Huddie Ledbetter's waltz "Goodnight Irene."

*Last Saturday night I got married*
*Me and my wife settled down*
*Now this Saturday we have parted*
*I'm taking a trip downtown.*

My father liked the big bands of the Dorsey Brothers and Benny Goodman, but it was my mother who brought rock and roll into the house on 78 rpm records of black acetate with brightly colored labels from MGM, RCA, Decca. Little Richard caterwauling "Tutti Frutti" like a tomcat, Jerry Lee Lewis preaching "Great Balls of Fire" like a demented evangelist, and Elvis crooning "All Shook Up" with what I would later identify as rampant sexual innuendo. These recordings would send me into innocent paroxysms of joy, rolling and shaking on the floor in a kind of religious ecstasy. She also brought home all of the Rodgers and Hammerstein albums from the Broadway shows *Oklahoma!, South Pacific, Carousel, The King and I,* Lerner and Loewe's *My Fair Lady,* and Bernstein's *West Side Story.* I played all of these records to death, falling in love with the meticulous ritual of removing them from their worn sleeves and dust jackets with my fingertips, blowing away the dust that had collected since their last outing, and setting them delicately on the turntable.

I had no prejudices about what kind of music I liked; I listened to everything with the rapt attention of a neophyte. Later, when I was learning to become a musician, I would play 33 rpm records at 45 rpm and hear the bass parts revealed, rescued from the bowels of the arrangement an octave higher, and the fast sections of the upper octaves on forty-fives so that they could be learned at a slower speed. I realized from these experiments that anything, no matter how complex, could be deconstructed and learned if you slowed it down enough to really hear it. The crude mechanics of the turntable allowed this, and while I listened to the comforting scratch of the needle before the opening notes of the overture to *Oklahoma!*, or the opening chords to Gene Kelly's "Singin' in the Rain," I was as much transfixed by the robotic slowness of the mechanical arm as it moved over the surface of the disc as I was by the music itself.

We live in a damp Victorian house without central heating. It is my mother who will teach me how to make up the fire in the living room, which is our only source of heat. We'd start with rolled newspapers, large sheets of the *Evening Chronicle,* folded diagonally into long tapers and then into compacted concertina shapes to ensure a slow burn, along with some egg cartons, a few sticks of kindling wood, and lastly the coal, laid like priceless black treasures atop the pile.

The matches are up on the mantelpiece, next to the chiming clock. I am seven years old now and tall enough to reach them if I stand on my toes.

"Can I light it, Mam? I know how to do it. Please! Can I?" I plead with her, desperate to temper my eagerness with a sense that I am now old enough to be responsible.

"You can light the fire, son, but don't leave the matches out for your little brother; always leave them up a height, do you understand?"

I love that expression: "Up a height."

"Now, make sure you light it from the bottom, not from the top."

"Yes, Mam."

"It will only work for you if you light it from the bottom, that's why we've built it this way. The coal will only catch if the wood's alight, and the wood will only catch if the paper's lit."

"Yes, Mam," I say again as I fumble with a box of matches and set last night's *Evening Chronicle* ablaze.

"Very good," she says with some pride. "Now help me tidy up, this place looks like a bloody tagarene shop." Another one of her expressions. I had no idea what a "tagarene shop" was, although it clearly described the disorder and chaos that always threatened to overwhelm the house if we didn't clear up after my mischievous younger brother.

"I'll swing for that little so and so," she would say.

Later she would teach me that even when a fire appears to be dying, a well-placed poker could bring it back to life. She warned me that once a fire is hot, anything that goes near it will be set alight. She taught me how to pack a fire for the night, starving it of oxygen without killing it, and how to revive it in the morning.

As a child I could spend all day gazing at a fire. I still can, lost in visions of crumbling towers, ancient glowing kingdoms, and cavernous cathedrals, indeed whole continents of imagining in its embers. My mother taught me this magic and it is still with me. She also taught me how to iron a shirt, fry an egg, vacuum the floor, all in the spirit of ritual and good order, but it was music and fires that retained an air of secret and arcane knowledge, which bound me to her like a sorcerer's apprentice. My mother was the first mistress of my imagination.

My maternal grandfather, Ernest, had something of a reputation in Wallsend, the town in which my mother's family lived, although the gossip about him may have been colored by his appearance. He was tall, unusually handsome, and rather too elegant to escape the attention of the whisperers in a small town. In my memory there was always something dangerous and romantic about him. He was not a local, another reason for suspicion. He hailed from the Isle of Man. In a photograph from my parents' wedding there is a knowing arrogance about the eyes, a quizzical and amused eyebrow, and the louche swagger of a ladies' man. He had little time for me and made a living as an insurance rep for Sun Life of Canada. He drove what people of the time called a "flash" car. I remember it well; it was a Rover and had running boards and bright chromium headlights on stalks. He was, to me, a mysterious and remote creature, but my mother worshiped him.

My only memory of my maternal grandmother is a shocking one. I remember her teeth in a glass by the side of her sickbed, a whole set, grinning at me with a malevolent rictus. I'm told that she adored me. I don't remember; she died before she was any more than a shadow to me, but her name was Margaret.

My dad was in his twenty-fourth year when he fathered me, the same age I was when I first became a father. He had completed his national service in Germany with the Royal Engineers. Photographs show him as darkly handsome in his olive drab uniform, a smiling Fräulein on his arm and a pint of ale and a cigarette in his hands. I liked to look at those photographs of my dad in his happier time, and wonder if I could see myself in those dark eyes or at least an intimation that one day I would exist, along with the frightening thought that so much of life could have gone on without me. I believe my father had the time of his life in Germany, and he often suggested that this was the case. He would often announce, rather grandly, that he had "occupied" Germany, perhaps to make up for the fact that he'd been too young to have actually fought the Germans, and that carousing with their women was a far better alternative. It wasn't that my dad was a braggart, he just wanted us to be proud that he'd "done his bit," seen some of the world, and earned his status as a man.

"Do you see that stripe there on my arm, son? Lance corporal, Royal Engineers, that was me. Build bridges, blow 'em sky high, and put them up again; I should have stayed in the army."

After a beer or two he would hark back to the promise of those seemingly carefree days like a golden age that the present simply couldn't live up to. And there was always the veiled accusation that he had been trapped in this life by us all, particularly my mother. But it wasn't until later, when things went wrong, that my dad would admit how much she had loved him in the early days. How she would wait for him every evening to return from work and throw her arms around his neck as he came through the door. Regret was a constant theme in my father's life until the end.

Born in the port of Sunderland in September of 1927, my dad was christened Ernest, sharing the name with my maternal grandfather. I imagine this sharing of names was a great topic at my parents' first meeting. I can see my mother getting home flushed with excitement, gushing to her sister Marion that she'd met a handsome man at the Saturday dance, and "Guess what his name is?"

My father's family were Catholic and my mother's were Anglican. So-called mixed marriages were still frowned upon by the church hierarchies, but not as much as they were in the previous generation, where the mixing of the faiths had been the cause of some historical controversy according to the hearsay of the family. Tom, my grandfather, had gone against the wishes of his staunchly Protestant father in marrying Agnes White, my grandmother, a young girl from an Irish family. Agnes had left school at fourteen to go into service in a "big house" and, being the daughter of an Irish stevedore on the docks of Sunderland, was considered beneath my grandfather in social status. She was the second youngest child in a stereotypical Irish family of ten brothers and sisters, fiercely intelligent, pretty, and devout. I can imagine her browbeating my grandfather into giving up his by now beige Protestantism and converting to the Roman church. Old Tom liked the quiet life, and Agnes always got her way.

The family controversy also concerned my grandfather's having given up his inheritance to wed the fair Agnes. The Sumners did have something to do with shipping, and there had been at least two master mariners in the family lineage in the nineteenth century, but whether this so-called inheritance was anything to speak of, I do not know. I suspect that the "family fortune" or "the shipping line" that my grandfather gave up for love may have suffered from a bit of grandiosity and romantic inflation. That he loved my grandmother was never in doubt, but the unvoiced motif remained throughout my grandfather's life, just as it did in my father's, that what he had given up in his past was not made up for in the present, that he too had been trapped in the institution of marriage and family, and there was no escape.

My grandfather Tom became a shipwright at the yards on the river Wear, fitting out tankers and battleships before they were launched and put out to sea. He and Agnes reared six children, two girls and four boys, of whom my father was the eldest. Her second pregnancy turned out to be twins—this had only become apparent during labor—and only one of them survived. Years later Agnes would tell my sister that she'd prayed God would take one of them away because she was afraid she wouldn't be able to feed them both. Her prayer seemed to have been answered. Gordon, the surviving twin, maintained his lust for life. My father told me he was always in trouble. His favorite pastime was lying between the tracks on the railway as the coal trains passed over his head. He must have imagined he was immortal. My uncle Gordon migrated to Australia before I was born to become a prospector in the desert surrounding the Darling Mountain Range, and I would be named after him.

My grandmother's Catholicism was a major part not only of her spiritual life but also the outer life of the family. She became the housekeeper to a young priest named Father Thompson, whom I came to know as Father Jim. He was an avuncular and saintly adoptee who had always seemed to me to be part of the family. Like a character from a P.G. Wodehouse novel, he had an impossibly plummy accent and the distracted air of a disheveled, displaced intellectual, shuffling into the house in his clerical collar, soutane, and biretta, Jesus-sandaled, black-socked, and bespectacled. Agnes seemed to be obsessed with Father Jim. The priesthood, and the good Father's innocent bookishness, combined with the fluted, stuttering tones of the upper class were a heady cocktail for a chit of an Irish girl from Sunderland. There was never a suggestion of something untoward in their relationship, but it was always "Father Jim did this" or "Father Jim did that," and poor old Tom rarely got a "look in" or a word edgewise. He'd just sit silently in the corner and pick out old music hall tunes on his mandolin, staring into the middle distance, always humming some wordless song.

By the time I was born, in October of 1951, they had moved to Newcastle with Father Jim, who had become the resident pastor at the Convent of the Good Shepherd in the northeast part of the city. He ministered to a group of nuns who looked after a school for wayward girls and ran a laundry that provided the local priesthood with clean sheets and altar cloths. I was never allowed near any of the girls, but my grandfather was in charge of the coke furnace in the cellar of the convent, and he ran the laundry vans picking up the soiled linens and delivering them back, pristine white. He rolled his own cigarettes and was invariably dressed in his old blue dungarees and black army beret. He was slyly laconic. Family lore has it that one day at lunch, Father Jim was musing aloud on what his Sunday sermon should be about.

"About five minutes," quipped my grandfather, just loud enough to be heard, earning a black and murderous look from Agnes and a puzzled one from the priest. My grandfather was a character, and I was fascinated by his long silences and the hairs that sprouted from his enormous nose and his ears, which grew ever larger as the rest of his body grew smaller.

A terraced house on the convent grounds went along with my grandfather's job (Father Jim was the perennial dinner guest). Next door lived the Dooleys, who ran the convent farm. Old man Dooley would take me to feed the pigs in the top field and would regale me with terrifying stories about big ugly sows that would gratuitously bite young lads in half just because they could. So I always kept my distance, especially as I was told that pigs were as smart as humans and just as mean. Even now I can see old man Dooley in his gypsy scarf, his rolled Wellington boots, and his enormous, piratical leather belt, which gave him the air of a swashbuckler. I supposed that walking into the pigpen was his equivalent of walking the plank.

Agnes didn't approve of the Dooleys. She thought they were wild and unkempt, while she aspired to some sophistication. She would complete the cryptic crossword in the *Times* every day, and subscribed to the condensed works of literature in *Reader's Digest,* explaining that as she hadn't had the benefit of a real education she would have to take some shortcuts. She had a lifelong interest in and love of books and encouraged me to have the same.

Agnes kept her books on shelves that ran from the floor to the ceiling in an alcove by the fireplace. She would spend much of her time in her armchair, a book in hand, her tortoiseshell reading glasses perched on her nose, with the tower of books looming behind her, a testament to her learning . She never threw a book away. But she lent me Robert Louis Stevenson's *Treasure Island* to read when I was barely seven, and with only a minimum of comprehension I would plow through it with the same bloody-minded determination that I would later apply to cross-country running. Not exactly an intellectual approach, but one that would prove useful in many other ways. Not least of all music. She also got me to read *The Lives of the Saints,* which can't have made much of an impression.

Agnes would often tell me that if I had any brains at all then I must have gotten them from her. And so it was largely through my grandmother's sponsorship and encouragement that I began to think of myself as bright.

My own family life began in a terraced house by Swan Hunter's shipyard in Wallsend. My mother was born and raised there on the north shore of the river Tyne, between Newcastle and the North Sea. Wallsend is where the emperor Hadrian decided to finish his wall after A.D. 122, when he visited this desolate northern limit of his vast empire. Hadrian's Wall winds like a giant snake for eighty miles over the moors and hills between Barrow-in-Furness, on the western shore, to the Tyne on the east. It is popularly thought the wall was built to keep out the Scots and Picts, but in reality it was built as a means of controlling the trade between north and south, and therefore the population of what would become the north of England. Translating the Latin description of *segedunum* into the depressingly prosaic Wallsend makes it sound like the end of the earth, and I suppose if you were a Roman legionnaire posted to this godforsaken wind-lashed spot in your little leather skirt, then you would agree. When the shipyard in our town was extended, in the early twentieth century, builders discovered the remains of a temple in honor of Mithras, god of light, a popular deity among the Roman foot soldiers, and a few years ago when they demolished my old street, they found an entire Roman camp beneath the cobbles.

When the legions eventually returned to Rome around A.D. 400, the area suffered constant invasions, mainly from across the North Sea by the Saxons, Danes, Jutes, Vikings, and Normans, as well as the Scots. Political ownership of the region changed hands so many times over the centuries that the local inhabitants began to feel that they belonged to no one but themselves, neither Scots nor English. We called ourselves "Geordies" for historical reasons that are still debated by local historians but have long been forgotten by most of us. What remains is a fierce regional identity supported in its uniqueness by a dialect that at times can be cannily unintelligible to the rest of the inhabitants of the British Isles.

Some famous ships were built on the Tyne. The *Mauretania,* built for the Cunard Line, held the record for crossing the Atlantic. Her sister ship, the *Lusitania,* was sunk by a German U-boat at the beginning of the First World War, which precipitated the U.S.'s entry into the conflict. The *Esso Northumbria,* in my own time, a quarter-million-ton oil tanker and the largest ship in the world at the time it was launched, was built at the end of my own street, where the shipyard was situated. The ship blotted out the sun for months before it was finally launched into the river and the North Sea, never to return.

There was something prehistoric about the shipyard, the giant skeletons of ships, and the workmen, tiny by comparison, suspended in an enormous cage silhouetted against the sky. The cranes too seemed like enormous prehistoric beasts, metallic monsters grazing thoughtlessly and moving with unnatural slowness over the busy yards and the acetylene flashes.

Every morning at seven A.M. the hooter was sounded in the shipyard, a mournful wail calling the workers to the river, and hundreds of men filed down our street in their overalls and caps and work boots. Across their backs many carry ex–army haversacks for their "bait"—sandwiches and thermos flasks. Apart from those who work in the coal pit or the rope works, everyone else in Wallsend seems to work for Swan Hunter's. As I watched them, I wondered about my own future, and what kind of job I would be able to do. Would I too join this vast army of men and live out my days in the bellies of these giant ships?

On Sunday mornings my dad would take my brother and me down to the quayside to look at the boats. The *Leda* was a Norwegian steamer that would sail weekly from Oslo to Newcastle and back again across the cold North Sea, plying the same route as the old Vikings. I remember my father gazing dreamily up at the wheelhouse and the ropes securing the bows of the ships to the quay. "Go to sea!" my father would always tell me, but I know now he was really speaking to himself as a younger man, and ruing his landlocked captivity.

Having received some training in the army, my dad then served his apprenticeship as an engineer's fitter at the De la Rue engineering works, where they built massive turbines and engines for seagoing ships. We were not a wealthy family, but my father was earning enough for my mother to stop work and look after me at home.

Three years after me, my brother, Phil, is brought into the family and my father will make another decision that he will regret for the rest of his life.

When I am five years old, in 1956, my father decides to leave his engineering job and take over the management of a dairy. The owner, a friend of my grandfather Ernest's whose name is Tommy Close, is retiring, and he needs someone to take over the business. The real incentive for my dad is that he will be virtually his own boss, and that along with the job there is a large two-story flat above the premises to accommodate our growing family—my sister, Angela, a year behind Philip, is on the way.

Below the house is a shop that sells milk, fresh ice cream, chocolate, sweets, and bottles of fizzy pop, Orange Crush, lemonade, and my favorite, dandelion and burdock. There are two assistants: Betty, a plump, hysterical teenage girl with a delinquent "teddy boy" for a boyfriend, whom everyone thinks beats her up, and Nancy, a sassy redhead who will become a close confidante of my mother's and something of an accomplice. Out at the back of the shop is the dairy yard, with two electric milk floats and a diesel truck called a Trojan on which the milk is delivered each morning. The town is split up into three delivery rounds by my father and two other milkmen, Ray and his younger brother Billy. Ray is a scurrilous, foul-mouthed dwarf of a man with slicked-back Brylcreemed hair. He shows me his hernia at every opportunity—"It's like a fuckin' orange, look." His gentle brother Billy is soft-spoken and prematurely as bald as a billiard ball.

From about the age of seven, on school holidays and at weekends I will go out to work with my father on his round in the High Farm estate and the miners' cottages at the north of the town. He works seven days a week, every day of the year but Christmas. My dad is the boss, but he can't afford to take a holiday. When I join him, he will shake me awake at 5 A.M., leaving my little brother in his slumbers, and I'll bundle myself into the warmest clothes possible. Sometimes, in the winter, it is so cold that there is frost on the inside of the window and I have to fumble to get dressed underneath the bedclothes as my breath condenses in the chill air. I stumble downstairs where my father is pouring the tea and I begin setting a fire before the rest of the family rise. We load up the van, wearing old leather gloves with the fingers cut out and lifting the cold metal crates as gently as possible so as not to wake the neighbors. Soon we are making our way through the dark empty streets. I learn to love the unique quality of the early mornings. When everyone else in the town is tucked up in bed, we move quietly like cat burglars and seem to own the streets, investing them with an exclusive and mysterious glamour that will vanish as the morning progresses. Even today I find it hard to lie abed. I'm always the first up—sleeping long will not become one of my talents.

The winters of my memory are grim, and there are mornings when I have no sensation in my feet for hours on end, my hands and face blue with cold. If the streets are icy, it makes it impossible for Bessy, as my dad affectionately calls the truck, to get up the steep banks near the river. I remember having to complete a lot of the round using my sledge. Sometimes the cold will force the cream at the top of the bottles to burst through the tinfoil caps and form solid tubes of frozen milk that protrude from the necks like strange mushrooms. We know that no one is going to pay for these, but what can we do? My dad puts a small paraffin stove in the cab on really cold days, but this makes getting in and out of the van extremely difficult.

Because my dad is tough and stoic I too never complain, or ask to be sent home. I want him to be proud of me. I also want to be like him, so I learn to carry six full bottles of milk at a time in my hands, and two under my arms. I learn the door numbers and how many pints each house receives, telling my father if there have been any changes. If so, he writes them in the book. I think I am good at my job, but he never praises me.

Every morning at seven-thirty we take a break and watch the smoke rise from the massive slag heap behind the pithead that looks like a man-made volcano. We sit silently eating cold bacon sandwiches, him thinking his thoughts and me thinking mine. My father is at times remote and taciturn, but I don't mind because the silences leave my imagination to run wild. I create all kinds of fantastical futures for myself as I run from door to door, my arms full of milk bottles: I will travel the world, I will be the head of a large family, I will own a big house in the country, I will be wealthy, and I will be famous.

\* \* \*

My auntie Amy, who was no relation, lived next door (every neighbor was your auntie in those days). Although she must have been close to retirement, she worked in the offices of the shipyard, and on launch days she would take me to see the enormous jeroboams of champagne, four times the size of a normal bottle, that would be shattered by some invited dignitary against the side of the hull as the ship was launched. She would stand me on the table, where the giant bottle, dressed in bright colored ribbons, would stand before the ceremony. I remember it being taller than me at the time. I also remember being distinctly afraid later as the bottle was smashed violently against the steel hull, the white foam flowing like spittle down the side of the ship, and the loud cheers of the men as the ship began to slide backward into the river drowned by a sickening cacophony of steel, wooden stanchions, and massive iron chains. The Queen Mother once came to the yard to launch a finished ship, and as she drove down our street in her Rolls-Royce, with motorcycle outriders followed by a motorcade of civic dignitaries in top hats, we all waved little Union Jacks, and I was convinced that she had smiled at me. The ships leaving the river would in hindsight become a metaphor for my own wandering life, once out in the world, never to return.

One day my mother and I are visiting Auntie Amy—she is one of Audrey's few friends in the street. I suppose she had become something of a mother figure for her after the passing of Margaret, her own mother. Amy is always well dressed, her hair always done, and in her flat-heeled brogues, thick winter stockings, and tweed skirts she exudes an air of middle-class respectability. My mother looks up to Amy as someone to aspire to, and over endless cups of tea they gossip about nothing in particular, at least about nothing that concerns me. I try to be as interested as a seven-year-old possibly could be under the circumstances but soon become bored and start to interrupt, asking questions like, "When will the next launch happen, Auntie Amy? Can I be there? Have you always worked at the shipyard?" Prattling innocently enough, but then letting my curiosity get the better of me, I ask, "Why don't you have a husband?"

There is a moment of stunned silence and my mother looks horrified, and I immediately know that I have said something terribly wrong. Auntie Amy looks nonplussed for only a moment but then quickly recovers her composure.

"I had a husband," she says, "but he died in the war." She gives me a kindly look. "He was a very brave soldier," she says quietly, and then she and my mother both begin to sip at their teacups as if synchronized with a choreographed ritual of suppressed grief and loneliness.

I am now too afraid to ask his name or if he is one of those listed on the war memorial, and I never mention it again.

Soon Auntie Amy will become ill and be unable to work in the shipyard, and each morning before school my mother will give me a cup of milky tea with one spoonful of sugar and a plain digestive biscuit in the saucer to take next door. I have a key and let myself in, careful not to spill the precious tea. I knock gently on her bedroom door with my free hand, and enter the dark room where there is a strange smell that I can't identify. I suppose it is the smell of sickness. She thanks me and briefly holds my hand. Weeks pass and Auntie Amy will be the first person I know in my life who will die. My mother cries all day and I can't console her. "So this is death," I say to myself, and I begin to have catastrophic fantasies, obsessing about my parents dying or that a war will suddenly break out and I will be left alone, but I do not share these thoughts with anyone else.

The back lane behind our house is cobbled stone and I will often find a wedge of grass between many of the cold gray stones. Perhaps the seeds have been carried by a bird or have been blown here by the wind. I often dream that all the tiny wedges of grass will one day join up and our lane will become a beautiful garden, green, green, green. But I'm always dreaming, and the landscape will remain resolutely gray, mitigated only by the muted plumage of those eking out a life among the bricks and stones.

There are two shops farther down from Auntie Amy's, a china shop that no one ever seems to frequent and then Trotters, the barbers, where my dad and I get our hair cut. We each get a "short back and sides," and because I am small, I have to sit on a plank across the arms of the barber's chair. I love the prickly chill as I run my fingers over the short hairs at the back of my newly shorn head. But most of all I am fascinated by the exclusively masculine smells and atmosphere of the shop: the leather straps where they ostentatiously strop the open blades; the flourish of the lathering brush; the bracing scent of hair tonic and pomade; the growing tumble of hair on the floor and the snip-snip of the scissors between the discreet, colorful language of menfolk away from the ears of women.

Next door to the barbers is the newspaper office, where a large and noisy printing press churns out the Newcastle *Evening Chronicle* in the late afternoon and the *Journal* in the morning. My best friend, Tommy Thompson, sells the papers on the corner outside the office to the shipyard workers as they come to and from work. Tommy and I have been friends since the first day of school. He has dark gypsy eyes and luxuriant black hair arranged in a sculpted pompadour quiff in imitation of his elder brother, who is a teddy boy. The teds are a dandified gang of toughs who terrorize the town, or at least like to think they do. While there is a great sweetness in Tommy, his studied pose as a hoodlum, a kind of precocious Gene Vincent, with an insolent swagger and an impudent face, seems to set him constantly at odds with authority. He rolls his own cigarettes, goes to school only when he feels like it, steals junk out of Woolworth's with a casual courage that beggars belief, and demonstrates a bafflingly exotic knowledge of sexual deviance with all of its appropriate vocabulary.

"Do ye know what a titty roll is?"

Shamed and fascinated in equal measure I reply, "No."

"A pearl necklace?"

"No, Tommy, I don't . . ."

"It's where a bloke gets his cock out, right? And sticks it in between . . ."

Tommy doesn't go to church, and claims not to believe in God. He is my first existential hero.

If I can manage to engage my most sophisticated friend in conversation long enough, he'll let me take over selling the *Chronicle* while he goes back into the office for a fag and a cup of tea. He teaches me how to call out the name of the paper in the street, elongating every vowel so that it sounds like "eevenaienn chroaniicaaell" sung at the top of my voice. I always have to be careful that my mother is never in the street when I do this because she thinks that it's common and people will think I've been "dragged up," but it is my first singing job.

On the opposite side of the street stands the Victorian-gothic St. Luke's Anglican Church, and farther down toward the river is Lloyds Bank, and then the post office, where, on Wednesday, I collect the family allowance, our weekly stipend from the government. The vicar from St. Luke's comes into the dairy every morning for a half-pint of milk, which he says is for his pussycat. This is his idea of a joke—I know he doesn't have a pussycat. He catches my eye with a wink and then looks quizzically at Betty's latest black eye. I like the vicar, I like his friendly smile, I like the white hair beneath his black hat, I even like his silly joke. He seems to be the prophet of a gentler religion than that of the Irish zealots who are beginning to terrorize me at the Catholic church two streets away.

Down from the post office is the railway station. Tommy's elder brother Mick works there, collecting tickets from the commuters rushing back home from their jobs in the "toon." In between trains I've often seen Mick hanging out the waiting room window high above Hugh Street, where he practices spitting across to the other side of the road. "Hey, Mick," I say.

He ignores me as if I'm some lower life-form, but manages to land a green gob close to my feet before the bell rings in the station to warn him that another train is coming. Every fifteen minutes an electric commuter train pulls in, but occasionally a noisy, prehistoric leviathan of steam will rumble over the bridge of Station Road and the small boy at number 84 will run out and experience the near-sexual thrill of the machine that made George Stephenson famous throughout the world. (Stephenson, the father of the steam engine, was born not three miles away, and probably was the only famous person ever to come from around here.)

My mother sends me underneath the railway bridge on Friday mornings to buy fresh cod and haddock from the fishwife. Her barrow is crudely hammered together with wood and nails atop an old set of pram wheels, which she pushes up from the fish quay. She wraps the wet, shining fish in old newspaper. Her fingernails are filthy, and her salt-and-pepper hair is pulled violently back from a face as wrinkled as a road map. She has one tooth. I'm afraid of the fishwife, because in my fetid imagination she is the evil spouse of a sea creature, and the twitching, openmouthed fish are her wide-eyed victims. I try to go missing on Friday mornings whenever I can or plead with my mother to let me go to the chip shop where the fish are already dead and battered and one sanitized stage away from the violence of the charnel house.

I attend St. Columba's primary school, which is housed in an old Victorian building next to the church where my parents were married and named after one of the wild Irish monks who converted the local pagans to Christianity in the fifth and sixth centuries. These monks must have had some serious "blarney" as well as "bottle" to set off from their monastery on the island of Iona to replace Odin and Thor with a God who turned the other cheek and preached love. Hundreds of years later our priests are still mad Irishmen and we still call the fourth day of the week Thorsday in the local dialect. Some things never change.

It was at St. Columba's that I began my lifelong fascination with religion and conversely my lifelong problem with it. All Catholic school children are taught the catechism, a little red book from which we are indoctrinated and expected to memorize verbatim, like proto-Maoists about to convert the world.

*Who made you?*

"God made me."

*Why did God make you?*

"To know him, love him, and serve him."

*In whose likeness did God make you?*

"In his own likeness etc., etc. . . . ."

Implicit in all of this was that God was a Catholic and that anyone who wasn't a Catholic would not be able to enter the Kingdom of Heaven and ought to be pitied or, if at all possible, converted to the true church. Luckily, being the child of a mixed marriage—my mother Church of England, my father nominally a Catholic—I didn't really swallow this idea whole. Consigning millions of lost souls to eternal hellfire just because they weren't members of the Catholic Women's League or the Knights of Saint Columba seemed hubristic long before I'd even heard the word. The concept of limbo, a place where unfortunate babies who hadn't been baptized into the Catholic and Apostolic Church were meant to sit out eternity, horrified me as much as hell itself (which one was signed up for immediately on missing mass on any given Sunday). In fact eternity, whether in purgatory, hell, or heaven, struck me as an appalling concept. Heaven to me just seemed like an endless boring mass while everyone I knew, including my parents, would be frying downstairs. I did become an altar boy, which paradoxically relieved some of the boredom of the liturgy. I could parrot the Latin mass with the best of them, although my understanding of the text was negligible. I'm sure I was far from alone in this, but I think I must have enjoyed the dressing up, a full-length black robe under a white surplice on a weekday and red on a Sunday—it was basically a dress—and the theatricality and the solemn pomp of the ritual must have appealed to the performer in me.

Since a genuine religious experience had up until then eluded me, I always felt like something of an imposter in the house of the faithful. I didn't quite belong. My biggest problem was confession. At the age of seven a child is supposed to know good from evil, but most seven-year-olds, as far as I know, don't commit evil acts. Yet the solemn sacrament of confession requires that, kneeling in a closed cubicle and facing a largely opaque scrim of canvas, you will confess your sins to the shadowy form of a seated priest on the other side.

The form of the sacrament begins as follows: "Bless me, Father, for I have sinned. My last confession was two weeks ago" (you see, you're supposed to go once a fortnight), but I had difficulties with both of these statements. As far as I was concerned, I hadn't committed any sins to speak of, but was too embarrassed to tell the priest that I was sinless, so the first statement that I had sinned was in itself a lie. I would then have to compound the lie by making up a catalog of venial misdemeanors like, "I have been disobedient" (I hadn't), or "I have told lies." Where the only lies I had been involved in had been told at my last confession, within the sanctity of the sacrament, compounding the lie with a sacrilege, which of course carried the penalty of eternal torment. This terrifying ontological conundrum and moral paradox was frankly too much for my seven-year-old brain, so I avoided confession like the plague, which of course made matters even worse. One is supposed to receive the sacrament once a year at least, under pain of excommunication (another offense carrying a statutory minimum of eternal hellfire). So, simply to avoid embarrassment in the confessional, I had condemned myself to life outside of the communion of the church as well as everlasting torment in the Joycean version of hell that our Hibernian priests favored. Either I was a very stupid seven-year-old or I was overthinking things.

I have carried such conundrums well into adult life, and sometimes they have served me well and other times they have not, but thought and torment seem to be inextricably linked and this is the lasting legacy of my Catholicism.

✦

Time has passed in the jungle church, but I have no idea how much time. Trudie looks peaceful and adrift in the sea of her own memories. A woman to my left and behind me is groaning softly in what could be pain or ecstasy, while to my right another woman is racked with weeping. I am silent apart from my breathing, which is long and steady, and I can only allow the medicine to take its course.

I am astounded by the seemingly limitless dimensions of

memory and visual metaphor that this experience is forcing me to address. Every relationship in my life seems to be under scrutiny: parents, brothers, sisters, friends, lovers, wives, and children all seem to be ushered into the court of memory and given their time in the witness box; and issues that I would normally avoid pondering—my failures as a son, a brother, a friend, a lover, a husband, or a father, or the dread fear of my own mortality—will not be pushed aside, but remain at the very center of my consciousness.

Although the darker, more violent images have largely subsided, this is no recreational experience; in fact it is deadly serious. I have had no choice but to surrender, and humbly accept that there must be a great deal of rage at the deeper levels of my consciousness and that these deeper levels are somehow being purged.

The young woman behind me to my right is still weeping, but more calmly now, while the one to my left seems to be experiencing a less than discreet sexual ecstasy. I recognize the music that is playing on the stereo; it is a female Brazilian singer called Zizi Possi. Her voice is passionate and filled with romantic and sexual longing. The song is one I have never heard, but is based on a classic piece by Heitor Villa-Lobos that I recognize, and is accompanied by a solo cello, deep and sonorous. The visions begin again.

The spiraling geometric entities behind my closed eyelids vibrate with the rhythm of the music and begin to morph into distinct humanoid shapes, dazzling, bejeweled, and specifically female. I have never in my life seen such gorgeous creatures and yet there is something intrinsically alien about them, something cruelly beautiful, almost insectlike and profoundly sexual.

I am being raised up into something like a vast elevator

shaft, surrounded and effortlessly supported by my mysterious, exotic companions. Up and up we go; I have abandoned all control and all resistance.

I am ushered into a large chamber, like the inside of a beehive at the center of which is a table with a chessboard. On the other side of the board is an exquisite female being of an even higher order of beauty and status than my attendant creatures, who bid me to sit down. They arrange themselves in an elegant circle around the table. In front of me are the white pieces. I am clearly expected to play.

I begin, moving the white queen's pawn two places. It is a standard opening and my opponent responds in kind. As the game progresses she neither looks at the board nor changes her expression, but keeps her eyes firmly fixed upon mine. Whenever I move my pieces, her responses are immediate and aggressive.

The music continues to drift into the room in undulating waves and the attendant nymphs begin to sway sensually at the urging of the drums. There is only the merest hint of seduction in the eyes of my adversary and a subtle mockery as she mirrors my moves on her side. The music vibrates with increasing urgency and swirls around my head like the swoon of perfume. The attendant's long fingers form delicate and intricate mudras, like temple dancers gliding in an encircling veil of eyes, lips, and insouciant faces. I must concentrate on the game, but the room has become a dazzling zoetrope of sexual images.

The female being in front of me is now a queen goddess of terrifying beauty and fearsome intelligence. I notice that as she places her ebony pieces on their squares, she twists them suggestively between her fingers as if she were screwing them into the board. This gesture is clearly designed to intimidate and unsettle me, and I am far from immune to its insinuation. This no longer feels like a game. I begin to feel as if I could be playing for my life. Beleaguered and outmaneuvered, I am becoming anxious and confused.

The dancing is becoming more and more erotic, the swaying curve of hips more exaggerated and flagrantly provocative. I am becoming flustered, making mistakes, mounting error upon error. I must think clearly but the dancers are now a frenzied blur of sexual energy. I am aroused and afraid at the same time.

Her attack is inexorable, destroying every defensive redoubt. I am given no choice but to move the king into the center of the board. He is exposed, out in the open field of battle, prey to the whims of the black queen and her cohorts, and now the rout has begun.

Arms outstretched, the dancers are like fabulous birds, a spinning latticework of arms and legs, like a tantric temple frieze, both elegant and lascivious in turn.

The black rook murders the white knight. Again the king is exposed, in mortal danger. Flagrant obscenities are being whispered in my ear. I can hardly breathe. A snakelike, insidious tongue thrills the skin of my neck below the ear, as the black queen presents herself to the wounded king. The word *check* echoes around the room with cruel insolence. The attendant nymphs move back.

I am in full retreat now, my enemy exquisite in all her malevolent glory. The black queen brushes the king with a mocking kiss and waits like a widow spider in the web she has so expertly spun, savoring the crude perfume of victory.

I am forced to retreat again and again, and again.

The music has now stopped. There is total silence in the room.

I am aroused, engorged, and utterly vulnerable.

The black queen smiles and moves one square to the side, mockingly, like a dancer at an Elizabethan court, opening a clear file along the edge of board.

My king has only one miserable move left, into the corner of the board. Black rook to H8, and checkmate.

◆

I LIE IN THE DARKNESS of my attic bedroom above the dairy, where I have successfully ejaculated into my hand for the first time.

Philip Larkin, in his poem "Annus Mirabilis," claimed that sex was invented sometime between the lifting of the ban on *Lady Chatterley's Lover* and the Beatles' first LP, but apart from Tommy Thompson's baffling intelligences, sex for me does not yet exist. Sex is never talked about in our house. There is no sex on television, and if there is any sex in the cinema, I haven't seen it. Christine Keeler and her friends may be entertaining the minister of defense, and about to bring the Tory establishment to its knees, but the newspapers don't know about it yet. The Lord Chancellor may be about to lift the ban on a dirty book that D. H. Lawrence wrote thirty years before, but none of this means anything to me.

I have no idea what it is that has exploded into my hand in the dark, only that it has the viscosity and temperature of blood. The delicious thrill of the moment is tempered with a terror that I have injured myself and that my body and the sheets of my bed will be a bloody mess in the light of morning. A light would waken my little brother. This is my secret, and already I can feel the welts on my legs from my father's hand. Fear, guilt, and fumbled ecstasy are already forming the seductive cocktail that will wallow in the warm pit of my loins long after this first intoxication.

My father is not given to outward displays of affection, and seems to regard hugs and kisses as needless and flamboyant affectation. He is of a generation for which this lack of physical warmth and intimacy is considered normal and manly; it is as if a society sandwiched between two world wars has unconsciously attempted to create a race of Spartans, inured to the hardships and emotional sacrifices of wartime. Anything that veers from this norm is considered sissified and effeminate; we don't cry, we don't run into each other's arms, and kissing only happens in the movies. My father is neither cruel nor sadistic, but he is a product of his generation; he is a good man who loves us profoundly in his heart but does not know how to show it; he is like a prisoner in an iron mask, increasingly sullen, desolate and utterly trapped.

My mother is a different animal entirely, spontaneously emotional, and as prone to tantrums and tears as she is to laughter and the joys of life. She craves romance and excitement. She is a rare and exotic bird, dangerous and unpredictable within the confines of her domestic cage. I adore my mother, but I'm also afraid of her.

On Sunday afternoons we watch old black-and-white movies, "three-hankie jobs," on the BBC: Trevor Howard and Celia Johnson in *Brief Encounter,* James Stewart in *It's a Wonderful Life.* My mother watches the screen with the rapt attention of a child, captivated by the shadowy images and more often than not awash with tears at the first hint of sentiment as the sad threnodies of violins and cellos pour into the room like warm syrup. As much as I am my mother's boy, I am also my father's son, and there is an ache at the back of my throat as I bitterly swallow the urgency to weep, to hold my mother in her sadness and wipe away her tears. My father is asleep as usual in the afternoons; he has no time for films. I sit like his deputy, grim and stony-faced, in what must look like suppressed fury.

My father's daily routine hardly varies. He finishes his round by midday, has his lunch, and then goes to bed for two or three hours. When he awakens, he reads the evening paper, then goes out to the pub—usually the Penny Wet on the High Street or the Rising Sun on the Coast Road near to where he delivers milk. He is not a boozer and will often complain of a headache when he has had one too many. But he never comes home drunk, nor does he come home late.

My mother does not drink and she never accompanies him to the pub. It is not considered respectable, and my mother definitely has "airs and graces." Only a common sort of woman would be seen in a pub, at least that's what was thought at the time. She spends her days looking after my two younger siblings, cooking three meals a day, shopping in the High Street or chatting and laughing with Nancy the redhead in the back room behind the shop. My mother does not work in the shop; she considers herself a lady and so does everyone else. We have a car now and a telephone, when no one else in the street does.

The back room is where we have the record player. My mother has taught me to jive to the forty-five of the Champs playing "Tequila" and slow dance to the Everly Brothers singing "All I Have to Do Is Dream" (it may be the first time that I've heard, or at least paid attention to, close harmony). We do the "twist" at Chubby Checker's urging and hula hoop till we collapse with exhaustion or pains in the chest. These are happy times; we laugh a lot, but in the afternoons we must be quiet so Dad can get his "shut-eye." During those hours my mother will sit behind the lace curtains of the upstairs window and watch as people pass by in the street.

Despite our relative prosperity there are clearly money problems.

On Saturday afternoons my dad, Ray, and his brother Billy bring the weekly takings into the back room. I am often put to work stacking pennies into piles of twelve, threepenny bits into piles of four, six-pences into twos, shillings into twenties, and florins, or two-bob bits, into tens. I even remember counting farthings, four to a penny, as well as ha'pennies and half crowns. But the figures often don't add up, barely covering expenses. I watch as Ray and Billy shuffle, ill at ease, from foot to foot as my father checks the numbers again and again.

One day four men arrive at the front door in brown overalls and manhandle the piano down the stairs. As they load it into the back of a blue van waiting at the curbside, I see something die in my mother's face. My father does not move to comfort her, nor do I.

Shortly after this, Billy goes missing. Ray turns up one morning saying he can't get an answer at his brother's door. He and my dad take the van round and knock for about twenty minutes, but there is no response. Ray and my dad split up Billy's round, and even though it's a school day I have to work. We don't finish until the middle of the afternoon. I go to bed exhausted along with my dad. Billy does not turn up the day after or even the day after that. Ray has no idea where his brother is. "Maybe he got a skinful, I dunno," he says with a shrug.

We never see Billy again, nor is he ever spoken of, and we must now find a replacement.

Some days later, a sad and far from inspiring procession of job ap-plicants traipses into the back room from the Labour Exchange. Nancy, standing in the corner with her arms folded across her chest and holding a half-finished cigarette, can barely contain her disgust at what she seems to consider such pathetic excuses for manhood and snorts audibly like a stage vamp. Betty is crying quietly in the corner, her face a picture of misery, wet with tears and made even more grotesque by an angry swelling on her lower lip from her tryst of the previous night. My mother attempts to comfort her without success. The Labour Exchange will send more men this afternoon, reminding my father that it is the winter and very few people would want to run around the streets in such weather.

"You can say that again!" I whisper under my breath.

Maybe it's the wisdom of hindsight, or memory conflated with imagination, but I can see this scene clearly. My father has gone to bed for his afternoon nap, having just chosen someone "presentable" to take over Billy's job. His name is Alan; he is a little younger than my dad with reddish blond hair, blue eyes, and regular, handsome features. Alan has come back to pick up a pair of overalls, the "round book," and a money bag. Nancy is in her corner having another cigarette—this time smiling her approval—Betty has been sent home, and in walks my mother.

I am invisible as time is frozen, and a look between these three is burned into my memory. It is a look of inexplicable mystery and power and stillness, and I am its witness.

✦

I open my eyes and look toward Trudie. My watch tells me that almost four hours have elapsed since we drank the ayahuasca, although it seems like a lifetime or at least a major part of it has flashed before my eyes. The others in the room are stirring. Trudie opens her eyes and greets me with a radiant smile. She tells me that her experience was extraordinary and wonderful and then, seeing my eyes red and swollen, asks me how it was for me. I tell her that I've been weeping most of the night. She reaches over, giving my arm a reassuring tug. "I'm sorry," she says, "I was off in another world. How do you feel now?"

"Wonderful," I reply, not quite knowing why.

The *mestre* calls the session to order and a final ritual song will close the proceedings. From our basic Portuguese we gather something about light, peace, and love, but little else. Everyone is now smiling, laughing, hugging, like shipwreck survivors who've lived through a terrible storm, and there is a palpable air of joy and community in the room. Trudie has been in a vast Neptunian palace, in the presence of a godlike deity, flowing beard and trident, sitting astride a massive throne and surrounded by the smiling faces of beautiful women. All of her visions seem to have been transcendent.

Our hosts are keen to know how we have fared. Was the experience too strong? Were we afraid? Did we see visions? Were we given insights? Did we meet our ancestors? Did we speak with God? But I am too bewildered to give anything like a coherent answer. Yet when we walk outside into the cool of the evening, the jungle is vibrantly alive, in fact disarmingly alive, and I have never felt so consciously connected before. I may be out of my gourd, but I seem to be perceiving the world on a molecular level, where the normal barriers that separate "me" from everything else have been removed, as if every leaf, every blade of grass, every nodding flower is reaching out, every insect calling to me, every star in the clear sky sending a direct beam of light to the top of my head.

This sensation of connectedness is overwhelming. It's like floating in a buoyant limitless ocean of feeling that I can't really begin to describe unless I evoke the word *love*. Before this experience I would have used the word to separate what I love from everything I don't love—us not them, heroes from villains, friend from foe, everything in life separated and distinct like walled cities or hilltop fortresses jealously guarding their hoard of separateness. Now all is swamped in this tidal wave of energy which grounds the skies to the earth so that every particle of matter in and around me is vibrant with significance. Everything around me seems in a state of grace and eternal. And strangest of all is that such grandiose philosophizing seems perfectly appropriate in this context, as if the spectacular visions have opened a doorway to another world of frankly cosmic possibilities.

I have to sit down on the steps of the church in dumbstruck awe at the beauty of the jungle and the stars above my head, but it is almost too much to bear. I lower my eyes to see a small gap in the stone steps, and there in the darkness, six inches down, at the bottom of the narrow crevice formed by the rough slabs of granite, grows an exquisite purple flower. It is like a forget-me-not, five petals of magenta radiating from the central mandala of a five-pointed yellow star, reaching bravely toward the light with an extraordinary life force and I am the sole witness to the courage of its struggle. In this moment I am led to an understanding that not only must such tiny, beautiful, and delicate living things be charged with love, but also the inanimate stones that surround them, everything giving and receiving, reflecting and absorbing, resisting and yielding, and I realize perhaps for the first time that love is never wasted. Love can be denied or ignored, or even perverted, but it does not disappear, it merely takes another form, until we are consciously ready to accept its mystery and its power. This may take a moment or an eternity, and there can be no insignificancies in eternity. And if this is true, then I must continue to remember my story and attempt to make some sense of it, to try to remake the drab prose of my life into some kind of transcendent poetry.

I will not sleep tonight but will lie awake in the darkness of our hotel room. It's as if a well has been sunk deep into the sediment of my life, an artesian well drilled into the stratified, impermeable bedrock of the past, and every memory that is forced to the surface breeds another ten in front of my eyes.

I watch as these memories unfold themselves on the ceiling above my head.

# 2

THE DAIRY ON STATION ROAD SEEMS TO HAVE RETURNED TO its normal routine and I go back to school with a letter from my mother to Mr. Law, the headmaster. It is not a truthful letter—my mother does a nice line in convincing sick notes, and she finds it easier to lie and say that I've had a "bilious attack" rather than admit I've been helping my father on his round. I think she believes that the word *bilious* gives the note a kind of medical validity, and she enjoys using it. She will use it in every letter that she will write for me, although I don't remember ever feeling bilious at all, or even sick for that matter. The reasons for this deception are complex, and involve some degree of shame and a social instinct to keep our difficulties private. I am, of course, complicit in this without being able to articulate it.

Some days I simply don't want to go to school. I'm bored there, and I find it easy to coerce my mother into letting me stay home. I think she is glad of my company, and after a statutory lying-in she'll allow me to get up and help her with the housework, or to just sit and watch the fire. Sometimes I'll close the curtains to a chink and watch the motes of dust floating like galaxies in the beams of the sun.

The Victorian building where we live is large and convoluted enough to find hiding places. A cupboard under the stairs becomes a priest hole, the space behind the dresser a hermit's cave. I sit on the slate roof of the dairy like a sentinel and imagine the house under siege. I'm a dreamer and my mother recognizes this, and she also recognizes herself in the faraway stare of the traveler lost in the world beyond the window. I return to school the next day with one of my mother's sick notes in my jacket pocket.

Sometimes a bank of fog rolls off the Tyne and you can't see a yard in front of your face. I love walking to school on mornings like this, when the world has disappeared and the ruined sides of houses loom like the ghosts of ships, or on bright spring mornings when the moon is still visible, hanging palely in the blue sky like a pared fingernail. But also along my route is a bomb site from the war, street after street of burnt-out houses that the Luftwaffe mistook for the shipyard a decade and a half earlier. There are shattered wooden staircases leading nowhere, bedrooms cruelly exposed to the sky, sad hangings of old buckled wallpaper and the musty smell of decay, broken floors and cross beams, redolent of a crucifixion.

I love the romance and mystery of the ruined streets, but there is always an uncomfortable spooky undercurrent, a dread that such impermanence and desolation can easily tumble over the perimeter of the bomb site and engulf everything around it like a poisoned cloud.

There is a general election coming up and the prime minister, Harold Macmillan, and his Tory Party have a new poster campaign.

YOU'VE NEVER HAD IT SO GOOD, it says in the confident guise of graffiti.

The local Labour Party have created their own posters using the same Tory slogan but crossing out the last two words.

It reads, YOU'VE NEVER HAD IT.

My father has gone to work. It is a school day and I have woken early. I get dressed and make my way downstairs to build a fire in the back room. As I turn the corner on the first landing, I hear a noise at the end of the passage that leads to a small porch and the front door. Crouching down, I see the shadows of two people behind the opaque glass of the porch. I move very quietly down the stairs, careful not to make any sound, supporting my weight on the wooden banister. I can hear soft moans and the quickening of breath from behind the glass door and see the shapes of two heads pressed together against the wall. I move slowly and silently down the long passage, not daring to breathe. The moaning is louder now, it sounds like pain, and as my hand reaches to open the door, I am terrified and fearless at the same time. I am driven by compulsion and curiosity and perhaps, although I haven't entirely thought this through, the need to rescue my mother from some terrible danger. As I turn the handle on the door there is a sudden panic on the other side of the glass. I manage to open the door only a crack before it is violently shut again.

"It's all right, it's all right." I hear my mother's voice trying to soothe me with the unconvincing tones of normality. Suddenly we are like a doomed family in a falling airplane, my mother desperate to hide the danger from me and desperate to hide her own fear.

I have seen nothing, but I run, and behind me I hear the front door slam. My mother doesn't find me when she comes up to my room. I am hidden, deep in my cave under the stairs, entrusted with a secret I don't understand.

I have no idea whether my father has somehow found out about the affair or whether he has had an intuition that something was going on and found some expedient reason to fire him but Alan is no longer with us. Nothing is said by anyone, nothing at all. Whatever the politics, I am relieved that perhaps now our lives can return to some sort of normality, but I am still in an emotionally disturbed state and becoming increasingly introverted and uncommunicative. I wonder if I am to blame, and I have no one to confide in or to reassure me that I'm not.

I do begin to spend more time at my grandparents' home, and while I don't feel I could share my secret with Agnes or Tom, I feel more secure within the stability of their cozy house and of all their years together. I also like to hammer away at the piano in the front room, which sits beneath a picture of the Sacred Heart, a portrait of Jesus with his organ of compassion glowing luridly and exposed within his chest and surrounded by cruel thorns. I've begun to miss our piano since they took it away, and Agnes's upright seems a perfect sounding board for my unspoken confusion and anger. This is the same room and the same piano where my mother accompanied my father in happier times, and the memory of "Goodnight Irene" lingers like a faded perfume. I close the sitting room door and draw the curtains across the window. With both pedals hard to the floor I attack the keys with a decidedly unmusical ferocity. Sweet harmony may be what I am seeking in my damaged world, but that is not what my unschooled hands are producing. It sounds like hell and strangely gives me some comfort.

Without the piano as an outlet for my aggression, I may well have become delinquent, vandalizing bus shelters, stealing junk from Woolworth's, and other petty crimes. God knows I had the contacts. This might have been some consolation for Agnes and Tom, who have to listen to this cacophony, if they only knew what was wrong with me, but they don't. No one does.

I can see my grandmother now, slowly opening the door to the front room. She is peering nervously over her tortoiseshell reading glasses. I stop midcadenza, as if I've been caught at something shameful.

"Eh, son, can't you play something nicer than that—" she struggles to find a word to describe my efforts—"that . . . that broken music?"

I lower my head, afraid now to look at her. "Yes, Gran, I'll try."

In spring the weather improved, so a replacement for Alan has been easier to find. Matters at home have reached a kind of détente. My parents are at least civil to each other, if not overly warm. The porch is no longer a safe place for my mother's assignations with Alan, and my mother has seemingly limited her social life to visiting Nancy at her house on Thursday nights, or at least that's what she tells us. She takes the car and my dad stays at home with us, sullen and silent. My mother may well have tried to end this clandestine relationship with Alan at various times, but her emotional needs and her romantic bond with him would have been too strong. She had found the love of her life, and she would be torn tragically between this love and the bonds of her family until she died.

It is Easter of 1962 and I have won a scholarship to the grammar school in Newcastle. There are forty other eleven-year-olds in my class, but only four boys and ten girls have sufficient percentages to qualify for a place in what is considered the top echelon of the school system of the time, the grammar school. My friend Tommy Thompson is not one of the chosen ones, although to my mind he's smarter than all of us.

My dad is never willing to spend money on anything frivolous, but my mother has convinced him that I should have some kind of reward for my academic efforts—I secretly think she feels guilty about Alan and wants somehow to make it up to me, without of course mentioning any of it. I have been hinting that I've seen a new bike in the bike shop—it's red with drop handlebars and whitewall tires and four gears. It costs fifteen guineas, a king's ransom. I know I'm chancing my arm, but I also know that I'll never be in this situation again. Ernie, with some reluctance, walks with me to the bike shop, which sits just off the High Street next to the funeral directors'. There it sits in the center of the window, like a prize in a TV game show—even my dad gets excited, the engineer in him marveling at the lightness of the frame, the gears and the brake system. Holding the handlebars I inhale its newness, and its chromium gleams like a promise of the future.

"Thanks, Dad."

"You just be careful now."

"Yes, Dad!"

Tommy lives on a council estate about a mile away, and this is my first trip on the new bike. It is spring and everything is new, the bike a shining symbol of adventure and escape. I park the bike at the side of Tommy's house, next to the cracked paintwork of the kitchen door.

I walk into the kitchen. "Is Tommy in?"

"He's watching the telly," says his mother. "He's not in a very good mood."

Undeterred, I march into the front room. "Hey, Tommy, I got a new bike."

The room is dark, as the curtains are drawn, and Tommy, seated in an armchair, is staring intently at a test card on the television screen. It's a black-and-white image of horizontal and diagonal lines, which is the only afternoon programming of the time, I suppose for the use of TV technicians so they can tune in this new technology that is bringing the world into our living rooms.

Tommy doesn't respond. He just keeps staring at the screen, his mouth set grimly, and now that I'm getting used to the gloom, I can see that his eyes are red and swollen.

His mother comes in from the kitchen. "What's the matter, our Tommy, cat got your tongue? Say hello to your friend."

"Shurrup, you!"

I wince, horribly embarrassed as she turns to me. "Oh, the tough guy's been crying 'cos he didn't pass the scholarship."

"I said shurrup," shouts Tommy.

The air is thick with the threat of violence but his mother will not be quieted now that she has me as an audience for her ranting.

"Oh aye, mister big shot, wouldn't go to school, playing the wag and smoking his tabs and God knows what else, but he was crying like a baby when he got the results. Weren't ye?"

"Fuckin' shurrup."

"Don't you set your cheek up to me, you're not too big that I can't hit you."

"You can just fuck right off!"

And with that Tommy leaps from the chair and bolts across the room. He is now framed cinematically in the kitchen doorway, and slowly turns toward me. "You coming or what?"

I sheepishly begin to follow him, trying to make myself invisible. "Er, good-bye, Mrs. Thompson."

"Good-bye, son," she says resignedly, and then screeches at Tommy's retreating back, "And you'd better be back before it's dark or your da'll take the belt to you. Do you hear?"

But Tommy is out the door, and so am I.

If he notices the new bike, he says nothing; there seems to be an instant and tacit understanding between us that he won't mention the new bike and I won't mention the redness of his eyes.

"Where shall we go?" he asks, and I'm somewhat taken aback, as it's always been Tommy who has set the agenda for our wanderings.

"I thought we could go to Gosforth Park," I venture.

"All right, let's go."

Tommy walks into a ramshackle wooden shed at the side of the house and emerges with the dilapidated old bicycle that he inherited from his sister. It has clearly seen better days. As well as having the lowered crossbar of a girl's bike, the front wheel is slightly buckled and has one or two spokes missing, it is far too small for him, and it has been hand-painted with black emulsion. It is, in short, an embarrassing joke, but not one I feel brave enough to share with my friend, who seems to be daring me to say something disparaging. He is still refusing to acknowledge the red trophy that gleams like an insult in my hands. I wonder if this is some sort of test. In my joy at winning the scholarship I suppose I'd assumed that Tommy had done the same; he certainly is smart enough. I had also forgotten about Tommy's ridiculous heirloom, but the effect of my friend's regaining his bravura despite the embarrassing difference between his steed and mine is a little like seeing Clint Eastwood in the first scene of *The Good, the Bad and the Ugly* astride a donkey: yes, the bike is ugly, but I wouldn't risk saying anything.

Gosforth Park is about five miles away to the north of Newcastle. There is a racecourse there, in a semirural setting that is the nearest thing we have to available countryside. We set off, Tommy behind me on the wreck.

We haven't gone but a few streets before it is apparent that Tommy's bike is no match for mine; at every corner I turn round to see him struggling with the tiny wheels and wait for him to catch up. My friend is now angry and getting more and more exhausted. The next time I stop to wait for him, I see he's furiously kicking the prone bicycle into the gutter. "Fuckin' piece of shit."

I ride back toward him, a vision of dazzling red and chromium.

"What the fuck are you looking at?" he explodes.

"Tommy, we're never going to get to Gosforth Park at this rate." I manage to suppress my impatience, and with a small hesitation and some steeling of resolve I say, "Why don't you take this one for a while and I'll take yours."

The effect is instant and for the first time he acknowledges the new bike, then looks at me with some suspicion. "Who bought that for you?"

"Me dad," I reply, reduced to wary monosyllables.

"Why, it's not your birthday?"

Now I don't know what to say.

"Did ye get it for passing the scholarship, did ye?"

I don't answer the question, but I do manage, "Are you gonna take the bike or not?"

He looks from me to the bike with calculated shrewdness, stroking the end of his chin with theatrical exaggeration.

"I'll give it a go," he says, with as much condescension as he can muster, putting himself astride my new bike and looking impossibly cool.

I pick up the ancient embarrassment from the gutter and we set off again, Tommy racing ahead and me soon struggling to catch up and cursing the wretched machine with its ridiculous pedals and its crooked wheels.

"Get off and milk it!" shouts some wag on the corner, which only adds a piquant shame to my exhaustion. I can hardly tell him that the gleaming red vision ahead with the whitewall tires is actually mine and that I'm doing my friend a favor.

It isn't long before I too am kicking the miserable crock into the gutter and cursing the man who made it.

"I suppose ye want your bike back?" says Tommy.

We eventually make it to Gosforth Park and back before nightfall, Tommy taking the last stage of the relay on the new bike, riding with no hands and circling me derisively.

We part at the corner of Station Road and West Street. He takes his pathetic excuse for a bike and I take mine.

There is only a slight hesitation as we make our way to our respective homes.

"Er, thanks," says Tommy.

"That's okay." I reply.

Tommy has been my best friend for almost six years, and over the next few we will drift sadly and inexorably apart, but it is during this period that I will find a friendship that will endure for a lifetime.

There was always music in my family; my mother's piano playing, my father's singing, even the submusical ramblings of my grandfather Tom on his mandolin engendered in me the belief that music was a kind of birthright.

Agnes's youngest brother, my great-uncle Joe, used to play the accordion. He would often say, with his customary and self-deprecating humor, that the definition of a gentleman is "someone who can play the accordion"—theatrical pause—"but doesn't!"

During the war my uncle Joe was "mentioned favorably in dispatches." His battalion was trapped on a beach in Crete, waiting to be evacuated by the Royal Navy. German Stukas dive-bombed them mercilessly for days. My uncle Joe played the accordion throughout the ordeal, and according to dispatches, "kept up the morale of the troops in the most trying of circumstances."

Uncle Joe was no blasé hero, he was as terrified as all the other boys on that beach, but I understand why he played that thing as the bombs fell, and I love him for it. He survived the war and played the organ in workingmen's clubs well into his retirement.

It is another uncle, although not a blood relation but one of my dad's oldest friends, who introduces me to the guitar. He is emigrating to Canada and needs to leave a few things behind and asks if he could store them in our loft. One of the items is a careworn acoustic guitar with five rusty strings. I pounce upon it like a starving man in a cake shop, as if it is mine by divine right. I have missed our piano, and I've stopped playing the one at Gran's, not wanting to upset her with my atonal experiments. My mother hasn't mentioned the piano since the day of the blue van, but I know she's sad.

The guitar needs new strings, and I need to figure out how to play this thing. Next to the Gaumont Cinema is Braidford's Music Shop. Mr. Braidford has thick pebble glasses, unruly and eccentric gray hair, and no roof to his mouth. Listening to and translating his utterances can take an agonizing length of time. He has a unique vocal argot that consists almost entirely of vowels. I have seen gangs of teddy boys in the shop, in their long velvet-trimmed jackets, slim-jim ties, and built-up "brothel creeper" shoes, entertaining themselves at his expense, snorting behind their hands as he struggles to help them in their spurious requests.

"Half a pound of sausages and two saveloy dips, Mr. Braidford."

The old man goes into one of his interminable stammers, as if the words themselves are fighting for breath. It seems to take an eternity but eventually, and with some anger, he is able to blurt out, "Aieees a oozic sho . . ."

"What's he say? Can't you speak proper English, old man?"

I desperately want to be brave enough to tell them, "He says it's a music shop, you fuckin' idiots."

But instead I'm silent and ashamed, ashamed of being young and ashamed of my cowardice. I'm terrified of the teds and they don't even register that I exist.

"All right then, how about a can of tartan paint? A packet of nail holes?"

But they're already bored and start to bundle out of the shop laughing and sniveling on the sleeves of their draped jackets, drunk on the delusion of their own wit.

I like old Mr. Braidford, and I like his shop. It's like Aladdin's cave to me. The window is full of long-playing-record sleeves and the latest single releases. As you walk in the door there is a mechanical bell and a *Melody Maker* chart of the top twenty. The Springfields, Del Shannon, the Everly Brothers, Billy Fury. On the wall are acoustic guitars, banjos, mandolins, and behind the counter, a couple of trumpets and a tenor saxophone, but the centerpiece of the entire shop is a Burns electric guitar, just like Hank Marvin's of the Shadows. I can't imagine anyone in Wallsend being able to afford such a thing, but people come from far and wide to see it, and wonder at its mystery. Not being privy to the science of amplification I imagine that you just plug it into the wall and out come the most wondrous sounds. I imagine myself standing on a riser above a sea of dry ice as a TV audience of young women screams hysterically at me on *Thank Your Lucky Stars*.

In a drawer behind the counter Mr. Braidford keeps sets of guitar strings. For the princely sum of two half crowns I purchase a set of Black Diamonds, and a further five shillings, begged from my mother, gets me *First Steps in Guitar Playing* by Jeffrey Sisley. This book will teach me how to tune the heirloom guitar and introduce me to the rudiments of strumming chords and reading music. I'm in heaven.

I become utterly obsessed with the guitar, and spend every available moment hunched over it, gazing into the sound hole, playing the same sequence of chords over and over again.

I've often thought that playing a musical instrument is an obsessive-compulsive disorder or a symptom of being socially inept, but I can't decide whether playing an instrument makes you socially inept, or you're a sociopath to begin with and you play an instrument as some sort of consolation. Needless to say, with the guitar, I become even less communicative at home during this period and can readily escape into the hermetically sealed world of my own making.

Because I've won the scholarship to the grammar school I have lost all interest in my junior school. I basically stop working or even pretending to. Mr. Law resents this greatly, as I'm one of only four boys to pass the eleven-plus examination in the whole class. "Arrogant," he calls me in front of everyone.

It won't be the first time that I'm accused of being arrogant, but I'm not arrogant at all, just lazy. Anyway, this school is boring and I'll be gone to another one soon.

Since my mother's love affair, sex seems to have sprouted up everywhere like an explosion of wild crocuses after a long winter. The headlines are screaming SCANDAL, PROFUMO, KEELER. Mr. Macmillan's government seems about to fall. Cinema posters have overnight become lurid sexual tableaux, advertising "naughty romps" and "bawdy tales." The newspaper shop in the High Street is awash with near-naked women leering invitingly from the covers of magazines and paperback books. At home we have an album of Julie London's; on the cover she is wearing an extremely low-cut evening dress. Put the edge of your hand over the bottom of the cover and she looks completely naked. This provokes such a stirring in my loins that I have to run outside and climb the lamppost in the back lane, but that only makes it worse. I can stay up there for hours. My nocturnal adventures too are becoming obsessive (now that I know it's not blood on the morning sheets) and my mother is too embarrassed or feeling too guilty to say anything about the less-than-discreet evidence of my activities. Besides, I'm still sure that this phenomenal discovery is mine alone, not having confided it to any of my friends, who I'm convinced simply wouldn't know what I was talking about, even Tommy. Confession is now utterly out of the question and I am privately exultant in my sin. I have a grossly inflated image of myself as one of God's fallen angels.

At school, besides Tommy (when he's there), I have befriended the more delinquent elements in my academic group, largely for protection but also out of a genuine fondness for and fascination with the underworld of smoking, swearing, and shoplifting. While I don't partake directly in any of these activities, my closest friends do, and I will often tag along like some sort of foreign correspondent, neutral and observant. Woolworth's on the corner of Station Road and the High Street seems to be the mecca for light fingers and deep pockets. The back of the Ritz is where the dexterous art of rolling your own cigarettes is perfected, soon to be superseded by the Rizla rolling machine, accompanied by much cursing and expert spitting. The only activity I will take any active part in is fighting, albeit unwillingly. I have been at least a head and shoulders in height above everyone in my peer group since I began school, and while this doesn't seem to bother the thugs in my own class, it really upsets the thugs in the older forms, especially the smaller ones. I am forced against my better judgment to fight these idiots after school behind the Ritz. As I have been lifting metal crates onto milk trucks since I was seven, the contest is usually somewhat uneven, and winning is only marginally less painful than losing.

But the Ritz is also the site of happier memories. I saw my first movies there: Fess Parker as Davy Crockett, Doris Day in *Please Don't Eat the Daisies*. My brother and I spent many afternoons there when Mum wanted us out of the house. We never called them movies at the time, we called them "the pictures." The town had boasted half a dozen picture halls at one time, but by the end of the fifties this had been reduced to two, the Gaumont and the Ritz. Philip and I went to the Ritz to see *The Guns of Navarone,* with Gregory Peck and David Niven. We even got in to see *The Carpetbaggers* by asking an adult in the queue to masquerade as a guardian so we could witness the forbidden decadence of a restricted film. On Saturday mornings the Ritz hosted what it called the "ABC Minors," showing children's cartoons and serials. This was a great treat, but in my usual overwrought and literal thinking I became convinced that my brother and I were there under false pretenses, imagining that you had to be the son of a miner to gain admission. We kept up the pretense, going unnoticed for a couple of weeks until my brother, who was given to violent and absurd arguments, got us both banned for life for a fracas during an episode of *The Cisco Kid*. The most striking memory of all of these films was the shock of Technicolor in the dark theater, which made the gray streets waiting outside in their drab monochrome even grimmer than they actually were. I began to believe that the world beyond the iron grays of the Tyne and the colorless battleship sky above it existed in a completely different universe of color, chromium and canary yellow, magenta and cobalt blue, which we would only ever see daubed onto these celluloid fairy tales that would so captivate and enthrall us on long wet afternoons.

I think I learn as much about the world from the pictures as I do at school, although I'm considered to be bright by most of my teachers, even by Mr. Law, who doesn't particularly like me. So I'm hived off with the other "bright sparks" to a special enclave on the right of the classroom, away from my friends and populated mainly by the girls. I sit next to Brian Bunting, a sweet, intelligent boy who "has a problem with his glands." Brian is extremely large and the butt of much sadistic humor from the thugs on the left. Because of my embarrassing height, I'm something of a freak myself, and have a degree of empathy and intellectual understanding with Brian that I don't share with the rest of the class.

One thing I do enjoy at school is singing. We learn hymns and carols and folk songs, which we chant in unison accompanied by an upright piano. I do have a voice, but when Mr. Law tests us in solo flight, I adopt the lumpen tones of my delinquent friends rather than reveal the voice that would lose me friends and influence. Mr. Law will often look up puzzled when he hears a clear and resonant soprano from somewhere in the back, but he never finds out who it is.

Brian and I and two other boys, as well as about nine of the girls, have won places at the grammar school. As a result there is an increasing sense of alienation from my erstwhile compadres, such as Tommy Thompson, who are doomed to the academic "poorhouse" of the secondary modern, where the thresholds for achievement and opportunity are depressingly low. They know this; the teachers know this; and so do we, the chosen ones. We shall wear uniforms that will set us apart, we shall learn Latin and calculus so that we think differently, we will be given expectations so that we will behave differently, and we will embrace this separation as our right. The scars of this institutionalized cruelty remain to this day, on both sides of the division.

By the time I begin my first term at the new school, Khrushchev and Kennedy will be facing off in the North Atlantic over some missile bases in Cuba and the short-lived détente at 84 Station will have come to an end. The world seems to be bracing itself for a descent into chaos and horror, while life in the house above the dairy will degenerate into a series of squalid, ugly conflicts.

Very little of what passes between my parents as conversation isn't freighted with sarcasm, acrid and barbed, and sadistically fashioned to hurt and gouge and scarify. My brother and I learn the terrible language of destruction. This is the trench warfare of our childhood as my brother and I sit out the poisonous clouds of abuse that explode above our heads, and we don't know when it will ever stop. When words fail her, my mother will throw whatever is at hand at my father's head, but he never retaliates, he will reply with a dark threatening look or a piece of quiet sarcasm, then silence, and this infuriates her all the more. Perhaps any kind of physicality was my mother's unconscious need, and perhaps my father in his own unconscious knew this too, and did not respond, but the child in me was grateful that blood was never spilled.

Today's row is about the car, the precious Vauxhall Victor. It's a Thursday, Mum is about to go out to Nancy's, she wants the car, and for some reason Dad is balking on the arrangement.

"Where you off to?"

"The same place I go every Thursday night," she replies.

"And where's that, then?" he asks, with a flimsy veil of politesse masking a truculent irony.

And then it starts, round and round the same circular carping, a thrust concerning her vagueness, a parry about his sarcasm, neither of them able to come out and say anything directly until, frustrated and cornered, my mother is screaming like a banshee and unable to counter my father's barbs, and nothing he can say or do will placate or please her.

While my little brother sucks his thumb I sit and play the guitar, silently praying that they'll stop. If they split up I'll stay with my father, I know I will. I love my mother deeply, but I trust my father with my life. He is a good soldier, brave and honest, grounded by the ballast of his stoicism, while my mother is already a shrieking ghost. I have a strange and terrifying prescience that she will die young.

My mother will win this particular argument purely on points for vitriol and high decibels, and storms upstairs to change. I leave by the back door unnoticed, and wait with my bike around the corner of Laurel Street.

After twenty minutes she emerges looking flushed and beautiful with a skittish energy like a hunted deer. As the car leaves I follow at a distance so she does not see me. Nancy lives a mile away to the east, but it quickly becomes obvious that she is not going in that direction at all. She has doubled back off the High Street and I follow, but with an increasing feeling of panic. I'm gaining on her, pedaling furiously. She has to see me in the mirror, she just has to. The car is now in high gear and I pedal faster as the exhaust fumes leave their blue trail in the air. I hear the accelerator and the noise of the transmission and the grinding of the gear box as she disappears down the road.

When I get home I walk past the closed door of my parents' bedroom. My father must be having one of his migraines, at least I think it's his migraine, as he is weeping softly, but I don't know how to comfort him.

# 3

I WILL BEGIN MY TIME AT ST. CUTHBERT'S GRAMMAR SCHOOL
in Newcastle in September of 1962.

I leave the house at eight every morning and catch the commuter
train to the Central Station. From here I catch a 34 bus up the West-
gate Road to where the school is located in the west of the city. It
takes me the best part of an hour to get there. The main building of
the school viewed from the drive is as grim and forbidding as the
opening shot of a horror film. The eye is drawn to the threat of dark-
mullioned windows in a towering and blackened fist of gothic ma-
sonry, and then to the dull gray classroom annexes that cling
awkwardly to the central structure like a spreading disease. This is
where I shall spend seven years of my young life, and my first day is
far from promising.

My mother is accompanying me as far as the school gates. It's not
that she's worried about me—I'm used to traveling alone, far and
wide—she's just curious to see the place. I know this is a mistake, as
is her insistence that I wear short pants and a ridiculous school cap.
I am furious with her all the way to Newcastle in the train, and even
more so on the 34 bus, where everyone apart from my mother is in
the claret jacket and striped tie that is my new school uniform. Like

most of my fellows, I have been culturally conditioned in the un-conscious mores of our society that this ritual rejection of the mother is an essential requirement of becoming truly male; that a man must not be tied to his mother's "apron strings," and that the consequences of such a connection for one's burgeoning "maleness" would be dire. I stare fixedly out the window, doing my best to dis-sociate myself from the pretty blond woman to my left who insists on paying my bus fare and talking to me incessantly.

By the time the bus reaches the Fox and Hounds pub, which is where we alight for the short walk to the school gates, I am insane with fury. I try to create some distance between myself and my mother by setting off at speed, hoping that no one will notice my at-tendant parent, but I can't shake her off until we reach the school gate. It is here where she seems to lose her nerve. We both wilt visi-bly at the sight of the grim institution at the end of the drive, but this does give me the opportunity to escape into the throng of stu-dents even though I feel like running back with her all the way to Wallsend. I don't look back though, and this must hurt her, to stand alone, abandoned at the gate without so much as a "bye." It must have been a long and sorrowful journey home.

Being accompanied by my mother on my first day of grammar school is the very least of my embarrassments. I am still a head and shoulders taller than everyone in my year, taller even than those in the year above. I look like a third year, and these short trousers make me look preposterous. I will suffer weeks of embarrassment over this, mainly from the older boys who see me as some kind of Nean-derthal throwback and an affront to their own manhood. I bristle awkwardly under the unflattering soubriquet of Lurch, the lugubri-ous giant butler in *The Addams Family*.

I somehow manage, through a combination of wit and diplomacy, to avoid beating the crap out of these morons or being beaten myself. It wasn't until winter that my mother agrees to shell out the money for some long gray flannels and I am grateful and relieved. But by then I have, after all, managed to quietly assimilate myself into this strange, eccentric place.

There are over two thousand boys at the school. The catchment area is unusually wide, as pupils are drawn from the parish schools as far north as the border hills. There is also a wide, middle- to working-class demographic, where the sons of Catholic doctors, lawyers, and the professional class are thrown together with the sons of coal miners, shipyard and factory workers—and one milkman's son.

Some of my new classmates live in Darras Hall, a well-heeled enclave to the northwest of the city, where at weekends I will be invited to large detached homes surrounded by landscaped gardens, with two-car garages, walk-in refrigerators, paintings and books, stereo systems, and all the accoutrements of the burgeoning middle classes. But while being taken out of the back lanes of my childhood and deposited on suburban lawns was, I suppose, an encouraging metaphor for the opportunities that my education would provide for me, it also made me feel inadequate and alienated, not quite good enough, marginalized, and resentful both of where I came from and what I was being led to aspire to.

St. Cuthbert's is run by a group of priests; the headmaster, the Reverend Canon Cassidy, is as fearsome a man of God as ever walked in a black cloak. A bald head and thick black eyebrows beetling over dark impenetrable eyes and a sunken cadaverous face give him an expression of permanent, theatrical anger, like a villain in an opera. I know of no one in the school who isn't deathly afraid of this man. I have absolutely no doubt that he is essentially a good and decent person with our best interests at heart, but the school is controlled by the threat of his demeanor and with an unyielding and harsh discipline. The headmaster's deputy is the Reverend Father Walsh. Father Walsh, as far as I know, does not teach, and his only apparent function in the school seems to be the caning of those boys unlucky enough to be sent to his office for offenses as minor as turning up late, excessive blotting of an exercise book, or the rare instances of cheek, swearing, smoking, or fighting. In one year I would hold the record for sustaining forty-two strokes of the cane on my rear end, in seven agonizing bouts, that for the life of me couldn't have been justified by my behavior. I just seem to have put myself in the way of trouble, been in the wrong place at the wrong time, with the wrong friends and the wrong look on my face.

"Six of the best" is a quaint euphemism for the ferocity of this excruciating torture. One is normally "sent up" to the main building after lunch. On the left as you enter is the school chapel, where a lingering trace of incense from Wednesday's Benediction gives the air in the narrow corridor an unmistakable fragrance: it is the sanctified odor of ritual sacrifice. There is usually more than one victim waiting in a sorry line outside the office. The school settles into an eerie silence as afternoon classes begin: the clock in the hall is ticking slowly; we wait like the condemned, not daring to speak. We continue to wait, and wait, and I know from past experience that this is quite deliberate psychological torture.

I project myself into an imagined future, years hence in the urbane security of an adult life, where I can look back upon this trial and others like it with a detached and amused nostalgia. "One day, this won't seem so bad," I tell myself, and this trick will work for me in a number of stressful situations, but only up to a point. The school clock is still ticking and the office door creaks open slowly. Sometimes I'm called first, sometimes in the middle, sometimes last. Perhaps it's best to get it over with, or then again, if you delay, there's always the chance that the good father may be called to a telephone and cancel the whole disciplinary session because his mother has just died, or perhaps an earthquake will shake the school to its foundations, and I imagine rescuing a grateful Father Walsh from the rubble of his office.

"There's a good lad," he'd say.

But despite my imaginings, it's a heroism of a different kind that is required here.

"Take your jacket off, and put it over the chair."

The study looks out over the playing fields, where I can see a football being lobbed effortlessly into the air and a straggling line of cross-country runners. No one seems to have a care in the world out there.

"Bend over, facing the window."

Sometimes, with some foresight you can be wearing an extra pair of underpants beneath your gray flannels, but this is as rare as it is unlikely, and an exercise book down your trousers only works in the comics. There is a sudden swish of air in the room behind you and then what feels like a cut from a rapier across the cheeks of your arse. The shocking pain reflexively has you standing bolt upright and winded.

"Bend over."

He can't possibly be going to hit me again.

*Whoosh!*

In almost the same place or at least within a millemeter he delivers a second stroke with quantum precision. Up you go.

"Bend over."

The man on the crucifix by the window averts his eyes from the torture; is this really being done in his name? *Whish!* Up you go.

"Bend over."

If there is any homoerotic component in all of this, it is totally lost on me, and I suspect totally lost on the good priest. Caning is simply stupid, pseudoacademic, pseudoreligious, medieval violence, mindless and institutionalized. *Whack!* Up you go. I swear that after four of these appalling deliveries, no matter how tough you may think you are, you will be crying, less from the pain than from sheer, bloody, murderous rage. Surely that is enough. What could I possibly have done to warrant this?

"Bend over."

That even the threat of this barbarity is effective in keeping us compliant, quiescent, and largely obedient is not in question. It is brutally effective. I just wonder whether those who suffered this painful indignity ever turned out the way they were supposed to. My suspicion is that, if we were to evolve into responsible and law-abiding citizens, we would do so despite this treatment, not because of it. Any idea that I would become an unquestioning and uncritical follower of the church's wisdom flew out the office window as the final swipe found its target at the seat of my resentment.

I'm happy to say that the school today by all accounts is a happier place, such barbarity having been outlawed for years, but there were also some fine teachers in the school, transcendent lights in the largely oppressive gloom that stalked the halls of the academy like a dark spirit. These men shone with an illuminating passion for the knowledge they were imparting; for them, standing in front of a class was as blessed a calling as the priesthood and far more than just a job. The best teachers were those who could galvanize an entire class solely with the charge of their enthusiasm, and it was these rare and exceptional men who would kindle in me an abiding and consuming interest in words, books, and the way of the world. I was inspired and infected by their energy, and I wanted to learn because learning seemed like an adventure, as if a dark continent were waiting to be discovered, dense, layered, and compellingly hidden.

Mr. McGough is a gaunt, stick insect of a man, well over six feet tall, with an enormous dome of a head that floats, disembodied and ghostly, over the lowing herds of schoolboys as they hurry to their classes along the dark corridors. He will be known, in a triumph of school irony, as Tiny, although I know of no one brave enough, or foolish enough, to ever call him by this name within earshot. A black gown hangs loosely over a gray three-piece suit molded closely to the angular wire of his body, and two or three books are as usual tucked under the crook of his long arm. If you dare to look as he makes his way through the halls his face is invariably set in a mask of displeasure and withering contempt, his dyspeptic, pitiless eyes observing and passing sentence on the world below. I imagine that from this Olympian height we must all look like pygmies to him, physically and intellectually stunted dwarves whom he is forced to live among like a sullen Gulliver in Lilliput.

Mr. McGough will teach us English literature with a fierce analytical precision, dissecting the language like a coroner laying out a corpse and then miraculously piecing it together and breathing it back into life. He can paraphrase the dense couplets of Chaucer and Shakespeare into clear modern English, coldly succinct but somehow with a conjuror's skill retaining the occult power of the original poetry. He will often halt in midsentence for seconds at a time, as the whites of his rheumy eyes disappear into the roof of his head, where he seems to search for and retrieve the exact word or phrase that will suddenly dazzle and enlighten the murky chambers of what he mockingly describes as our intellects.

From dread of this awkward, eccentric man I will come to revel in the privilege of his tuition, awed by his austere and devastating command of a language that he wields like a weapon.

That there is some undisclosed sadness in this man's life is never in question, and he seems to have few if any friends among the staff. What is known among the whisperers of the school is that he has no wife or children and lives alone with his father, an unusual arrangement for a man in his fifties, and in more prurient times would beg questions about sexuality and definitions of normality. We are thankfully innocent of such prying, and although I am intrigued and fascinated by his aloneness I have no desire to pry further. Many years later I will hear that he returned home one evening to find his father dead and half incinerated in the fireplace, having fallen unconscious, and it is that macabre image that will remain, strangely conflated with the dramas and tragedies that he had guided us through as if he were a boatman on a mythical underground river.

He will take no part or interest in the disciplinary fetishes of the school, he has no need to, and seems to live exclusively in a realm of words. He will guide us through the barren landscapes of Eliot's *The Wasteland,* Dante's *Purgatorio,* and the hellfire of Joyce's *A Portrait of the Artist as a Young Man.* He will help us uncover the human tragedies of Shakespeare and the petty moral foibles of Chaucer's *Canterbury Tales.* He will instruct us how to decode the parables of Sergeant Musgrave's *Dance* and Swift's misanthropic *Gulliver's Travels.* He will teach us to unravel the plot complexities of Fielding's *Tom Jones,* and expose us to the subtle aesthetics and social sensibilities of E. M. Forster.

I will become so swept up in these journeys of discovery that I will continue to read and read, long after the academic need has passed. There are no books in my house apart from a Bible and some equally unfathomable engineering texts from my father's apprenticeship, but soon books will become for me an acquisitive passion filling up rooms and rooms with their dusty and inert bodies. Like my grandmother, I will never throw a book away, storing dog-eared paperbacks from school or college, year after year, stacked like hunting trophies on makeshift shelves in my rooms. For to sit in a room full of books, and remember the stories they told you, and to know precisely where each one is located and what was happening in your life at that time or where you were when you first read it is the languid and distilled pleasure of the connoisseur, and this lifelong pleasure I owe to Mr. McGough and others like him.

Even from the earliest days of my education, I never had much of an affinity for maths. Numbers were cold and cruel abstractions whose only seeming function was to torture hapless souls like me with their strange, puzzling tricks and pointless adding and subtracting, multiplying, dividing, and extrapolating to fearful infinities. I feared them instinctively the way wild animals fear sprung traps. No one in my entire school career so far had ever managed to demonstrate the beauty of an equation to me, or the elegance of a theorem, nor had anyone had the foresight to point out the clear parallel between numbers and my passion for music. My scholarship exam had fortunately concentrated on general intelligence and not math skills, and I'd survived from year to year in a kind of skulking dread of each new mathematical instrument that seemed designed for the sole purpose of tormenting me with its abstract and baffling technology.

Bill Mastaglio had taught maths in the school for enough years to be considered a legend. Of Italian extraction, he had the face of a tough Roman centurion or a Neapolitan boxer, with his broken nose and his sleek black locks combed back severely from a receding hairline. Bill, and we always called him Bill, tested the whole class at the beginning of the autumn term. He hadn't taught any of us before and wanted some guide as to the problems he would be facing in the coming terms. I struggled through the paper and waited anxiously with the rest of the class for the results at the end of the week.

Bill walks in on Friday morning with a face like a burglar's dog, throwing the pile of papers onto his desk with a resounding slap, as if he is delivering a fiat from Rome announcing a mass execution. This is not looking good.

He proceeds, with an increasing vein of irony, to read out the percentages achieved in Monday's examination.

"Hanlon 75 percent, Berryman 72, Taylor 69 . . . Hornsby 25, Elliot 23 . . . and lastly, Sumner 2—yes, that's right, 2 percent.

"Do you know why you got 2 percent in the maths exam, lad?"

"Er, no, I don't, sir."

"Because you managed to spell your bloody name right."

"Thank you, sir."

There are some titters from the back of the class.

"Would you mind telling me how someone like you could have survived in this bastion of academic excellence with such a paltry and pitiable knowledge of basic mathematics? I have a cat at home who knows more than you do. How have you survived?"

"Native wit, sir?" There are more titters from the back of the class.

*He survives by native wit* was the phrase that my previous teacher had used to describe my faltering progress through the school in my last report. I took it as a kind of compliment and had even shown it to my mother, who gave me one of her wry smiles.

To Bill's credit and my eternal gratitude from that day on, he literally took me under his wing. Perhaps he saw me as some kind of tabula rasa upon which he could inscribe the unique signature of his craft, like a missionary teaching a savage to read the word of God. Or perhaps he was just a damned good teacher with a job to do. Once he had set the other geniuses in the class to work he would call me over to his desk, sit me down, and painstakingly, day by day and week by week, reveal the hidden magic of the logarithm tables, the balanced perfection of quadratic equations, and the graceful logic of the theorems. A whole continent was revealed before me, until then concealed under a dense cloud.

As well as being a fine teacher, Bill was also a hell of a storyteller. When things were going well in class, it wouldn't take much of a hint to start him on one of his sagas. He had fought with the eighth army in North Africa, and marched with Field Marshal Montgomery fighting Rommel, the Desert Fox, and his Panzer divisions from Tobruk to El Alamein. He had changed his name from Mastaglio to Massey in case he was ever captured by the Italians and shot as a traitor. I think Bill taught us almost as much modern history as he did mathematics. Two years later I managed to achieve a surprisingly decent pass in a subject where I had expected to fail miserably, and I owe that to Sergeant Massey, aka Bill Mastaglio, or just Bill.

Two terms at the grammar school will isolate me even further from my parents. Neither of them has ever read a book to speak of, or understands a word of any foreign language. Apart from my dad's spell in the army, they have never been out of England. I, on the other hand, learn to conjugate Latin verbs, write in basic French, tackle the rudiments of physics and chemistry, read literature, and study poetry. I may as well have been sent to the planet Neptune for an education, for all the comprehension my parents have of the work I bring home. This is no fault of theirs, but with only a paltry amount of learning I have managed to become a ridiculous, intellectual snob. The education that they had so wanted for me becomes yet another barrier between us, a Berlin Wall of indecipherable textbooks, theorems, languages, and philosophies, which must hurt and baffle them.

My parents are far from stupid, but in my arrogance and anger I begin to treat them as if they are. Sullen, uncommunicative, and lonely, I have become increasingly restless, trapped in a claustrophobic house in a small town and unable to share my frustrations with anyone. Neither is there any improvement at all in the relationship between my parents, just a grinding war of attrition that wears us all down.

In addition to all of this, my alienation from my old school friends is now total. One evening as I walk home from the station I see Tommy selling the *Chronicle* on the corner. He has a sheaf of newspapers under his arm and catches sight of me trudging up the hill in my uniform, a satchel of books on my back. We had been close for six years, but our friendship cooled in the aftermath of the scholarship results and I haven't seen him since I started at the grammar school and he went up to the secondary modern. He is wearing blue jeans and shiny black "winkle picker" boots with a Cuban heel. There is nothing remotely fashionable about my claret jacket, my careworn gray flannels, and my hideously sensible shoes. Even a hundred yards away I recognize him, and I can also see a vague sneer playing around his lips. As I get closer he looks me up and down with barely disguised mockery, killing dead any idea of a greeting. I am suddenly angry and ashamed. Our eyes meet for a second and we both look away in confusion. As I walk past him toward the dairy I feel his eyes on my back.

From then on I will avoid the corner of the *Chronicle* office by using the tunnel to the other side of the station, walking four streets and doubling back. I don't see Tommy for a long time and we never speak again.

It will be almost ten years later, when I am at college, that Dad asks me if I've heard about my friend Tommy Thompson. He still thinks that we are best friends even though I haven't seen Tommy in years.

"He came in from the Penny Wet on Saturday night, must have had a skinful, got home, put the gas fire on, forgot to light it, and fell asleep. They found the poor lad dead next morning."

I will take myself down to the river with my thoughts, and from the ferry landing look across to the town of Hebburn, ghostly under a veil of fog on the other side. The lapping of the slow gray waters seems to soothe me as they move inexorably to the sea. When I was younger and listening to the pulpit brogue of the Irish priests I would confuse Hebburn with the heaven that would be our promised reward for remaining good "Catlicks."

"Is that where ye are, Tommy?" I whisper quietly as if he could hear me, but there is no answer.

The boy who was my best friend has died, and for the first time I am aware that there is a strange and terrible guilt attached to death and its survival. Part of you rejoices that it was not you who was chosen, part of you is ashamed and regretful that you made no effort to rebuild a bridge to someone whom you've had the privilege of knowing intimately, and now it can never be built again.

Music has always been my refuge from sadness. The guitar I inherited from my uncle John now has decent strings, and I'm no longer making the "broken" music that so upset my grandmother; in fact I'm making a lot of progress, but the limitations of my first instrument are holding me back. There are things that I simply can't do with this primitive heirloom.

From the money I earned on the milk rounds I have saved up enough for a new acoustic guitar that I've had my eye on. It has been hanging from the wall in Braidford's Music Shop for three months now. I go and see it after school every evening, praying that no one has bought it. It is a beautiful steel-stringed instrument with a blond finish, an ebony fingerboard, and delicate marquetry inlaid around the sound hole. It costs me sixteen guineas, which is a large amount of money, but I'm in love for the very first time.

I first heard the Beatles in my final year at junior school. I remember being in the changing rooms of the swimming baths. Mr. Law had just supervised one of our chaotic and impossibly noisy trips to the baths—by "supervised" I mean that no one had actually been drowned. We were drying ourselves off and, as was our custom, flicking towels at each other's genitals. It was at this point that we heard the first bars of "Love Me Do" from a transistor radio in the corner. The effect was immediate. There was something in the sparseness of the sound that immediately put a stop to the horseplay. John's lonely harmonica and Paul's bass played "two to the bar," and then the vocal harmony moved in modal fifths up to minor thirds and back again to a solo voice on the refrain. Not that I could articulate any of this at the time, but I recognized something significant, even revolutionary, in the spare economy of the sound, and the interesting thing is, so did everyone else.

By the time "She Loves You" reached number one in the charts I was already at the grammar school, but it wasn't the confident primitivism of the "yeah yeah yeah" chorus that excited me so much as the G major chord with an added sixth that colored it at the end of the coda. An old dance band cliché, but when the Beatles used it there seemed to be a subtle irony at work. Again, I couldn't articulate this then, but I knew instinctively that it was pointing to a level of sophistication that I hadn't been aware of in pop music until then. The Beatles would succeed in manipulating as many musical forms into their songs, whether classical, folk, rock and roll, the blues, Indian raga, or vaudeville, in a dizzying and seamless pastiche of ideas and cultural references. It was music without frontiers and the ubiquitous soundtrack for a generation that thought it could change the world.

Jim Berryman, in his otherwise excellent biography, *A Sting in the Tale,* claims that I was outside the City Hall when the Fab Four played there in 1963, and that I managed to grab a lock of McCartney's hair. This is of course fantasy, and would have been out of keeping with the budding intellectual pretensions that I was nurturing at the time. But it is impossible to stress too much the influence that the Beatles had on my early life, and the fact that they came from a similar background to my own was fundamental to the vague plans of escape and glory that I was hatching in my imagination. Lennon and McCartney were both grammar school boys from humble roots in Liverpool, a town not dissimilar from Newcastle. From their initial chart successes they went on to conquer the world with songs that they wrote themselves. This gave an entire generation of musicians the confidence and permission to at least attempt the same feat.

I pore over Beatles albums with the same obsessive and forensic scrutiny that I'd applied to Rodgers and Hammerstein, only now I have a guitar. I have an instrument that can reproduce the practical magic of the chord structures and the network of riffs that their songs are built on. And what songs, one after the other, album after album. I learn to play them all, confident that if I persevere, what I can't play immediately will yield its secret eventually. I will reapply the needle of the record player again and again to the bars of music that seem beyond my analysis, like a safecracker picking a lock, until the prize is mine. No school subject ever occupies as much of my time or energy. I'm not claiming that any kind of prescience about the future is at work here, but there is something in the driven and compulsive nature of this obsession that is unusual, something in the unconscious saying, *This is how you escape. This is how you escape.*

It is 1966 and England, having won the World Cup against Germany that summer, is at last enjoying the fruits of the postwar boom and is considered to be, in the quaint argot of the time, "swinging." In Newcastle, however, the hedonism of social change and cultural revolution is limited to a small enclave surrounding the university. King's College gives the pubs and clubs and bookshops an air of musty intellectualism and bohemian sophistication. Wittgenstein, of all people, is supposed to have spent some time in the city during the war—I can just see him trying to explain the more difficult passages of *Tractatus Logico-Philosophicus* to the coves in the Haymarket snug in a blue haze of Woodbines and brown ale.

The Club A Go-Go is above some shops in Percy Street, behind the Haymarket. It was originally a jazz club catering to the sophisticated tastes that developed in and around the university. The Go-Go is where the Animals had their residency before they hit the big time, and living proof that the Beatles miracle could be repeated, even in Newcastle. When I am fifteen years old, the first live band I ever see is there: the Graham Bond Organisation. It is a fortunate introduction. Graham Bond is a big round-faced man with long greasy hair and a mandarin mustache. He plays Hammond organ and alto sax and sings in a gruff and passionate baritone. His band contains figures who will soon become legends: Jack Bruce and Ginger Baker, who will become more famous as members of Cream, on bass and drums respectively, and Dick Heckstall-Smith on tenor. The music is harsh and uncompromising and I'm not sure if I like it, but I have a strong sense that what is being played has a weight and a seriousness that will later be characterized and then caricatured as "heavy." Graham Bond would later become obsessed with the occult and end his own life under a train in London's Underground.

I go to see John Mayall's Bluesbreakers, again at the Go-Go, although I don't remember which of their subsequently legendary guitarists was on duty that night. It certainly wasn't Clapton, though it may have been Peter Green. But it wasn't until December of that year that I really had my mind blown.

I would watch *Top of the Pops* with a religious devotion at 7:30 every Thursday evening. I loved this show with a passion. Almost forty years later I can still see a picture of the DJ, Jimmy Savile, standing in front of a large chart of the top twenty, circa 1966, and am able to sing a line from every entry. Such familiarity with the music of the time could not, however, have prepared me for the whirlwind, the tidal wave, the earthquake, the force of nature that was Jimi Hendrix.

The Jimi Hendrix Experience appeared on *Top of the Pops* in December of 1966 and changed everything. Hendrix had transformed "Hey Joe," an old folk song, and propelled it by the elegant ferocity of his guitar playing into a sassy, bluesy vehicle of awesome power. His vocal was as sulky and offhand as it was passionate and openly sexual, and as the three-piece band stormed through the three-minute song, I imagined everyone in whole country in front of their tellys sitting bolt upright in their chairs.

*Wow! What the fuck was that?*

It seemed only days later that he would be booked to appear at the Go-Go. The excitement in the town is palpable. I am technically too young to gain admission to a nightclub, but because of my height I can easily pass for eighteen. I have brought a change of clothes in my schoolbag, a pair of Levi's and a white Ben Sherman shirt with a button-down collar. These are the "coolest" clothes I have, and look fine under my school overcoat. I change out of my uniform in the toilets at the Central Station, trying not to breathe. The lavatory is foul with the pungent stench of urine and sadness. I dress with mesmeric slowness, not wanting to drop any of my clothes on the filthy floor, beneath a faded Ministry of Health poster warning of the dangers of VD. Some hope! I still haven't come close to having sex. There are no girls at school, and most of my evenings are taken up traveling home on trains and buses. When I do get home, I usually have a punitive amount of work to do, and when on those rare opportunities I do meet girls I am painfully shy and haven't a clue what to say. But the other reason is music; I already have my passion. I stow my bag in the lockers at the station and set off at a brisk pace for Percy Street, breathing in the crisp air of the evening in grateful gulps and anticipating something extraordinary.

There is a long queue stretching around the corner. I tuck myself into the end of the line and wait. I imagine I'm one of the youngest people there, although my height allows me some anonymity in the crowd. They are mainly boys, dressed much the same as me, although a few dandified "exotics" have managed to purchase Afghan coats and are sporting droopy Zapata mustaches and spiffy desert boots. The girls all have the same style, hair parted severely in the middle and falling in lank sheets to the shoulders of black leather coats. There is an atmosphere of seriousness, though, that pervades the crowd, as if we are about to witness an event of high cultural significance. Hendrix will play two sets. I manage to scrape in for the first one, which is fortunate, as I would have had to find some convincing excuse to stay out so late for the second. My parents have no idea where I am, and I have no wish to tell them. One of the dividends of my alienation is that I don't have much explaining to do and am pretty much left to my own devices.

The club is tiny and I secure a pitch for myself halfway between the stage and the back wall. I will have no trouble seeing. The band of course are late. The crowd waits patiently.

They say that "if you remember the sixties, then you weren't there."

Well, much the same could be said of this gig. The Jimi Hendrix Experience was an overwhelming, deafening wave of sound that simply obliterated analysis. I think I remember snatches of "Hey Joe" and "Foxy Lady," but that event remains a blur of noise and breathtaking virtuosity, of Afro'd hair, wild clothes, and towers of Marshall amplifiers. It was also the first time I'd ever seen a black man. I remember Hendrix creating a hole in the plaster ceiling above the stage with the head of his guitar, and then it was over.

I lay in my bed that night with my ears ringing and my worldview significantly altered.

I did enough schoolwork to get by, but no more. All I wanted to do was play the guitar and listen to records. I listened exhaustively to Dylan and memorized great tracts of his lyricism, from "The Lonesome Death of Hattie Carroll" to "Gates of Eden." I also learned to like jazz, the hard way.

I developed a number of friendships with older boys in the school who recognized the seriousness of my musical obsessions. One of them lent me two albums by Thelonious Monk, *Monk Live at Olympia in Paris* and *Monk Solo*. I was at first baffled by the angular complexity of the melodies and the density of the underlying harmonies, but had an inkling that there was something important here. I persevered, in the same way I persevered with the books my grandmother lent me, or the way I figured out how to play the guitar pragmatically, unschooled but determined. I had no intellectual approach, just sheer bloody-mindedness. I would come home from school, put Monk on, begin my homework, and let the music teach me by osmosis as I struggled with some abstruse geometry proof. When I heard Miles Davis and John Coltrane, I realized that these musicians were exploring the outer reaches of human understanding like physicists in a sound laboratory.

I wonder if I would have developed even a small understanding of such music if I hadn't first put the time and effort into listening. I am no jazz musician, but I've put in enough work to have some understanding of it and develop a common language with those who do play it.

By 1967 my parents have saved enough money to move the family to a semidetached house near the coast in Tynemouth, only a few miles downriver from Wallsend. After all these years they're miraculously still together, or at least nominally so, being under the same roof. Divorce simply isn't an option for people like us, either financially or socially. It just isn't done. I'm relieved that we haven't had to deal with the seismic upheaval of a divorce, but sometimes, exhausted by the constant emotional static that crackles and then festers just below the surface of the house, I wish the whole thing would just blow itself sky-high, once and for all.

I am too awkward and clumsy to be much good at football, but I can run. No one has ever beaten me over one hundred yards at any of the schools I have attended. I am big-boned and strong from all the exercise I get working with my dad and, of course, all the free milk.

I hold the school record for the hundred yards and have qualified for the Northumberland County championships in Ashington. It is the summer of 1967 and I am sixteen. This is the biggest race of my life. I can recall the nausea of waiting for the starting pistol, the agony of the silences between the instructions: "On your marks . . ." My spiked feet in their blocks, measuring the distance between my left knee and my fingertips. "Get set . . ." Now an eternity as I raise my head and push back on my hips and stare down the long tunnel to the finishing line. *Bang!*

I return home that evening flushed with pride and victory, having won the race by a good length and blurting out the news of my triumph to my father, who is rousing himself from his afternoon sleep on the sofa. "That's very nice, son," is his only response, before he drifts off to the kitchen to make himself a cup of tea. I am at first deflated and then angry at him. He is too embedded in his own unhappiness to be able to really share in my success or take pride in it as something that he himself helped to create. His pride in me will continue to be ossified in the bones of his sadness, unvoiced. I understand this now, but I didn't then.

My running career ends that summer after I am beaten for the first time in the early rounds of a national tournament. I have lost heart in the sport, consoling myself with the knowledge that there is no strategy involved in sprinting, no real tactical training. You are either born with the right musculature to be the fastest, or you are not. Excellence in sports is cruelly definitive, and this is the nausea in the pit of your stomach and in your throat, this is the fear—that you will not be good enough, that you will be beaten, that you will fail.

I begin to fantasize that I will no longer seek my father's attention, and yet a lot of my life has been nothing but a vain attempt to find approval, to find acceptance. And no matter how full my belly, I wonder, will I always feel hungry?

While I despise the new house and its suburban pretensions, it does have a garden, which my dad loves though he has to get up even earlier and drive back to Wallsend to do his round. He builds what he calls a conservatory in the back garden, but in reality it's a jerry-built shed with windows. He spends most of his days in there with the spiders and some sad-looking cactuses.

My mother still goes out on a Thursday night to an undisclosed location assumed to be Nancy's house, but nothing is ever said. The walls are too thin for voices to be raised. We are like a family of Trappists, cloistered in our own silences. I can't be much of an elder brother to my siblings. I'm sure they're as confused as I am, because when I'm not actually missing from the house, I'm just emotionally absent, for although I love them dearly, and I think they love me, I can't really express any interest in them or risk any emotion. They must think I'm a cold fish, but I have no idea what they know or what they can tolerate. I share a back bedroom with my brother and a view of the ocean—that is, it has a view of the ocean if you climb on top of the wardrobe and peer over the rooftops, and there in the distance will be the gray, forbidding horizon of the North Sea. I get out as much as I can. I will use up whole days wandering up and down the beaches from Tynemouth to Whitley Bay, drifting with the tides, aimlessly walking and thinking.

I begin to spend a lot of my evenings at the YMCA in Whitley Bay, and befriend two brothers, Ken and Pete Brigham. Ken, like me, goes to a grammar school in Newcastle. He is an excellent musician and plays piano and guitar. Pete, who is a couple of years older than we are, is an apprentice chef and plays the bass. Pete has actually built this instrument himself, and I am stunned by his ingenuity. The bass is functional without being crude, utilitarian without being ugly. He explains to me the electronic mysteries of the single-coil pickup, the mathematics of scale length and the crucial distances between the frets on the fingerboard. This will be my first introduction to the cult of the bass guitar. I have not really taken much interest in the instrument, regarding myself exclusively as a lead guitarist because I could now make passable attempts at Hendrix riffs, using this new skill to inveigle my way into the coterie of young musicians who gather in the music room most weeknights. I am the kid who can play "Purple Haze," and this becomes my calling card. From such small beginnings reputations are made. I probably teach that riff to half the kids in the YM.

One of these kids is Keith Gallagher, who will be the best man at my wedding, as I will be at his. A lifelong friend and an early supporter, it is with his enthusiasm and encouragement that I dare to imagine that I have something that sets me apart as a musician, that somehow the dream can be nurtured into reality.

Keith has a practical nature. He is apprenticed to an engineering firm in Newcastle and attends night school. He also had the ambition and tenacity to get a good degree and eventually become a leading consultant engineer. Although my convoluted route to success will be far less structured, we must have recognized in each other similar traits, similar desires to escape the confined world of our parents. We walk the beaches together, talking and fantasizing, sometimes until the early hours of the morning. Keith is the first person to hear my early songwriting efforts, and although they are probably awful, he shows just enough interest to encourage me to carry on. (He did remind me recently that one of my earliest efforts concerned a flower in the desert. I had long forgotten this before I came to write a song called "Desert Rose," which would sell over a million copies thirty-five years later. It still seems fantastic to me that something as private as a song can become public property, but maybe all it takes is just one person to believe in what you are doing to give you the confidence to keep trying.)

While Keith is my Svengali it is Ken, the younger of the Brigham brothers, who will be my mentor. We learn old Freddie King numbers like "The Stumble" and "Hide Away" note for note, and play these tunes ad nauseam. Brother Pete plods away on the bass while Ken and I wheedle and deedle our way through the blues. We go to see Peter Green in Fleetwood Mac, Stan Webb in Chicken Shack, and John Mayall's Bluesbreakers, feeding our fantasies that we too can become bluesmen. When we aren't playing in the YM we are practicing up in Ken's bedroom, which is in the attic of a Victorian terraced house near the seafront. One night Pete has a date and won't be able to do the honors on bass, so I nobly volunteer to take up the support role while Ken wheedles and deedles.

The bass feels strange in your hands when you've been used to the smaller instrument with its narrow strings and short neck. The bass has a weight and a heft to it that feels like a weapon, yet there is a quiet beauty to it as well. This instrument is the root of all harmony, the bedrock at the bottom of the stave upon which music is constructed. When I accompanied Ken, I realized that whatever he played was harmonically defined by the notes on the bass. If he were to play the upper partials of a C chord on the guitar, it would only be a C chord if I played C in the bass. So I began to form in my mind what I can only describe as a strategy. A vague one, but nonetheless a strategy that the bass, while being far from flashy, would suit the covert side of my personality much better than the guitar. It would be a quieter heroism I would seek, stoic and grounded like my father's. My ambitions would become concrete from the ground up, hidden yet effective. I would suppress my desire to shine spectacularly in favor of digging deep and marking time in what I somehow knew would become a long campaign.

* * *

Did I really imagine that I would somehow become a successful musician? I wasn't even in a working band, but I sauntered into my A level exams with as cavalier an attitude as I could muster. Academia seemed as much of a fantasy as music, and in my final and crucial year at grammar school, I do very little but mark time. Other than playing and listening to music, I would while away the late afternoons and evenings in the amusement arcades of the "Spanish City" in Whitley Bay. I was not alone in being blasé about my A levels. Two of my fellow cavaliers were Paul Elliott and Hughie McBride.

Paul is a damned good drummer with a great ear for harmony and, like Keith, is one of those people who somehow believe in me, or, at least, in my musical ability. He has an infectious enthusiasm and a lust for life but suffers from being unable to step out from the shadow of his successful and wealthy father. His critics would disregard him as a child of privilege, but he is my friend and I know how hard he has fought to keep the fire in his belly when much of life seems to have been handed to him on a plate. There are no easy childhoods, though, and Paul likes to get drunk as often as possible. I too am self-medicating with alcohol but I don't have Paul's constitutional tolerance. I will be retching yellow bile in the street behind the pub while my friend is getting in yet another round.

Hughie is the eldest son of a large Irish family, impossibly handsome, with the blue eyes and chiseled features of a film star. He is charmingly shortsighted, while also being a terrific center back on the football team and the school captain. He can also drink as much as Paul without the slightest change in his agreeable personality.

The day after the exams we are standing on the West Road out of Newcastle, spaced a few hundred yards apart with our thumbs out for a lift. Sleeping bags and a change of clothes are stuffed into our haversacks. We have agreed to meet up in Stranraer, where we will take a ferry to Northern Ireland.

Three weeks later it is midnight and we are standing together in a bunker on a golf course in County Down. Behind us are our sleeping bags, where we will doss tonight. The Americans are about to land three of their astronauts on the moon, and we can barely stand up. I think "legless" is a suitable term to describe our state, although Hughie and I have managed to carry Paul from the pub to the golf course, and dropped him only once.

We have been hitching everywhere, sleeping on park benches, in farmers' fields, a couple of uncomfortable nights on Dun Loaghaire Pier. The year before, we three had hitched to Polperro in Cornwall and spent the summer living in an open shelter on a cliff top. We were supposed to be on our way to the Isle of Wight to see Dylan, but somehow we got diverted and had a great time anyway.

We always hitch separately, being "pros" (no one's going to pick up three guys), and we agree to meet up in the evening in whatever the next big town is. We head west toward Limerick and Kerry. One day a farmer picks me up outside of Tralee. He too is legless drunk and has a sow and a couple of her piglets in the backseat. He tells me that the only thing the English gave the Irish was the pox. I tell him that it takes two to tango as well as make a bargain, which he thinks funny.

Paul, Hughie, and I get as far as Dingle, in the southwest. Every night we get out of our minds on pale ale and Bushmills, and sleep wherever we can. We have successfully avoided being arrested for three weeks. We head back to the north to catch the ferry home at Larne, having scaled the mountains of Mourne, blind drunk.

Here we are roaring on a golf course under a full moon. I swear I can see some activity up there in the Sea of Tranquility. A small step for them, a giant step for us.

\* \* \*

My A level results are waiting in a nondescript brown envelope when I get home from Ireland. I avoid opening it for a whole day. But eventually I succumb. The narrow white slip of paper tells me that I have three passes in English, geography, and economics, but the grades, apart from a quite reasonable mark in English, will not set the academic world alight, nor will they get me into university without at least two resits. I decline the option and set myself adrift.

Over the next six months I will drift in and out of half a dozen jobs. The first is as a bus conductor. I quit, and sign on the dole, and then I get work as a laborer on a building site. Winter is approaching, and we are laying hard-core foundations for a shopping center in Byker. It is hard work, cold and unfulfilling. On my first day my always well-meaning mother will come up trumps again. She had offered the night before to make me some sandwiches for my lunch, which she would wrap and seal in a Tupperware container for me to take to work next day. The first morning has gone pretty well. I know how to use a shovel and a pickax but I covet the dumper truck job. All the driver has to do is wait for us to fill up the waiting bucket while he warms his hands on the running engine, then he's off, a master of the universe in a noisy blue cloud of petrol fumes, nonchalantly trying to attract the attention of the office girls across the road. I want his job, badly.

It is now lunch break, and there are about twenty of us on the gang stuffed into a wooden hut at the edge of the site. These are tough burly men crammed onto wooden settles. Everyone lights up and starts reading the *Mirror,* the *Sun,* and the *Sporting Life* while tucking into massive doorstep sandwiches and swilling down great mouthfuls with scalding tea and rude laughter. We are surrounded by a fog of cigarette smoke and the steam from a battered metal urn on the table. Being new, I take my place quietly in the corner. Famished, and with frozen fingers, I prize open the Tupperware container and stare for a brief second with horror at its contents. My darling mum has made me a selection of delicate cucumber sandwiches cut into finger-size fours that would not be out of place at a vicar's garden party, but exhibiting them here, in this Dante's Inferno of a builder's shed, would be tantamount to wearing a pink tutu and pearl earrings. I shut the plastic lid quickly before anyone can see the source of my embarrassment, but maybe too quickly.

"Wozza marra?"

"Not hungry," I reply, none too convincingly.

I will pack my own lunch from now on.

Weeks pass and I find myself digging a trench in the clay with a lad my age. It's cold and miserable and my back is sore and the skin on my hands is cracked and broken. When the gaffer's back is turned we talk and somehow we get onto the subject of education. He's a secondary mod kid, left at fifteen, and when he hasn't been on the building sites he's been on the dole.

"My life's a fuckin' joke," he says, glaring at the shovel and the splits in the palms of his hands. "How about you?"

I'm reluctant to tell him my life story, but as he's been so candid with me I don't feel like spinning a yarn.

"I went to a grammar school in town . . . seven years," I add, I suppose, to make it sound like a prison term, which in a way it was. But he is having none of it.

"Then what the fuck are you doing here?" he says.

"What do you mean?" I bleat defensively. "Don't you think I can do the work?"

"Oh no," he says. "You can do the work all right, it's just that you don't fuckin' need to. You can do better than this."

I can't disagree with him, but I carry on digging in the sodden thankless clay. A few days later I get to drive the dumper truck, but the weather will take a turn for the worse after this, and a lot of us get laid off two days before Christmas. I can't say that I'm sorry.

On Saturday nights I usually go to the dance at the Plaza on the seafront at Tynemouth, a huge white elephant of a dance hall above the beach. This is where my parents met for the first time some twenty years before. You might think this would put me off, but courtship is not really the first thing on my mind. I've really come to see the bands. Three local bands usually take the stage, playing an odd selection of psychedelic anthems, Motown classics, and long indulgent twelve-bar blues encompassing a normally appalling drum solo that only the drummer seems to get off on. I will eventually work up the courage to ask a couple of the pretty girls to dance, just for the sake of form. But it's usually a waste of time. I ask, they grunt their approval, and then they ignore me for the duration of the song, staring at the ceiling, glaring at the ill-suppressed giggles of their friends, checking the location of their precious handbags, in fact looking anywhere but at me. I'm frustrated, they're indifferent.

When all else fails there are always the plain girls. They are usually ignored in favor of their prettier sisters and are often happy to be asked. They are much more fun, having been forced to develop personalities, unlike the stuck-up virgins tottering around their handbags in the center of the floor.

That winter I become very friendly with a girl called Mavis who is actually gorgeous but has somehow developed a sense of humor and a sophisticated view of the world that doesn't revolve around her makeup mirror. Mavis can also open a brown-ale bottle with her teeth. Of course I am smitten. We share some blissful weeks together and then she goes off to live with her sister in London. We exchange letters for a while but then I never hear from her again.

Deborah Anderson is my first real girlfriend. We met on a double date with a friend of mine from the YM, John Madgin. I went off with her friend, who had a terrible cold and spent most of the night snuffling into her sodden handkerchief. Apparently John didn't have much luck either. We all meet up a week later in a pub and somehow it is Deborah who ends up in my arms, and John will walk home alone.

Deborah is a beautiful girl, tall and shy. She stoops a little, embarrassed because of her height, but she has a wide full mouth and a smile like a toothpaste model's, skinny legs, and long dark hair. Despite our star-crossed beginning, she and I adore each other from the first moment and it is obvious to everyone who sees us together. We had explored our first intimacies like children making blood promises in the dark, attempting to secure the volatile cargoes of the future in the fumbling, silent exchanges of our lips and hands. These were the tacit contracts of sexual risk, the unspoken bonds of shared danger and novelty and longing. You possess this innocence but once, like a memory of Eden, and that it had come so late in my teenage years made it so much more poignant. My mother, hopeless romantic that she is, recognizes in Deborah and me the idealized picture of love that she had craved and been cheated of. She embraces Deborah like a daughter, and she too makes emotional down payments on a future that can never be. But walking back from Deborah's house in those early days would eventually become a song, for being in love is to be relieved of gravity.

Deborah works as a secretary in the offices of a legal firm in Newcastle. She doesn't seem to have many ambitions other than to get married and settle down. Although we've never actually discussed this, marriage is the standard subtext that would underlie all relationships between the sexes, for people of our age and class at that time. I will acquiesce in this, while a part of me knows it to be expedient. We will have one false pregnancy scare before I eventually drift away from her for a headmaster's daughter, and four years later, she will be dead and I will be haunted by her memory to this day.

After my time on the building sites and my spell as a bus conductor, I decide I will try for an office job; at least I won't be cold, it will please my mother, and I can pretend that I'm using what I cynically call my "brilliant mind." I see an ad in the *Evening Chronicle*: USE YOUR A LEVELS, JOIN THE CIVIL SERVICE, and I apply in my best handwriting for a job with the Inland Revenue. I dig out my old school tie, my herringbone suit, my most sensible shoes, comb my hair and get the train to Manchester for a twenty-minute interview in front of a board of disinterested middle-aged men who ask me questions like, "Do you have any hobbies?"

I'm tempted to lie and say I like fly-fishing, but that will probably get me into trouble if he asks me if I tie my own flies, or what's the best trout stream in Northumberland. Of course I could have said music, but I would resent calling it a hobby—an obsession, yes, but hardly a hobby. So I decide on walking as my hobby.

"And where exactly do you walk?"

"Oh, I'll walk anywhere" is my less-than-inspired answer.

"Well, there won't be much walking in this job, Mr. Sumner."

"No, I don't suppose there is."

"And what newspapers do you read?"

As I am now in Manchester: "The *Guardian*?" I say, which raises a few eyebrows, and I wonder if they think that that's too left wing, "And the, er, *Telegraph*."

"Very balanced, Mr. Sumner." They know I'm lying.

Frankly, I reckon I would have gotten the job if all they'd done was put a mirror in front of my mouth and checked it for condensation—that's how challenging the interview was.

"So this is the civil service," I say to myself.

So I drift into a desk job as a tax officer in much the way that I've drifted in and out of the others. It is a miserable job for which I have absolutely no aptitude and even less interest. While it is virtually impossible to be fired from government employment, my position as a tax officer quickly becomes untenable. My in-tray becomes a towering steeple of abandoned files, while sad dog-eared folders containing the tax histories of thousands upon thousands of employees line the walls in oppressive ranks of clerical misery. That those whose tax affairs I'm supposed to supervise have jobs just as desperate and unfulfilling as my own is absolutely no consolation. I will often arrive at my desk as much as an hour late. My lunch breaks begin to telescope into the afternoons and I'm always the first out of the door at 5 P.M. after which my real life begins: dragging Deborah to see bands in pubs and clubs and dance halls. Rod Stewart and the Faces at the Mayfair, Fleetwood Mac, Julie Driscoll, and Brian Auger at the Go-Go. She patiently indulges my fantasy of being able to break into this charmed circle of working musicians, and listens to my prattling on the bus home, on and on about the merits and demerits of this band and that band. And then it's back to reality and work the next day.

One Mr. Wilson, who has worked in this office for over twenty years, tells me that Alan Price, the keyboard player in the Animals, sat in the very desk where I'm sitting now before he found fame and fortune. Mr. Wilson, as well as being custodian of office lore and history, is also the wry office rake: he watches slyly as the girls retrieve bare armfuls of brown and pink files to distribute to the designated work stations in the long room. He will invariably turn in his chair to sharpen a pencil and stare absently in the direction of the shelves whenever the lovely creatures have to reach up in their miniskirts and heels for the highest folders. As there is little else to relieve the boredom of these fruitless days I begin to mimic this artful choreography of swivel chairs, pencil sharpeners, and absent stares. We move together effortlessly like synchronized swimmers in a sea of longing. Not that the girls seem to mind, they're as bored as we are. A couple of these office sirens are disarmingly pretty, but I suspect that if I succumb to their easy charms, I will be trapped here forever and dwindle into a Mr. Wilson, tied to his work station like a sad Priapus in the temple of the senses.

This soul-destroying day job actually catalyzes me. I realize I must find a way to nurture my musical ambitions within some kind of institutional framework. In the seventies, a student grant, while hardly allowing one to wallow in the lap of luxury, at least provides a subsistence level of financial support to keep a roof over your head, a couple of eggs in the frying pan, and maybe a quid or two left over for a pint in the union bar. I may also find some people of like mind.

After six wretched months I will be gone from the Tax Office and enrolled in Northern Counties Teachers' Training College. And it is there, in the fall of 1972, that I will meet a brusque and bluntly spoken Yorkshireman who, in the years that follow, will become my mentor, musical guide, partner, and rival.

# 4

GERRY RICHARDSON IS IN THE YEAR AHEAD OF ME AT COLLEGE. We have a lot in common. Like me, he has been adrift since leaving grammar school, bouncing from one dead-end job to another, just as desperate to break into music, but needing some sort of institution that would allow him the time to figure out how it's done. Born and raised in Leeds, he'd played the piano from an early age, and both of his parents are musicians. As a musician he is streets ahead of me, but when we meet our friendship will be grounded in two things: that music is our singular passion and that neither of us has the slightest desire to become teachers. That said, in a teacher's training college it is possible (or it was then), with only a minimum amount of academic work, to keep your head above water and off the chopping block, which of course leaves plenty of time and energy to "gig."

Gigging is all we really want to do. To make a living playing music seems, if not the noblest of ambitions, then something pretty close. To gig night after night had an honorable and romantic tradition, at least it appeared so to us. It is Gerry who is the pioneer, the pathfinder into the fabled realm of clubs and cabaret, where if you can play well and are versatile enough, you might be able to join that illustrious brotherhood, that select band of musicians, who provide the backing behind crooners, jugglers, strippers, magicians, and singing comedians. To be a professional musician, a journeyman able to sight-read sufficiently to hold down a job, to play in whatever style was required—this was the ultimate goal, and Gerry, with his prodigious skills, could do all of it. I was in awe of him.

Today, becoming a better musician is still an all-consuming ambition: to practice daily, to read better, to be intrigued by the ever receding mystery of music, and to be chasing this elusive knowledge until your last breath. It was my friend Gerry who initiated and inspired me in these ideals, though he'd be unlikely, in his modest and down-to-earth way, to admit it, even now.

The teaching course would give us a three-year period in which to set ourselves up not as teachers, of course, but as musicians in some form or other, and if we should fail to "make it" within that period, then teaching would be the fallback, nothing more. However, even as a fallback, with its short hours and long holidays, teaching would provide, so we thought, a nominal financial safety net as well as a respectable front for more gigging until a lucky break would, as the fantasy went, propel us out of semi-pro-dom and into what we imagined was the big time.

We met at the college folk club one wintry Sunday night in my first term. The folk club repertoire was normally limited to reasonably close if uninspired interpretations of songs by Ralph McTell or Cat Stevens, or some doleful renditions of Leonard Cohen's oeuvre, performed without much skill, or any of the original irony.

I decide one night that I will get up and perform, and I spice things up a bit with a song from the film *M*A*S*H,* called "Suicide Is Painless." From there I take a nifty segue into "King of the Swingers" from Disney's *The Jungle Book,* then add a couple of my own improvised lines with the odd Anglo-Saxon expletive thrown in for good measure. This eccentric choice of songs and their ironic juxtaposition attracts the attention of Mr. Richardson. Being a York-shireman, he finds it difficult not to vent his feelings, especially when he feels that his musical sophistication is being insulted by the hapless innocents who normally grace the folk club's stage. As a result, he has developed a reputation as a harsh and abrasive critic.

With a pint in one hand and a cigarette in the other, Gerry makes his way over to me at the end of my performance. He has a fine beard, like an art teacher's, and is squinting at me through a bohemian swag of dirty brown hair as I put my precious guitar into its case.

"Well, that was slightly more intriguing than the usual shite that gets served up here on a Sunday night," he says.

"Er, thanks," I say, not sure whether to be flattered or relieved.

"Gerry's the name, piano player. Come over to the bar, I'll buy you a pint."

"Thanks."

I follow in his wake, guitar case in hand, maintaining a respectful distance behind him.

"Nice chords in that song from *M\*A\*S\*H*," he says, turning to see how far behind I am. "Been playing long?"

"Yeah, a while now, but I'm really a bass player."

We've now made our way through the throng to the front of the bar.

"Really, who do you play with? Two pints of special, please, Ken."

"Nobody really, some friends from school, that kind of thing."

"That'll be 40p, gentlemen," says Ken the barman.

"Do ye know any drummers?" says Gerry, feigning to have mis-laid his cash.

"Yeah," I say, reaching for my own and unwilling to risk remind-ing my new friend that it was he who invited me for a drink.

"There's this guy I play with, Paul Elliott, plays a Slingerland kit."

Gerry nods sagely as we both begin sipping the warm beer from our pint glasses.

"He's got his own van," I say, trying to give my situation a professional gloss, and Gerry, who has been Mr. Fucking Cool up to this point, is now spluttering beer.

"A van, really? Does he wanna join a band?"

"What band?"

"The college band, we need a drummer."

"I'm sure he'd be happy to, but how do you know if he's any good?"

"He's got a van, hasn't he?"

"Oh, I see."

This guy is clearly an operator, and aware that he may have seemed a little too venal, he softens a little. "Oh yeah, I'm, er, looking for another bass player."

"What's wrong with the old one?"

"Oh, nothing, it's just that he doesn't have a friend who's a drummer with his own van."

We both crack up.

Ensconced in the union bar we talk music—what we like, what we don't like—until they throw us out around midnight. We continue to talk music all the way back to Gerry's flat in Jesmond, a bohemian enclave of student digs and quaint pubs in the northeast of the city. Gerry shared the flat with a fiddle player named Brian, who was the brother of local folk legend Johnny Handle, who would become a founding member of the Killingworth Sword Dancers. Brian would refer to Gerry as "the jazzer," in an affectionate, mildly insulting way.

The flat, situated in a leafy Victorian terrace, is strewn with unwashed plates and coffee cups, cigarette ends, empty beer bottles, dirty laundry, dog-eared paperbacks, and old album sleeves. It is, in short, a student garret, a wild profusion of half-finished meals, half-scribbled essays, half-read newspapers, and is halfway between a slum and an encampment, as if an unruly army had suddenly been called away to do battle.

Gerry pulls an old Dansette record player from underneath a pile of books and papers, then leafs deftly through the pile of record sleeves and removes Miles Davis's *Bitches Brew* from its protective sheath. In all of this untidiness I recognize the ritual slowness and care with which he places the needle on the edge of the turning disc and then lies back indulgently on a pile of cushions to observe its effect on me, as if he's just administered a powerful drug. I was familiar with Miles's previous incarnations as the arch–high priest of "cool," and his masterly interpretation of Gershwin's *Porgy and Bess* was a personal favorite, but I am not familiar with this new recording, which shows the great trumpeter embarking on an innovative path that would come to be known as fusion music—I suppose because it would fuse together primitive rock elements with jazz improvisation and virtuosity—but indeed its effect on me is immediate and profound, and during the next hour I fall under its narcotic spell.

Many years later I meet Miles Davis for the first time. I am invited into his studio in New York City. Sometime before this I had stolen one of his excellent musicians for a project of my own and it was this musician, Daryl Jones, by then a member of my Blue Turtles band, who brought me to face the music.

The great man fixes me with his eye.

"Sting, huh?"

"Yes sir," I reply.

"Sting," he says again, savoring the word in his mouth like a gob of spit, "you got the biggest fuckin' head in the world." His voice is no more than a malevolent whisper.

I'm a little shaken by this, to say the least. "What exactly do you mean, er, Miles?"

"Saw ya in a fuckin' movie, man, and your head filled the whole fuckin' screen."

I don't know which of my movies Miles is referring to, but his comment provokes a wicked cackle that infects the whole of the room. Everybody's laughing but me. I must look a little uncomfortable, not to say hurt, so Miles, I suppose in an attempt to make amends, says, "So, Sting"—he rolls another gob of spit around that famous embouchure—"speak French?"

"Yes," I answer, a little warily now.

"Okay, translate this."

He hands me a copy of the Miranda rights. "Anything you say can and will be used against you . . ."

I gulp at the task in hand, my French being only rudimentary and just good enough to get me into trouble and nowhere near good enough to get me out of trouble. At the same time, the great Miles Davis has set me a task, and I desperately want to please him.

"How long have I got?"

" 'Bout five minutes," he shoots back.

"Okay."

I'm in a blind panic. I run to the studio reception desk and ask if I can use the phone. I call my home in London praying that Trudie will be there. She speaks French like a native. My housekeeper answers.

"No, she's not in, she went to the Bullock Cart in Westbourne Grove—you know, the Indian restaurant."

"Shit." The minutes are ticking away.

"Can you get me the number, Carol? It's a bit of an emergency."

Shit, shit, shit, she's taking an eternity. Eventually, she returns with the number and I dial.

"Hello, I'd like to speak to one of your diners, she's blond with green eyes, probably in a short skirt with high heels, very pretty."

The seconds are ticking away, Miles's assistant leans his head into the room. "You done?"

"Yeah, just a second."

"Hello, Trudie? Please don't ask me any questions—can you translate this?" I read the statement to her over the phone.

" '*You are under arrest. You have the right to remain silent. Anything you say can and will be used against you . . .* So shut up!' "

Minutes later I run back into the studio, victorious with my little sheet of paper.

"Okay, follow me." Miles beckons me into the vocal booth. "When I say so, shout this French shit at me as loud as you can, okay?" he says.

"Okay."

I'm standing in a vocal booth with Miles Davis, one of my boyhood heroes, I'm about to scream the Miranda rights at him in French while a driving funk track is playing in the phones. Miles nods at me. Here goes: " '*VOUS ETES EN ETAT D'ARRESTA-TION, VOUS AVEZ LE DROIT DE GARDER LE SILENCE, TOUT CE QUE VOUS DIREZ POURRA ETRE RETENU CON-TRE VOUS.' ALORS TAIS-TOI!*"

Miles responds, pointing to his crotch, "YEAH? *TAIS-TOI* SOME OF THIS, MOTHERFUCKER!!!!!"

Minutes later I'm out on the street. I feel like I've been mugged, but I'm gloriously happy and proud. I'm on a Miles Davis album. It's called *You're Under Arrest.*

"What do you think?" says Gerry as the record finishes and I drowsily emerge from my dream state. And regardless of where the music had taken me in my head at that moment, or the extraordinary turns my life has taken since, or how I wish I could have said, "Oh, I just projected myself into the future, you know, where Miles was really pissed off with me and made me shout at him in French during a funk track on one of his albums." "Shite and bollocks!" would have been Gerry's reply.

Paul and I join Gerry's band at the college. In addition to ourselves, there is a gentle Italian trumpet and flügelhorn player named Aldo, and Steve, an opinionated but unarguably talented tenor sax player. I will play bass and sing backup. The band will be called Earthrise, which is Aldo's idea, inspired he says by the picture of the earth taken from the moon by the Apollo astronauts.

The singer is Gerry's current girlfriend, Megan, although, due to a combination of Gerry's bohemian insouciance and my attraction to striking women, she will very soon become my girlfriend and not his. Gerry seems bafflingly unconcerned. Needless to say I am still going out with Deborah, and she attends a few rehearsals with me at the college but is so intimidated by Megan that she soon stops coming with me, and our relationship enters a kind of twilight of vague doubts that are unspoken and small deceits that go unchallenged. We will part soon, but the break is far from clean.

Megan is not shy, has a fine singing voice and, with her startling blue eyes, porcelain complexion, and luxurious shoulder-length blond hair, a confident sexuality. She is also from Leeds and, like Gerry, blessed with that same forthrightness that is guaranteed to make the more circumspect among us blush. She is highly educated and well bred, but when she speaks, the normal sensibilities of polite conversation are somehow swept aside in favor of bald and often brutal statements of honesty.

"You'll have to change the bloody key, Gerry, I sound like a screeching bloody parrot up there in B flat."

"But . . . but I've already written out the arrangement, love," pleads Gerry. "And the horns, they hate playing in sharp keys," he adds, hoping, I suppose, to baffle her with theory.

"Then they can bloody sing it, 'cos I won't. And don't try and patronize me with that 'love' shit, either."

Gerry glowers at her darkly but nonetheless begins to cross out the arrangement he has painstakingly been working on all morning, grumbling sotto voce about women in bands and the trouble they cause.

I note with some interest that while Gerry is no pushover when it comes to music, he is no match for a woman with attitude. Soon, though, I begin to understand that Megan's toughness, while effective, is only a well-crafted outer shell that armors a much more sensitive and insecure soul than the one she presents to the world. She will, nonetheless, be the second person to break my heart.

As this is essentially Gerry's band there will be no guitarist and the music will be oriented around jazz-tinged piano voicings rather than the cruder modal shapes of guitar-driven pop. One of the first tunes we rehearse is Graham Bond's "Springtime in the City." Megan's strident, uncompromising contralto lends an authenticity to "Cry Me a River" and "The Letter," even though we have culled the arrangements straight from Joe Cocker's *Mad Dogs and Englishmen* album.

We don't have much equipment to speak of and gigs are hard to come by. We play a few support spots for the bigger bands that drive up from London to perform at the students' union on Friday nights.

We acquit ourselves pretty well, but apart from the odd club date outside of the college, we don't seem to be able to get the thing off the ground. Megan, despite her seeming fearlessness, suffers from debilitating bouts of stage fright which she usually manages to disguise behind a smoke screen of irritability mainly directed at Gerry. I begin, with Gerry's encouragement, to take over more and more of the singing duties when Megan is indisposed, but I can see the whole enterprise falling apart long before it finally does.

We struggle for a year until Gerry is offered a nightclub residency in Bristol, working six nights a week with a trio and a girl singer. He decides to quit college, and the band, and I more than anyone else am bereft, as without its presiding genius the band will fold. Paul will go to work in his father's business, and Aldo and Steve will take up full-time teaching. Megan and I, with another year to complete at college, will stay together for a little while longer but not before I receive a bitter dose of my own unpleasant medicine.

Deborah had become a surrogate for my mother's longing and it may have been this primitive but mutual understanding between them that provoked the stirrings of a deep rage in me, as if I were being led unconsciously to act out some vague, confusing myth of betrayal and revenge. Whatever the psychological truth of the matter, and whatever unread myth was being played out, the scene was set and Megan would make her Amazonian entrance into the overwrought emotional theater inside my head. Infidelity became an engrossing aphrodisiac and a mentally exhausting game of timing and lies. I was smitten in a way that was totally novel to me. The gentle innocence of my first love had been swept aside by a close-to-profligate wantonness that seemed modern, unsentimental, and refreshingly cold. But it was a lust that was more than sexual, there were social elements of class and education, and this was my coldness, that a part of me saw Megan as a resource, as an escape route and a weapon.

Afternoon lectures are soon replaced by languid hours in Megan's room in the halls of residence across the campus. The line from Leonard Cohen's "Hey, That's No Way to Say Goodbye" that describes "her hair upon the pillow like a sleepy golden storm" will always remind me of Megan in these days.

Her shelves are lined with the plays of Genet and Ionesco, the novels of Sartre and Camus, and while her library and tastes are not exclusively French it is the exoticism of these names that will attract my attention before I've even heard of existentialism or have begun to identify with the muted and lonely heroism of *L'Etranger* and *La Nausée.* After our first afternoon session she will lend me *Iron in the Soul,* telling me that if I like it she'll give me the first two books of the Sartre trilogy, and only now does that seem like a strange and quite deliberate initiation. But our relationship was in many ways something played out and explored backward, from sudden and shocking intimacy to a slowly revealed understanding.

I will sustain my double life for a term and a half until the strain becomes unbearable. I will painfully break with Deborah, but that is only half of my purpose. Introducing Megan to my mother will complete the circle, and while this will bring me no obvious joy it is somehow bracing, like the cold thrill of steel.

When I bring her home for the first time the occasion, while cordial, is hardly warm. Audrey is clearly put out while maintaining an innocuous if prickly humor, and Megan bristles quietly without a contentious word being said. They exchange bland pleasantries while sipping tea and I begin to understand that women are able to communicate in subtle codes beyond the ken of mere males. Still, by the end of this uneasy summit, I am confident that Megan knows my mother and that my mother knows Megan.

It is my dad of all people who warms to Megan; her sassy confidence gives him license to flirt and I see a part of my father's personality that I had assumed dead brought back to life. But he is still a handsome older man and she, being the smart girl that she is, plays her coquettish role with some elegance and a confident ease. There is something protean in Megan's personality: she has an actor's talent to be all things to all men, and I am falling in love.

She and my father had first met in distinctly odd circumstances.

At 5 o'clock one morning some weeks earlier, I am standing in a red phone box in Front Street, Tynemouth. I call my father at home, knowing he will be cooking a couple of eggs and a rasher of bacon for his breakfast before he sets off for work in the car. The phone rings three times and I imagine the darkened hall and my father's puzzled expression as he makes his way from the kitchen to pick up the black handset. I'm praying that no one else answers.

"Hello?"

"Dad, it's me."

"Where are you?"

There is only the slightest hesitation in my voice. "I'm at the Spanish Battery."

"Oh aye?"

The Spanish Battery is the site of the old gun emplacements at the mouth of the Tyne, and my father knows that there is only one reason why a young man would be in such a place at five in the morning. He must be up to no good.

"Who are you with?"

"A friend," I reply, desperately trying to sound casual and move the conversation to the point and away from embarrassing revelations.

"Oh aye? And who might that be then?"

"Look, Dad, do you have your towrope in the boot?"

"Aye?"

"Well, could you bring it down to the Spanish Battery?"

"What for?" He is being quite deliberately obtuse. I try to ignore his unhelpful and spurious questioning, and at the same time try to maintain a polite calm.

"I need a tow, I'm stuck."

The simple facts of the matter are this: after a night of torrid and in my case, to be honest, rather inexpert lovemaking with my new "friend," I have decided in the interests of romance and local pride to show Megan the magnificent view at the mouth of the Tyne. Below the eleventh-century abbey on the cliff top is a narrow causeway leading up to a roughly circular headland, where gun batteries that had defended the river since the time of the Spanish Armada, through the Napoleonic Wars and against the threat of German invasion in the twentieth century, have been replaced by a rather fine car park. While less imposing than the artillery emplacements, the car park does maintain, as I said, a magnificent view of the twin piers and their respective lighthouses, which sit like sentinels on either side of our famous river. However, the Spanish Battery, having lost its strategic, defensive importance, is still celebrated locally as a "snogging pitch," where the steamed-up windows and the gentle rocking of cars on their chassis, under the moonlight and the ruined abbey, are merely the outward signs of a thriving fertility cult that has probably been celebrated covertly on this site since old King Oswald was a lad. Well, at least that was the pseudohistorical guff I was feeding Megan to get her to come down here in the first place. We had driven the seven miles from her rooms at the college to the coast, in my 1964 Reg. green Mini with the fiberglass bonnet, and every movable part having been replaced or repaired at some time by my good self.

I am driving with a newfound assurance, the proud captain of my own fate, flying into the teeth of the hurricane, the radio blaring some late-night jazz, with my new girl, smart and secret and so sexy. I take corners and roundabouts a little too fast, hoping that she'll notice my expert double-clutching and my predatory watchfulness. "You're safe with me, baby" is the desired subtext for all of this nonsense. "I'm fucking James Bond and at your service."

A half-moon sails above a flotilla of dark scudding clouds and hides itself behind the ruined walls of the old abbey. It has been raining heavily and the road is slick in the moonlight, but the sky is now almost clear and I can see the brightest planet, Venus, on the eastern horizon.

There is a steep road from the seafront down to a narrow isthmus that connects the headland with the shore, where the road rises on the other side to a surprisingly empty car park. We descend quickly and as we do so, one of the black clouds obscures the bright moon and we are in sudden darkness but for my headlights. To my horror the twin beams wanly reveal that the narrow causeway has disappeared under half a fathom of seawater, but by this time it is too late. We hit the obstacle at speed, and freezing water is now flooding across the transom of the engine and into the cab of the little green car. In this sudden shock we find ourselves up to our knees in the flood and the car is still, dead in the water, and so am I.

I look with horror at Megan, who is utterly stony-faced. She turns to me slowly. "Boy, you know how to show a girl a good time, don't you?"

I must be blushing redder than the lighthouse because her face suddenly begins to break into a faintly amused smile and then she drops her head back to release a raucous and derisory laughter that fills the car. This laughter is so rude that were I not so relieved I would be totally crestfallen. My embarrassment is tempered only by the fact that we are still alive and, apart from the freezing estuary water around our knees, unharmed. When I at last see the headlights of my father's car descending the narrow road toward us, Megan is seated on a nearby bench, dripping but still surprisingly elegant in her leather boots, and smoking a thankfully dry cigarette. My car is marooned in the center of what looks like a lake, the salt water lapping gently at the windows.

My father gets out of his car and takes in the whole scene immediately. With an infuriating smile he walks to the rear of his car, takes out a length of towrope, and hands it to me without a word. Then he takes a seat next to Megan and lights up his own cigarette. It is clear he is not going to help me.

As I struggle in the moonlight with the two cars and the towrope, Megan and my father watch with a detached amusement. They make charming conversation, as if they are guests at a cocktail party, my father making sly asides, I imagine at my expense, as Megan releases another of her awful laughs. My father seems hideously urbane and at ease. My humiliation is complete and absolute.

Perhaps there is some large element of the instinctual competition between alpha males here, but it is only in seeing my father's spirit aroused in this way that I realize, after I have calmed down, that I am falling more deeply in love with Megan than I had ever intended.

When Gerry leaves for Bristol, he doesn't leave me entirely without opportunities. He has kindly fixed me up with auditions for two of the bands with whom he'd been moonlighting when Earthrise were short on gigs. One is the Phoenix Jazzmen, and the other is the Newcastle Big Band.

My tenure in the latter will be commemorated by a picture, on the front page of a local paper, of the entire band outside of the University Theatre. We normally play here on Sunday mornings to a packed audience in the bar, but this particular morning, for legal reasons, we are playing in the car park.

My amplifier is plugged into the battery of my new car, a Citroën 2 cv. Don Eddie is behind his drum kit to my left and beyond him is John Hedley on guitar, and then three ranks of musicians: five trumpets, five trombones, and six saxophones, two altos, three tenors, and a single baritone. Standing in front of us and waving his hands in the air is Andy Hudson, the bandleader. Andy is a walking homage to tried and failed fashions of the sixties. A jaunty blue ascot at the neck, an oversize sweater, tight hipster pants secured at the waist by a wide and piratical-looking belt, and suede loafers, all topped off with one of those ridiculous nautical hats that people wear at boat shows. The rest of the band are dressed a little more conservatively but not much better, come to think of it, nor am I. This snapshot of the band is unusual in that it includes the local constabulary, as we are all about to be arrested, and not just for our crimes against fashion.

In the foreground are two officers from the Northumberland Constabulary, who are trying to stop Andy waving his arms, in the vain hope that this will stop the unholy row that we're making. We are apparently in contravention of the Sunday Observance Act, which forbids the playing of secular music in public places on the Sabbath. This is a bylaw concocted in the nineteenth century, I suppose by local fundamentalists to stop people having fun. The fact is, we have been playing inside the bar of the University Theatre every Sunday lunchtime for over two years now. The bar has been packed with over two hundred "punters" paying a pound a head to listen to big band arrangements by Stan Kenton, Neal Hefti, Count Basie, Duke Ellington, and Johnnie Dankworth. We may play them in a manner lacking the tonal subtleties and elegance of the original versions, but this is more than made up for by sheer brute force and disarming enthusiasm. The Newcastle audience, while never being exactly a pushover, become less and less discriminating as copious amounts of brown ale and lager are consumed and a great deal of "ungodly" fun is had by all.

However, it is a Sunday, and although none of us could be described as observing the Sabbath in any traditional sense, it is not the church that has complained. In this instance it is a rival bandleader, embittered and driven by jealousy that we can pull a large, enthusiastic crowd every Sunday morning while his "superior" orchestra, who play at the posh Park Hotel on a Saturday night, are lucky, in Andy's quaint phrase, if they can draw "two lesbian nurses and a Labrador."

This rather sad individual, whom I had the misfortune to work for but once, must know someone on the board of magistrates, because a "cease and desist order" is served upon Andy, and the theater bar is forced to close its doors. That is why we are here, set up in the theater car park. We are unbowed and defiant and, if it's possible, playing even more loudly than usual to a displaced if cheerful audience, when the gentlemen from the constabulary arrive.

The Newcastle Big Band had been started by a group of university students in the late sixties. Andy Hudson, who was reading chemistry at the time, met up with Nigel Stanger, a brilliant if rather dissolute student of English. Nigel was an extraordinary saxophonist and pianist who could quite easily have carved out a professional career for himself if he'd had a mind to. When I join the band, he is following a career as an architect and Andy is carving out a living as an entrepreneur. These two had teamed up with the tall, patrician-looking John Pierce, who as well as being a lawyer was a damn fine trumpet player and an ambitious arranger. While Andy could play the piano, no one would ever have described him as any more than simply proficient—he could tickle the ivories but no more. However, Andy is one of those fortunate individuals who upon recognizing their limitations in a particular field are then able to devote all of their remaining energies into something for which their talents are far better suited.

Andy Hudson is a brilliant bandleader and he has taught me a great deal. He has irrepressible energy, he is innovative, he is urbane, he has charm, and he seems to have an eye for talent, an ability to see promise in the most unlikely places. My audition for the band is a case in point.

The Big Band by this time had become something of an institution, playing in the upstairs room of the Gosforth Hotel. They had been without a bass player for a number of weeks now. The band would share the proceeds of the door money, and less committed members were often poached away into more lucrative situations.

I had seen the band on a couple of occasions when Gerry had played with them, and it seemed to me that everyone was having a great time, being trapped in a "time lock" somewhere between 1940 and 1959. I would love to play with this band, and I feel that I could learn something within their ranks that playing rock and roll in a garage will not give me. On Gerry's recommendation I turn up at the Gosforth Hotel with my bass and my amp to audition.

There are few things more intimidating than the sounds of a big band warming up. They are a cacophony of flashy runs and arpeggios, trills and riffs, quotes and improvisations all designed to put the hapless auditioner as far from ease as possible. I watch everyone very carefully, looking for an ally, a sympathetic glance, or a gesture of welcoming kindness for a stranger, but nothing comes my way.

Almost everyone in the band is at least a generation older than me and had been playing many of the tunes for years. I set up my equipment at the back of the room, where shortly a pile of charts are thrown in my direction. They are covered in beer stains and crossings out, where codas have been moved, whole sections transposed or quite simply missing, so that the charts, while having begun life as guides to the music about to be played, are anything but. I manage to look confident despite my apprehension as the band swings into a Woody Herman tune called "Woody's Whistle." It is essentially a twelve-bar blues, so I can busk through the changes without having to refer to the chart, which by the way looks as if it has been written by a spider on acid.

I believe, by the end of the tune, that I have managed quite well, although there were vaguely disgruntled noises emanating from the trumpet section when what I had obviously improvised did not exactly tally with the notes that had been written. I also manage to busk Ellington's "Take the 'A' Train" without being derailed, although I can now see a few unconvinced and shaking heads in the saxophone section.

Disaster, though, is just around the next bend. Nigel Stanger, who seems to want to get this torture over as quickly as possible, calls out a tune by double bass legend Charles Mingus: "Better Get Hit in Yo' Soul." I don't yet know this tune, and what is more, it is played at such a lick—in double 6/8 time—that I simply can't keep up. Within sixteen bars it is apparent to everyone, including myself, that I am no Charles Mingus, or anything even close. I abandon even attempting to read the chart and while the " 'A' Train" may have safely reached its destination we are now in the wreckage of a full-fledged, high-speed rail crash. The band collapses in a disheartening heap of broken saxophone runs, comical trombone glissandos, and the tragedy of soaring trumpet lines brought disastrously to earth.

I may as well pack up now, this isn't going well. There are now open smirks displayed on my behalf. I actually overhear "The kid didn't make it," I think because I'm meant to, and "Nigel doesn't want to play with 'people like that,' " with nods in my direction in case I have missed the point. I am mortified, ashamed, and utterly embarrassed. Andy makes his way over as I am absently shuffling the useless parts and looking out the window.

"That's a difficult tune."

He smiles, but all I see is the face of an executioner.

"I'm sorry." I feel like crying, but Andy says he liked what I was playing in "Woody's Whistle" and that I obviously have a good ear. At least he's a diplomat, I think, but here comes the ax. . . .

"If you took these charts home you could probably learn them by next week, couldn't you?"

I can't believe my ears, but I grab the pile of useless hieroglyphics in front of me before he changes his mind. "You bet"—and I'm out the door.

I don't know what it was that Andy saw in me on that first day. It was a terrible audition, but I was determined that I would try and live up to his inexplicable faith in me, and the following week, after managing to decode the semiotic charts, I got the job.

I will spend the summer holidays living with Megan's family; her parents have given me a room in their home in Leeds. Megan has gotten both of us jobs at a frozen-vegetable factory in Hunslet. The seasonal workforce is entirely made up of students, who work twelve-hour shifts, seven days a week for a month, coming on at 8 A.M. to take over from the night shift. We will be paid sixty pounds a week, which is more money than I have ever earned.

Megan is the middle child of a large, successful, Catholic family. Her father is a grouchy and irascible headmaster of a secondary school, and he dominates the family with a zeal that oscillates between the warmth of his paternal devotion and the extravagance of his foul tempers. Megan's beautiful mother has an Italianate elegance and a calm grandeur that is the perfect foil for the father's Celtic unpredictability. They are clearly devoted to each other and exhibit a proud tactile sensuality between them. I am enthralled by their affection for each other and realize that Megan's toughness seems to have been bred in her to survive the noisy commerce of this extraordinary family—an older brother and sister, no longer living in the house but still drawn by the gravitational pull of the family and the rituals of Sunday lunch, and two younger siblings of school age. Arguing seems to be the family sport, but it is not the destructive bickering that I became used to as a child in my own family, it is instead a game of mental agility, vibrant with passion and love and ideas, and the ability to articulate them. I can no longer distinguish whether it is Megan's family I'm in love with or her.

There is a factory tea break in the morning, a lunch hour, and another break in the afternoon, but for most of the twelve hours I am pushing armies of green beans off a conveyor belt and into a freezing plant. Megan works with the rest of the girls downstairs in the packing department, all dressed in blue overalls and white cotton hats. We see each other only during the breaks.

The noise in the factory is excruciating and talking is near impossible. With only the relentless marching of the green beans to watch, I very quickly begin to hallucinate and imagine massed battalions of marching insects being carried irresistibly to an apocalyptic battle, and myself armed as I am with a long rake as a sort of grim reaper mercilessly sweeping the combatants to their doom. And apart from daydreaming about sex with Megan, this is the only fun to be had, except that at the end of this purgatory I will have enough money to buy a Fender Precision bass, which has become something of a fetish for me.

I have had my eye on a secondhand Fender in the back of Barratt's music store in Newcastle since the beginning of the summer term. It is a careworn relic of the sixties, the fingerboard scarred with overuse at the third and fifth frets, the paintwork ruined and the varnish flaked and piebald. Among all the shiny others on the wall there is something orphaned, something life-scarred about this instrument that appeals to me. I have absolutely no desire for a new bass, I want something with a history, where every scratch and dent in the varnish has a tale to tell. I try to imagine all of the music that has been played on its sculpted surfaces and what the musicians must have looked like and thought about, holding this thing in their hands night after night, gig after gig, road trip after road trip. What were their dreams and their aspirations and how close did they get to realizing them? Why was it sold, and what were the circumstances? No one in the shop remembers, but I am convinced that I can pick up the trail where it was left and if I have as much skill in dreaming as in playing, I will dream up a new and glorious future that the past has only hinted at.

I return to Newcastle a week before the new term, leaving Megan in Leeds, and when I arrive at my parents' house I am shocked to find my mother and the lovely Deborah sitting together in the kitchen.

I hadn't seen Deborah in almost a year. Precisely what my mother's plan was, I have no idea, and I doubt if she did either. It's not something she would have thought out. Yet she had obviously engineered this meeting in one of those ill-conceived, spontaneously romantic gestures that she'd dredged up from an imagination fueled almost exclusively by old movies. Old movies that we'd watched together on rainy Sundays, which fed an appetite for turgid sentimentality and trite perfect endings. Not only is she unwilling to let go of her own emotional attachments, she can't let go of mine either. Suddenly she's the expert on affairs of the heart, the fixer of broken dreams, the facilitator, and though there's no real malice in it, this is dangerous meddling. I wonder if unconsciously she wants to bridge the chasm between us by putting me in her position, suspended between love and duty, idealized romance and practicality. We have never discussed this between us, and neither of us has the verbal skills or even a common language to match the complexities of the situation: we share no fund of literature that parallels and articulates our lives, and it is as if I have to become her to understand her. We are like characters in a primitive masque, but it is a dumb show, and a mystery play without an author.

So now the star-crossed lovers are reunited, and of course, my mother knows me well enough to guess that I too am far from immune to the promptings of this same sentimental and childlike vocabulary.

Perhaps it is the scarcity of vocabulary that is the root of the problem. *Love* seems like such a deeply inadequate word for a concept with so many complex shades and shapes and degrees of intensity. If the Inuit have twenty words for the concept of snow, then perhaps it is because they live in a realm where the differences between each type of snow are of vital importance to them, and the minutiae of their specific vocabulary reflects that central importance. Yet we, who spend vast amounts of our time, energy, and ingenuity thinking about love, being loved, loving, longing for love, living for love, even dying for love, have no more than this paltry, troublesome word that is no more descriptive or effective than the word *fuck* is for expressing the wonderful and infinite varieties of sexual congress. It's rather like a city dweller looking at the jungle and dumbly grunting the word *trees* for the manifold diversity that faces him. There are plants out there that can feed him, plants that can cure him, and plants that can kill him, and the sooner he identifies them and names them, the safer he will be.

However, as I've allowed my emotional evolution to be stunted by the shallow and tepid waters of popular culture, I can only throw up my Neolithic hands and grunt. Besides, Deborah, following her stage directions to the letter, looks stunning, like a film star. All that is missing are the violins, but the tears flow all the same, and she is suddenly in my arms, and my mother's crying, and I'm in trouble. Thanks to my mother's intervention I will have to break with Deborah all over again and the second time is even harder than the first, but at this time I'm convinced that I love Megan and that she loves me.

I move into Gerry's old flat in Jesmond at the beginning of the autumn term, while Megan lives a few miles away with a couple of girlfriends. Although we don't live together we are considered an item, a recognizable feature on the landscape of the college.

The danger of premature parenthood is never far away—every month we will go through the torture of anxious waiting. The years of safe sex and condoms being years hence, we live with a libertine fatalism and I'm too ignorant and horny to calibrate my amors to the female cycle. But when a few days become a week and the next morning is accompanied by an undeniable nausea, Megan is convinced that our days of freedom are numbered. She takes to her bed and I leave for college where the day's lectures are just a background drone to the drama playing out in my head: *We'll have the baby, we'll get married, I'll get a job, and somehow everything will be okay.*

I have a gig that night, playing at a dinner dance with an ancient pianist and an even older drummer. They are both well past retirement age and stooped over their instruments like wizened relics. The pianist has wisps of baby silver hair combed artfully in a swirl from just above his left ear to the other side of his shining, freckled pate, while the drummer is wearing a ludicrous bouffant of a toupee, so dark and rich in texture against the pallor of his skin that he looks as if he has a cat on his head. Apart from the barely perceptible movements of their wrists they are utterly still. The toothless "Gerontius" behind the kit seems to be whisking an egg with his brushes and looks as if any further effort will give him a seizure, while the piano player stumbles and shuffles through an hour-long medley of standards, fox-trots, quick steps, and waltzes. The only indication as to what comes next is a faint signal from the pianist's right hand. If the next key is to be G major, he will raise one withered finger to indicate the one sharpened note in that particular key. If he raises two digits we will enter the key of D, three for A, and so on. The flat keys will all be indicated by a subtle finger pointed at the floor for the key of F, two for B flat, etc. There is no other communication between us. I have to recognize the tune within two bars and busk the changes through to the middle eight until the next key change. These two have probably been playing these same tunes in the same order since the thirties. I listen with the concentration of a safecracker, trying to second-guess changes in the harmony before they occur. This is not easy work.

After an hour we retire backstage for a drink and a sandwich break. The two musicians sit and eat their sandwiches silently, as I imagine they have done for year after year, decade after decade, the same tunes, in the same keys, wearing the same tired dinner jackets, gig after gig after gig. I'm afraid to ask where the normal bass player is tonight; I suspect that he may have died. Part of me feels privileged to be learning this arcane craft with this geriatric duo, while another part of me wonders what the hell I'm doing this for, and shouldn't I be spending more time with people my own age?

When the break is over, we continue to accompany the dancers gliding across the chalk floor in their shiny shoes. This kind of event always ends with the "Bradford Barn Dance," the "Hokey Cokey," and gratefully, the last waltz. I pack up my equipment and the pianist slips me two five-pound notes and croaks that, "busking is all very well, but you should learn the proper changes to 'Stella by Starlight.' " The drummer adjusts his toupee and gives me a thumbs-up and a gummy grin. I drive back into town with the two crinkly notes in my pocket and wonder if I could support a family this way, doomed to play dinner dances until I too have one foot in the grave. I shudder at the possibility, and think about poor Meg in her sickbed. What am I going to do?

On the way back I pass a big roundabout at the end of the Coast Road. It is March, and the roundabout is covered in daffodils. I circle it twice, an idea forming in my head. I park in a nearby street. It is early morning and there is no one around. I check for police cars and head across the road to the roundabout.

Half an hour later I let myself into Megan's flat and slowly open her bedroom door. My arms are full of daffodils, maybe a hundred all told, their drooping yellow trumpets lighting up the entire room. Meg starts to cry, and so do I. The next morning our prayers are answered, but our relief is mixed with a subtle, unspoken regret.

\* \* \*

There are no publicity shots of the Phoenix Jazzmen, and for good reason: no one in their right mind would ever have employed us on our looks. It's the spring of 1973, and I've started playing with this band on weekends. Our uniform consists of pink nylon shirts and gray slacks. I am the bass player, and at twenty-one the youngest and least experienced member of the band. It is Gordon Solomon, the bandleader and trombonist, who will give me the name Sting.

The Phoenix Jazzmen have been playing together since the "trad" boom of the fifties. The music of Louis Armstrong, King Oliver, Sidney Bechet, and Bix Beiderbecke, much of it recorded before the war, had inspired countless British admirers and imitators, among them George Melly, Humphrey Lyttelton, and Chris Barber. Theirs seemed to be an atavistic reaction to the smooth big band sound of the forties epitomized by Glenn Miller and the Dorsey Brothers.

Trad, or traditional New Orleans–style jazz, was raw and authentic, closer to its blues roots than the sophisticated dance music that followed it. This quest for authenticity led many musicians to the smaller band format, usually comprising a rhythm section and three front-line players, trumpet, clarinet, and trombone. More often than not the trumpet would take the melody while the other two instruments would weave around the main tune in a kind of improvised fugue. (This music would evolve and eventually reach its apogee in the bebop improvisations of Charlie Parker, Dizzy Gillespie, and Thelonious Monk, but this development was to a large extent ignored by enthusiastic British amateurs who were trying exclusively to re-create a music that belonged to a bygone era.) These small bands thrived in the pubs and clubs of Newcastle, the tradition kept alive in the music of the River City Jazzmen, the Vieux Carre

Jazzmen, and the Phoenix Jazzmen. I would play in all of these combos at one time or another and developed a deep fondness for the raucous polyphony of these bands in full flight. It was every bit as exciting and visceral as rock and roll.

We would hurtle through "Twelfth Street Rag," "Tiger Rag," "Beale Street Blues," "Basin Street" with wild evangelical zeal even though, at the time we were playing it, the music was hilariously unfashionable. The early seventies were really the era of glam rock with David Bowie and Marc Bolan at the high end of the spectrum and Gary Glitter and the Sweet at the other. I had no interest in any of it.

I would wear the band's hideous pink nylon shirt with a certain amount of perverse pride. We would turn up at workingmen's clubs on a Saturday night, and following the bingo would ply our archaic and often anarchic music to a largely indifferent clientele of miners and their wives in Cramlington, shipyard workers in Sunderland, or the chemical workers of Teeside. These were tough rooms by anyone's standards, but we believed that our enthusiasm and passion would blind the audiences to our total lack of contemporary style, either in the way we looked or in what we played, and largely we got away with it. We were thrown out of a club on only one occasion, as I remember.

In a workingmen's club in the north of England, the central event of the evening's entertainment is not the act, or the "turn," as it's known, but the playing of bingo. Everything is organized around this quasi-religious ritual. The bingo caller is the high priest of the ceremony and sits at the center of the stage behind a large Perspex box filled with luminous colored Ping-Pong balls, numbered from one to a hundred. Inside the Perspex box is an electric fan that, when turned on, causes the balls to tumble attractively before they are randomly sucked into a tubular column from which the caller removes them, one by one. He reads the numbers out and places the balls neatly in a waiting rack.

"Kelly's eye, number one."

"Doctor's orders, number nine."

"Downing Street, number ten."

"Two little ducks, twenty two."

"Two fat ladies, eighty-eight."

"Was she worth it? Seven and six."

The bingo caller, usually the club secretary, will read out these numbers with the solemnity of a hanging judge, and importantly for this story, what prevents the colored balls from being spewed out into the room is a tiny plastic membrane over the mouth of the tube, which secures each ball until the caller is ready to remove it.

The occasion of our ignominy takes place on a Saturday night in the Red House Farm Social Club, Sunderland, in the middle of a tough working-class area in the north of the city. The Phoenix Jazzmen will perform at 9 P.M., after the bingo session. It is the early part of the evening and we are lounging in the dressing room, which we also share with the Perspex machine.

We are all there:

Gordon Solomon, or Solly, the bandleader. His boyish, rather innocent chubby face is belied by a mischievous and sadistic wit. He is also a fabulous trombone player.

Don Eddie is one of the maddest drummers I ever worked with, and also one of the best; playing with him is like being tied to the front of an express train. He is a big man in his forties with a bald head and a handlebar mustache like Flying Officer Kite. He is also a functioning alcoholic.

Graham Shepherd is the clarinetist. He is an eccentric, closet intellectual, music student, and ladies' man. His feature in the show is "Stranger on the Shore" by Acker Bilk. Graham hates this tune with a passion, and Gordon, being the kind, considerate bandleader that he is, forces him to do it every night. It is this same sadism that will force me to sing "Never Ending Song of Love" by the Seekers. I dread this moment in the set but I do it all the same.

Finally, there is Ronnie Young, trumpeter and vocalist, and a sweet, sweet man on the wrong side of fifty who sings much better than he blows his horn. There is a tradition among Jazzers that when you are given a solo, you are expected to improvise, to create something fresh, something extempore. Ronnie is to the art of improvisation what the pope is to belly dancing: he can only play what he knows, note for note, night after night. He plays the exact same solo in every song, and this we all learn to hum, sotto voce, behind him, note for note, night after night. Ronnie doesn't mind the ribbing about his horn playing when he can scat like Satchmo and croon like Sinatra.

Gordon is going over the set that we will play tonight.

"Ronnie, could you try not to crack that high note in 'Caravan' again tonight? Or I'm gonna start calling you the Cruel C."

"Don, do you know what they call somebody who hangs out with musicians?"

"No, boss."

"A drummer! And while we are on the subject, 'Tiger Rag' is not a race. I thought the club was on fire last night, the way you were playing it."

While our fearless leader is giving us our nightly pep talk, he is leaning casually against the bingo machine and absently playing with the delicate plastic membrane at the end of the tube, the one that holds the balls in place.

"Sting, dear boy . . ." He's been calling me that for weeks now. I must have worn the damned sweater but once, and yes it did make me look like a wasp, with its black-and-yellow hoops, but this stupid name is beginning to stick. "Would you mind terribly . . . ?"

*Snap!*

There's a sound like a starting pistol in the tiny room.

"Oh shit!"

The tiny and crucial piece of plastic has snapped in his hand; all of us are in shock. This is not just vandalism; we are in a workingmen's club and we know this to be nothing less than mortal, bloody sacrilege. Gordon's expression has lost all of its irony. His mouth hangs open in horror, with the doomed and piteous look of the condemned.

Just at this point the club chairman, an officious sneer of a man that Gordon refers to as the Syrup (so black is his hair, and in so much profusion for a man of his age, that it can only be a wig), bustles into the dressing room with two of his henchmen. They have come to wheel the precious bingo machine out onto the stage, handling it as if it were the Ark of the Covenant.

Gordon is like a rabbit in the headlights of an oncoming truck, but before he can explain the awful tragedy that has occurred, the club chairman, hairpiece ever-so-slightly askew, is already launching into him.

"Now, you lads had better be playing some tunes from the hit parade tonight, so the lassies can dance, none of that jazz rubbish you played last time you were here."

Gordon bravely tries to set things to right, "But . . . but . . ."

It is too late. The Perspex box is now being wheeled into its place in the center of the stage. The pompous chairman gives us one final glower before he strides out like a tragic actor.

The noisy club is immediately hushed as the chairman braces himself in front of the mike.

"Ladies and gentlemen, you will be entertained tonight, if I can call it that, by the Phoenix Jazzmen. They're not exactly my cup of tea, but some of you may like them."

Gordon whispers to Ronnie to go out and start the van in the car park while we watch aghast as the disaster unfolds before us.

"And now, without further ado, the high spot of the evening, for a cash prize of one hundred pounds . . ."

The club secretary is seated behind the machine. He has the switch between his fingertips as the audience sit, poised and expectant with their bingo cards and ballpoint pens. The atmosphere is charged with high drama.

"IT'S EYES DOWN FOR A FULL HOUSE, MR. SECRETARY. PLEASE, THE SWITCH."

The switch is pulled, the fan begins to whir, and then all hell breaks loose. The horrified audience are bombarded by a relentless hail of luminous Ping-Pong balls, landing in glasses of beer, lodging themselves in wigs and cleavages, and bouncing disastrously under the feet of tumbling tray-laden waitresses.

The Phoenix Jazzmen are frozen at the open door between the stage and the dressing room, and there is the unmistakable look of guilt and shame upon all of our faces. The club chairman, with a face like death, slowly raises an accusatory finger at the doorway and now we hear a primal and gut-wrenching howl of outrage from the floor that wouldn't be out of place at a public hanging. We run for our lives.

My final year at college has settled into a routine of lectures, essays, and working weekends with the Phoenix. I have one more teaching practice before I qualify. They send me to a little village in the Lake District called Threlkeld, lying on the northern slopes of Blencathra, the forbidding and broody mountain fell known locally as Saddleback.

Megan's teaching practice is in Wallsend, of all places, and we have to accept that we won't be seeing much of each other for about five or six weeks.

Threlkeld sits in a wide glaciated valley between Keswick in the west and Penruddock to the east. Behind it and to the north are the dramatic fastnesses of Blencathra and Skiddaw, and a mile across the valley, the gentler slopes of Clough Head. The schoolhouse is a dry stone structure of local granite and slate and comprises only two classrooms and a gray schoolyard beneath the shadow of the mountain. The school has been there for most of the century and can't have changed perceptibly in all of that time.

There are two members of staff. The headmaster, Mr. Sturridge, a craggy, kindly man in his sixties looking forward to retirement next year, and Mrs. Anders, a cantankerous though not too unfriendly spinster displaced recently from Keswick by the "droves of summer tourists" who descend on the town like locusts in their hiking boots and anoraks. She prefers Threlkeld, a backwater by comparison, nestling discreetly and quietly on the lower slopes of the mountain. Mr. Sturridge has been teaching here since the war, and in the muted gray tones of his clothes and hair, and the sculpted angles of his face, he seems to be cut from the same rock as the dry stones of the school wall. The children seem well adjusted and happy. It's easy to imagine them remaining in the valley always, leading uncomplicated country lives watching the busy traffic on the main road to Keswick with a calm indifference and a shrug of the shoulders. I quickly fall in love with this place, and take to "fell walking" every night after school, turning from the climb every few steps to look back at the distant stillness of the valley under the sweeping clouds.

At the weekends I return to Newcastle, spend Friday night with Megan, and play Saturday with the Phoenix in some social club for a tenner. Sunday lunchtimes I'll play with the Big Band at the University Theatre and then on Sunday afternoon drive back across the Pennines to my digs in Cumberland. The road over the hills is usually empty on Sunday evening and after it has ascended steeply to its summit at Ambleside there is a good fifteen-mile stretch of meandering downhill curves where the gradient is gentle enough to turn off the engine and coast with the handbrake and the roof open all the way to Penrith. I've saved enough money to buy a new car, and it feels like I'm sailing in a land yacht. I'm so happy with the wind in my face and the sun's rays spreading below the cloud base to the west and the car running silently all the way down to the waiting valley.

The teaching practice is a success, largely because Mr. Sturridge seems to like me, so much so as to offer me a permanent job there in the autumn term. He tells me that the kids like me too. I'm very flattered and I thank him for the compliment, but ask for some time to consider the offer.

That evening I climb up to the top of Clough Head. On the crest of the high ridge I turn back and I can see my life spread out like the valley below me: growing old like Mr. Sturridge, a village teacher, gray-headed and stooped, with worn leather patches on the elbows of my jacket, going home each night to a stone cottage on the hillside with an older Megan standing in the garden, roses in a trellis around the front door, a wood fire in the hearth, my books and my music, idealized, peaceful, devoid of complexity or worry or the vanity of ambition. Whatever is comforting about this image of a possible future, however different it is from the harsh industrial landscape of my childhood, it holds me for no more than a moment and then it is gone. I know the answer I shall give the headmaster, and as the evening draws in I make my way at a brisker pace down the mountain to my digs in the village.

> **Diary entry, summer 1973.**
>
> *It may be there in a distracted glance out of an open window or in the split second of an absent look when you speak to her, or in the guarded inflections of her voice as she replies, or in the subtle chemistry of touch or smell or the taste of her skin in your mouth, or in some unspecified sixth sense that you can't name, but when love is over, its signals are louder than disclosure, if only you are willing and open enough to acknowledge them. But of course we shake off these feelings as if they were mere irritations, as if they were unimportant and uninvited guests at a feast.*
>
> *"Not now," you say, fobbing them off with shallow excuses and feigning more urgent business elsewhere. But they linger long after the party, and skulk in a corner where they plot and fester and return to ask their impertinent questions in the still of night, when she's sleeping and wearing her child's face. When she looks so beautiful and vulnerable with her mouth slightly open, and her hair a mess on the pillow, but as you reach to touch her, she turns unconsciously away toward the window, and then the questions start again, and you can't sleep. . . .*

It's a Friday evening; I've driven back from the Lake District having completed my teaching practice like everyone else in our year, and there will be a small celebration at our friend Tim Archer's flat.

Tim is one of the stars of Megan's drama course. He has a streak of charismatic madness, which may or may not be a studied pose, is balding prematurely in an interesting, intellectual sort of way, and displays a permanent manic energy, like a demented marionette, but I suspect it is Tim who is pulling the strings. He is wearing a homemade badge with the name M. PROUST stenciled on the front. Megan and I are both very fond of him, and his pretensions are invariably self-deprecating, if not always amusing. Just about everybody in my year is there, the boys nursing cans of lager, the girls sipping cheap wine, Bob Marley singing "No Women, No Cry."

Meg is chatting animatedly with Derek, an old friend of Gerry's from Leeds. He's ruggedly handsome, with a straggly geography-teacher-cum-mountain-climber's beard and piercing blue eyes. I am talking with two girls from the English course. In such social circumstances, Meg and I feel that we don't have to be hanging on to each other for dear life; we try as far as possible to exude an air of sophisticated ease with each other, to be able to flirt without provoking comment or jealousy. I will admit that Meg is far better at this than I am, but I'm learning.

We are all comparing notes about the tribulations of what looks like becoming our chosen profession. I'm still wistfully hoping that something will turn up to prevent me having to teach, as I cast what I think is a subtle albeit proprietary glance toward Derek and my girlfriend.

Everyone gets a bit drunk and we dance a little, talking until the early hours and aware that after one more term our carefree student days will be over. I'm both relieved and in dread of the prospect of teaching full time.

Megan too has had a very successful teaching practice in Wallsend, and later that night she tells me that she was surprised at just what a tough place my old hometown is. I tell her about my job offer and my idealized vision of the future, and she smiles in response, kissing the side of my face, but says nothing.

On most Saturday evenings at around six o' clock I meet up with the other members of the Phoenix Jazzmen in the bar of the Douglas Hotel near the Central Station. We normally have a drink together and then take a couple of cars to whichever club we are playing at in the area. The drives are rarely more than an hour and I often share my car with Ronnie and Don. This is usually hilarious in that they each compete with the other about who can tell the most outrageous stories from the old days. Bands they played in, women they'd known, and ridiculous venues at which they'd performed.

"We once played a gig at a nudist colony in Cleethorpes, and they wouldn't let us wear our band uniforms, I mean I was all right being behind me drums, but poor Ronnie here with only a piccolo to protect his manhood. . . . Well, there were this old bird in t' front row with an enormous pair of . . ." etc. etc. etc.

Whether any of these stories was true or not was beside the point, they were remembering what was for them a golden age when they were young and wild, and I wouldn't have questioned the veracity of their stories for all the world. We would laugh all the way to Teeside some nights and often all the way back.

This night Ronnie and I are already in the Douglas bar playing a quick round of dominoes when Gordon, our fearless leader, walks in with a crestfallen expression on his normally impudent face.

"I've just called the agent, which is lucky because the club's double-booked us. Bastards! Anyway, we've saved ourselves a drive to Stockton. Where are the others?"

Gordon is gutted, for while we don't make very much for our efforts on a Saturday night, usually about a fiver each, it definitely keeps the wolf from the door.

"Can't the agent get us another gig?" I ask.

"Nah, it's too fuckin' late."

We resign ourselves to the luxury of a Saturday night off and wait for the others.

When it looks as if my elders and betters are going to make a night of it in the bar, I make my excuses and head off home to surprise Megan, although by the end of the evening I'll wish that I had stayed.

"What do you mean you didn't know?" says Gerry, incredulous. "I knew about Meg and Derek weeks ago, and I was in Bristol."

We are sitting in the Cradle Well bar in Jesmond, it is almost two weeks later, and there are two half-finished pints on the table between us. Gerry has quit his nightclub job in Bristol and is looking for work playing music in Newcastle. And despite the gloomy cloud that Megan has cast over my life I'm glad to see him, although he's hardly a ray of sunshine.

I suppose my old friend is trying in his own way to be helpful in pointing out my near total blindness with regard to Megan, whom I had begun to think of over our almost two years together as my soul mate and my happily-ever-after. The fact is he's making me feel a lot worse, if that's possible. I haven't eaten in eight days, I've lost nearly a stone in weight, and I haven't shaved, which is pathetic because I'm beginning to look like that bastard Derek.

"Anyway," says Gerry, "she was my girlfriend. You stole her off me."

"She was only your girlfriend for five minutes and I did not steal her off you."

He lights up a cigarette and thoughtfully blows the smoke right in my face. "Look, cheer up, it's not the end of the world."

"Isn't it?"

"No, it's not. Listen, I've heard about a gig, Andy Hudson told me, a real gig, playing in the pit in the theater. How's your reading now?"

"It's all right," I reply sulkily.

Gerry leans closer and looks around as if to make sure no one's listening. "They're doing a revival of *Joseph and the Amazing Technicolor* whatsit at the University Theatre and they're looking for a younger band, and it's real money."

"Real money?" Now it's me looking around furtively. "How much?"

"Sixty a week, for six nights and a matinee, two weeks rehearsal, and a month minimum. You in?"

I lean back in my chair, balanced on its back legs, and weigh up the paucity of my options. I haven't made sixty quid a week since Megan and I worked at the frozen bean factory.

"I'm in."

The weeks that follow are not the easiest of my life. A college is a very small place for two lovers and a cuckold, and I'm getting sick of the whispering noises behind me whenever I walk by, and even sicker of the pitying looks, heartfelt advice, and amateur psychology that comes my way between classes. Even the teaching staff are starting with their kindly wisdom routine. It's infuriating and I'm utterly miserable. When I do eventually see my mother she is shocked by how much weight I have lost and cooks me an enormous supper that I can't eat. She has the good sense not to ask what is wrong, and I don't have to tell her; she has seen the movie a hundred times. So having successfully played my mother's role in the eternal triangle, I'm now forced into playing the bitter role of my father.

◆

*Joseph and the Amazing Technicolor Dreamcoat* was written by Tim Rice and Andrew Lloyd Webber when they were still at school, and it is arguably their best work. Based on the Old Testament story of Joseph and his coat of many colors, it is retold in a series of musical tableaux, charting the fall and subsequent rise of the favorite son, who enrages his jealous brothers, is sold into slavery in Egypt, becomes chief advisor to the pharaoh, and finally is reconciled to his astonished and repentant family. Now, that's a rock-and-roll myth if ever I've heard one. The music is perfectly charming if flagrantly unoriginal, being a camp pastiche of fifties' pop, simply arranged and sweetly unpretentious. The show, expertly directed by Gareth Morgan, will be a massive success, the huge and unexpected hit of the 1974 season, and will more than double its projected run to ten weeks, each performance selling out more quickly than the last.

I am so proud that after all this drifting and treading water I have a professional, well-paid job making music. This was my ambition, and here I am turning up every night under the enormous steel structure of the stage set, finding my own music stand, its tiny light glowing among the wires and equipment and the parts for the show, waiting in the darkness as the audience files in for the evening performance.

Excitement and expectation are humming in the auditorium, in the cavelike mystery of the theater. I love the frenzy of the backstage before the show, the swirl of costumes and makeup and the glare of the mirrors as the actors transform themselves into heroes and villains, old men and vamps, calming their nerves with outrageous camp and last-minute cigarettes. I fall in love with this magic of the theater and become intoxicated by its tawdry glamour and cheap illusion, its noise and its pretense. It's not that I have any desire to be an actor, I just love being here at the center of it all, playing the bass in my dark cave. I grandiosely imagine that the whole artifice is being constructed on the subterranean foundation of this sound, the steady, grounded, invisible pulse from the instrument in my hand.

For when the lights go down and the conductor raises his baton in the silence before the first bar, nothing else exists and I am ridiculously happy.

Ewan Williams is the show's giant, bumptious teddy bear of a musical director. Ewan will wave his little white stick at us while watching the TV monitor and listening to the lighting cues on his headset as if they are the messages of God. Local legend John Hedley will be on guitar, and the equally legendary Ronnie Pearson on drums. John, who'd moonlighted with the Phoenix Jazzmen for a while, had previous to that enjoyed a briefly stellar sojourn in London with Blinky Davison's band, and long before that had been one of my favorite players on the local blues scene. John looks like a blond Hendrix, with his shock of frizzed-out white hair framing the long, lugubrious features of his face. His body is painfully thin, like that of a great skeletal bird atop two long spindly legs. He is a delightful person and an extraordinary guitarist with a wry, wizened sense of humor. John seems to have rolled with some of life's hard knocks and fallen back on simple philosophy and the therapeutic discipline of music.

Ronnie Pearson, so legend has it, turned down the Beatles when they were struggling in their early days to find a drummer. Ronnie did hail from Warrington in Lancashire, only a few miles from Liverpool, and would be about the right age, but I would never probe him about the details of this fabled story for fear of its veracity dissolving in the cold light of scrutiny, and also wanting to maintain my own thrill at this proximity to greatness. The problem for Ronnie was that this "nearly was-ness" would become a recurring motif in his life. He had walked out of the Teeside band Back Door just as they were beginning to make a name for themselves, and then later, regarding my own success, he felt he'd been left behind yet again. Ronnie is a great drummer—and that was never in dispute—always in demand as a session musician, slick, professional, able to play in any style, and is considered even among other drummers to be the best. Gerry and I are very proud to be playing under the same stage with such luminaries.

On the romantic front, having recovered from my humiliation over Megan and Derek, I am now stepping out with a girl named Lizzy, a tall willowy blonde and undoubtedly the prettiest girl in the college. This provokes an interesting reaction in my former girl-friend. Whether things aren't working out with Derek or whether she is merely chagrined at being replaced in my affections by the spectacular Lizzy, I shall never know for certain, but when she pleads with me to come back, I have the exquisite pleasure of informing her that such a thing will never happen. Straight out of the script from one of my mother's dreadful movies I tell her that I couldn't risk any more pain, where the truth is I'm infatuated with Lizzy and the wheel just keeps on turning. My heart is like a revolving door in a cheap hotel, and though Liz and I stay together off and on for a while, I am not prepared to make another commitment. It is the romance of the road that is calling me.

# 5

IT IS 1974. THE WINTER IS DRAWING IN AND HIGH ABOVE THE
city geese are migrating south, instinctively drawn by the rhythm of
the seasons and the magnetic fields of the earth. Gerry and I know
that if we don't leave soon we never will. He has become unusually
reflective lately and I know he is hatching a plan. He wants to enlist
both Ronnie and John in his new project. He already has the name
of the band. We will be called Last Exit after Hubert Selby Jr.'s har-
rowing novel *Last Exit to Brooklyn*. I suppose Gerry is hopeful that
the name will be prophetic of our final escape from the claustropho-
bia of our limbo into the big world and not of our fall into moral
and spiritual degeneracy. But the first step will be to convince our
elder brethren, John and Ronnie, to join the crusade because without them, and the legitimacy of their virtuosity, we will be a
nonstarter. Convincing them will not be so easy.

They are both a generation older than Gerry and me, and it is unlikely that either of them would give up steady professional work for
some vague promise of glory farther down the line. It isn't that they
are jaundiced, just more cautious, having grown-up responsibilities
such as mortgages and hire purchase payments. They can make a

reasonable living doing sessions and backing the better acts in local night clubs; why would they want to rough it in a van and flog their carcasses around the country for next to no money, with just the promise of an adventure? This will be a difficult proposition to sell to our two reluctant hobbits, but we do manage to coerce them into a couple of rehearsals.

The seed that would grow into the idea for Last Exit had been sown about a year before on a disastrous gig with the Big Band. We'd been booked in a support slot at Newcastle Polytechnic for a band called Return to Forever, led by jazz piano legend Chick Corea. Chick was an alumnus of Miles Davis's *Bitches Brew* sessions, but even that knowledge didn't prepare us for the coming onslaught. We had bumbled through our usual set of big band covers in a kind of swooning stupor that approximated swing but more often than not drifted like a listing galleon in a storm, three sheets to the wind. The cavernous sound of the hall didn't help either, and the rare moments of subtlety that escaped from the arrangements became lost in the vastness of the room. A few isolated hand claps from the indifferent student audience witnessing this pathetic spectacle meant that the evening was a thoroughly dispiriting experience, not least because what followed forced us all to recalibrate the scale upon which we had measured our competence as musicians.

Watching Lenny White attack the drums with an unbelievable ferocity and technique demolished our drummer's pretense that he was any more than a noisy builder of sheds, and Andy our pianist and leader was simply agape at the dazzling, even inexplicable pyrotechnics of Mr. Corea at the Fender Rhodes. We thankfully had no guitarist at the time, as I'm convinced that there would have been a slashing of wrists should any hapless twanger have witnessed Bill Connors in full flight. But it was the bass player who utterly demoralized me. Stanley Clarke, as far as bass playing was concerned, had reinvented the wheel. Pops and growls, thumb slaps and startling runs of semiquavers had vaulted the bass, often merely the plodding supporter of harmony, to the front of the band. For much of the music, Clarke's bass had become the lead instrument, with a baffling array of effects that I couldn't even imagine emulating. The one saving grace for me was that no one in the band was singing. If I could bring the level of my playing up to a quarter of what Mr. Clarke had demonstrated, and sing at the same time, I could maintain the belief that I could still be a contender in this wholly redefined universe.

Last Exit would be loosely based on what we had witnessed that night—the same instrumentation, with a similar basis in jazz fusion and the addition of a singer.

As soon as the *Joseph* run was over we began rehearsals at Ronnie's house. Our jazz rock pretensions were laced with songs by Bill Withers and Marvin Gaye, "I Heard It Through the Grapevine" becoming Ronnie's chance to sing, while I inherit Graham Bond's "Springtime in the City" from Megan and Neil Young's "Don't Let It Bring You Down." We rehearsed long and hard, even attempting some Chick Corea compositions, with bombastic sci-fi titles like "Hymn of the Seventh Galaxy," aping our heroes note for note. Being the least accomplished member of the band, I was indulged by the three others for the length of time it took me to perfect these tunes, but they must also have been struck by my tenacity.

The manager of the Gosforth gave us the upstairs room every Wednesday night for as long as we could fill it and make it worth his while to pay an extra hand to open the bar. Our first-night audience was made up entirely of friends from college and drum pupils of Ronnie's, who sat in the front and marveled at his awesome skills. My confidence as a singer was improving, and serving an apprenticeship in Andy Hudson's big band had given me an appreciation of the importance of talking to the audience. And that inclusive and self-deprecating humor between numbers could make the punters feel that they were part of the adventure, which of course they were. Ronnie and John reveled in the almost cult status that they began to command among the budding musicians who frequented the room on a Wednesday night, while Gerry and I were content to man the engine room and concentrate on writing new material for the band.

Gerry and I had moved in together in a flat in Heaton. It had two bedrooms, a living room, and a kitchen with an old miner's fireplace that had a built-in oven. Some college friends of ours named Jim and Stef had lived upstairs for a year. They were a very respectable married couple, and when they informed us that the downstairs flat was up for rent, they also told us the landlady was only interested in another married couple to take over the rooms. Short of one of us dressing up as a woman, there was no way Gerry and I would qualify, until Gerry had the brainwave of asking Megan to help us out. Megan, who'd since split up with Derek, was, despite our estrangement, kind enough to masquerade as my wife, for old times' sake, as she put it. The irony was not lost on me that the woman I'd fantasized about marrying was now using all her acting skills to pretend that we were in fact respectably wed, even borrowing Stef's wedding ring for the evening.

The ruse worked. In future, whenever the landlady turned up for the monthly rent Gerry and I would be out, and I'd leave the rent with Jim and Stef upstairs, promising via hurriedly scribbled notes that I'd see her next month, which, naturally, I never did. Gerry and I must have lived there for over two years and the landlady, whose memory I now confuse with her near-doppelgänger Mrs. Thatcher, never even knew he existed. Of course, she never saw Megan again either.

Our narrow hall was always filled with equipment: Gerry's Hammond organ, his Fender Rhodes, my bass cabinets and amplifiers, assorted mike stands, and whatever pieces of PA systems we'd begged, borrowed, or stolen. Gerry and I lived in pseudo wedded bliss, seriously falling out only once, as I remember, when I resorted to my mother's habit of throwing plates. The rivalry between us was intense, never over women as one might expect, but in our mutual quest to write new material for the band and entertain our growing audience at the Gosforth. Each of us would try to come up with at least a song per week. I always felt it was a little easier for me to write songs because Gerry didn't sing, and I could write things that were tailored for my voice, whereas Gerry could only hope that I would do justice to his compositions. We wrote in all styles and the fads and fashions that engaged our interest, often highly derivative but no different from anyone learning a craft, by imitating and shameless borrowing, even from each other. Gerry could flesh out even the crudest of my musical ideas so they would be presentable to the elders at the next rehearsal, but week by week by sheer and persistent dint of numbers my songs began to find their way into the band's pad more often than Gerry's.

It would be disingenuous to pretend that what became an increasingly uneven competition did not cause friction between us. It did. But to Gerry's credit, this didn't distract him from the band's mission. Gerry and I believed the band could make it, whoever wrote the songs. The other two may have been humoring us to a certain extent, as they never offered up any material themselves, but the band slowly began to get a reputation and the upstairs room at the

Gosforth Hotel would become packed to the gunnels every Wednesday night. We would split the door takings at a pound per head, half of which went into a kitty to buy equipment while the other half would cover expenses. It was hardly a living wage but we supplemented our incomes with other bands and club work at the weekends.

In the late summer of 1974, I receive a mysterious telephone call from a nun. Sister Ruth, now a headmistress at a school in Cramlington, a mining village north of Newcastle, had taught my youngest sister, Anita, who had been a virtual paragon of academic virtue from her first day at school until achieving a very impressive M.A. in English from Leeds University. The head, having seen my name on a list of those who had qualified to teach that year, called to ask if I was related to the aforementioned paragon. Upon hearing that I am in fact a very close relative, she invites me to the school for an interview. This development has taken me totally by surprise. I am somewhat flattered to be head-hunted in this way, even though it has more to do with my sister's prowess than my own. Up to that moment, I've had no intention of going further in the teaching profession. Then a quick glance at the dwindling balance in my current account and the unlikely prospect of a recording contract appearing miraculously out of nowhere catalyzes me into finding a decent tie, a sports jacket, and a clean shirt so that I could turn up for my interview at St. Paul's First School. I try to get out early the next morning before Gerry catches me, but to no avail.

"Where the hell are you going looking like that?" The first cigarette of the day is already burning in his hand, and his hair, while never neat, looks as if it has been ironed asymmetrically by a demented Dadaist. He is wearing an appalling floral dressing gown that would have looked too camp on Noël Coward, and an ancient pair of faded tartan slippers with a hole over the left toe. He is, in short, a sight, and he of all people is questioning my appearance. However, having been caught on the back foot, I decide honesty is now the best policy.

"I'm going to get a job."

He gives me one of his looks, as if appraising my chances, inhaling casually on his cigarette.

"Good luck!" he says, with an infuriating and unmistakable sarcasm, as he heads for the bathroom in a cloud of blue smoke, chuckling to himself like some sort of Mephistopheles.

The interview goes well despite Gerry's sarcasm, and after it I find myself with the unexpected offer of a teaching post. This is, after all, what I've been training to do for four years, to take over a class and teach them everything from basic math to soccer. I do have to remind myself that this is still part of a long-term strategy to make it in the music business, even though from the outside it probably looks as if I've caved in, buckling under the weight of conformity. I'm preparing my defense to Gerry on the way home: I know that a teacher's hours will still allow me the time to maintain my commitment to the band. Long holidays will allow us to travel farther afield. A teacher's wage, while hardly substantial, will allow me to pay the rent until the band is really up and running. There is, of course, a certain amount of fantasy at work here, sustained partially by our burgeoning popularity as a local band. In reality, though, we have as much chance of winning the lottery as we have of being signed to a recording deal. Nonetheless we manage to sustain the fantasy while the fantasy sustains us.

In September of that year I take up my position at St. Paul's wearing the same jacket I wore for the interview. Sister Ruth introduces me to the rest of the staff, a gaggle of middle-aged women in a fug of hot tea and cigarette smoke. A couple of them peer skeptically over their spectacles at me from the rustic warmth of their Fair Isle sweaters, their flat shoes, and their tweedy skirts. Their homeliness is in direct contrast to the stark severity of the sister's wimple of white linen and her black cassock. She stands there erect and defiant like an exclamation mark in a field of dull prose, a missionary from a strange and distant culture, tolerated but hardly welcomed. There is clearly an uneasy truce at work here, just below the surface of civility. I immediately sense a tension in the room between the head and her lay staff, and I realize from old experience that if I choose to survive in a situation like this, then I will need to be circumspect as well as charming.

I wonder why I have been brought into this odd little tableau. The headmistress presents me to the others like some kind of awkward trophy, and their scrutiny, while certainly not unkind, is curious and guarded. I feel like a marine exhibit in the wrong tank. Have I been brought in to break up the hegemony of this group, a joker in the pile, a wild card and something of a creature? Am I here to be the head's creature?

Perhaps I should have made a living as a spy. I say this because in my life, as I've described it so far, I would often feel that I was some kind of impostor, showing all the outward signs of conformity but holding on to a stubborn, persistent knowledge that I wasn't showing my true colors. That, inside, I simply didn't belong. Here I was masquerading as a teacher, just as I'd playacted being an altar boy, or a civil servant, or a student. I would maintain my cover for as long as possible and then it would all fall apart. Many years later I will frequently be asked if I somehow knew that I would succeed in my ambition to be a performer; I had no such prescience. It was just that nothing else I'd ever tried was going to work, I was merely treading water, but as there is some degree of performance in the teacher's craft, I didn't feel as if I was entirely wasting my time, or the children's for that matter.

There are thirty or so eight-year-olds in my class, boys and girls, the grandchildren of a coal-mining community that had been set adrift by the pit closures of the fifties and sixties, and whose parents had sought work on the new industrial estates dedicated to light engineering and office work. The unifying cohesion of a community linked almost exclusively to the mining of coal had all but disappeared, as had the colliers' cottages, the tin baths, and the mountainous slag heaps that would burn continuously night and day. There are no more appalling respiratory diseases, no more black lung, no more mining disasters, collapsed underground tunnels, or gas explosions that could wrench the heart out of entire villages, where men and boys could be lowered into the shafts in the morning and hauled out as corpses in the evening, or when the fires had died down, if they were ever found at all. The town, like my own, has a long history of bleak heroism in the face of such conditions, and it is easy to imagine the faces of these children in front of me covered in nineteenth-century grime and working ten-hour shifts in the terrifying darkness.

In spite of my worries about pretending to authority, to knowledge, to enthusiasms that will hopefully inspire the students to teach themselves, I do enjoy reading to them resonant fantasies of escape and adventure, *The Iron Man,* by Ted Hughes, *Elidor,* by Alan Garner, *The Hobbit,* by J.R.R. Tolkien. I will play the guitar for them and we'll learn folk songs, calypsos, Christmas carols, and I will encourage them to sing their favorite pop songs, from Gary Glitter, Suzi Quatro, Mud, et al., and I will recognize shy kindred souls who will be transformed by the act of performing. I borrow a pile of wind instruments from the Big Band and the kids and I have a riotous time figuring out how to get a noise out of them. We create a festival of farts and squeaks, and room-shaking blasts mixed in with a little of the basic physics of sound, but not too much. There is a noisy anarchy in the class, and while I have no idea how much the children are actually learning they seem to enjoy my company, and I like theirs. We paint and we draw and I try to have as much fun with them as I possibly can. The head will often sit in on my classes and seems to be indulgent of my method, but I do have an inkling that some of the other teachers don't altogether approve of the levels of noise emanating from 4B on the top floor.

Meanwhile, in the evenings, Last Exit are playing to packed houses. The barman is run off his feet every Wednesday night. There is a constant flow of pint glasses and empties being relayed across the room, there is laughter and applause, and just below the mist of the cigarette smoke I can see the pub manager's Cheshire cat smile, the smile of a man who has just seen a marvelous invention of his work like a charm. Gerry and I add new songs and arrange a cover or two so that the crowd doesn't see the same show week after week. There is considerable pressure on us to write new material, as it is virtually the same audience every week, but neither of us mind in the least. We both feel this is our true calling. I'm also beginning to realize that singing is the most exquisite joy. When I sing, I have total freedom to soar and swoop; it's a little like being able to fly. Of course my band mates aren't entirely convinced of my abilities, particularly Ronnie, who would prefer to sing everything himself, but I prevail because I've now written most of the original material and I'm improving week by week.

After school on Wednesdays I drive back to the flat, load Gerry's electric piano and the PA system into the back of my car, and drive back up the A1 to Gosforth, then carry the gear up the stairs, set it up, and return home to pick up my bass amp and speaker cabinet and make another journey north. It is backbreaking work that only visionaries or the insane would consider worth the effort, especially since we have to do the same thing in reverse after playing and singing for two hours. We'll usually get home around midnight, and after we've stowed the gear in the passage I'll start a fire on the old range, Gerry will break out a couple of cans of lager, and we'll perform a postmortem on the entire gig. Which songs worked and which did not, who played well and who didn't. We plot and we plan and we fantasize as we watch the glowing coals in the old fireplace until we can no longer stay awake.

The flat is full of old *Melody Makers* and the *New Musical Express* and *Sounds,* and we pore over the music press as if the keys to success are somehow encrypted in the record reviews, the tour dates, the album charts, the gossip of this magical and exclusive world. In the classified sections the small ads are of particular interest. *Wanted. Singer for heavy rock band. Recording deal, agency, management. Must have image and own PA for immediate work. No time wasters.* There is something tempting about the idea of simply walking into an established situation instead of having to build one yourself from the bottom up, but neither Gerry nor I ever answer these ads, assuming they're all placed by dreamers like us. Besides, I'm always put off by the insistence on image—*must have image.* I don't have an image. I don't have long flowing hair, and I would look stupid in the girl's clothes that seem to be de rigueur among pop's current denizens like David Bowie and Marc Bolan. Gerry and I will not satisfy anyone's fashion criteria for stardom. We look rough and unwashed. However, there have been a number of rather attractive females turning up at our gigs in the Gosforth Hotel, and although they have generally disappeared by the time we finish packing up, their numbers are increasing. I begin to practice piercing and hopefully smoldering glances from the stage and, when I feel their eyes upon me, the studied pose of the serious poet tortured by the vicissitudes of life and love.

One night Ewan Williams turns up at one of our gigs to see if we are interested in a six-week run for sixty quid a week—it is always sixty quid a week—playing for a new musical. Because *Joseph and the Amazing Technicolor Dreamcoat* had been such a financial success for the University Theatre, the board of governors have decided that another hit musical will swell the coffers sufficiently for them to continue to sponsor serious theater in the area. (Serious theater being the kind that plays to half-empty houses, by playwrights like Ibsen and Strindberg and Chekhov.) Another lowbrow musical will help them fund their highbrow mandate.

So when Ewan turns up to see if we might be interested in being the band for the show, and with such a princely sum of money on offer, our brows are as low as is anatomically possible, in fact he's lucky we don't bite his hand off in gratitude.

The projected musical will be written by Tony Hatch, pop genius and writer of classic sixties' songs like "Downtown," a huge hit for Petula Clark on both sides of the Atlantic. The production will be called *Rock Nativity* and the book, written by David Wood (one of the young actors in Lyndsey Anderson's *If* ), will tell the story of the birth of Christ, from the Annunciation to the Epiphany, in three acts. Mr. Hatch has a reputation for being a hard taskmaster, but we are full of bullish confidence and very excited at the prospect of working with a genuinely famous person like himself. We are full of projected fantasies that this will be our chance at the big time, believing that fame is a kind of positive contagion and that we too will become elevated in status by mere proximity to someone as esteemed as Tony Hatch.

There is one small problem. While the other three members of

Last Exit are self-employed professional musicians, I am now a schoolteacher. Playing for *Rock Nativity* will entail a Wednesday matinee, when I would normally be teaching in class. I say nothing to the others, because I think I can sweet-talk Sister Ruth into giving me Wednesday afternoons off and much of the run will take place during the Christmas holidays. I'll figure it out somehow.

Rehearsals begin a few weeks later. We are given the parts to learn. There is nothing particularly difficult to read but there is one passage in the overture that has me playing a repeated eight-note minor scale at an impossibly fast tempo. I put a lot of hours in practicing that scale, playing it slowly at first, and then faster and faster, but I'm still nowhere near the required speed.

Our first rehearsal is on a very cold mid-October evening. The band is set up in a large gothic hall in King's College behind the theater, and we quietly run through the parts. A 6/8 gospel ballad called "Open Your Heart" is the first song up. It is absolutely freezing in the old Victorian hall and I can see my breath in clouds in front of me. The ancient radiators are as cold and dead as dinosaur bones. I am wearing a green woolen balaclava, and all that can be seen of my face are my eyes. I think we must be nervous. Ronnie is tightening and retightening his hi-hat, John is restringing his Les Paul, and Gerry and I are staring fixedly at the parts and making sure that there are no hidden surprises. I start blowing on my fingers to warm them up, and I suppose in this hat I must look like a nervous Edmund Hillary about to tackle the South Col of Everest. This is probably why Ronnie gives me a disparaging look and a long-suffering shake of his head, when Mr. Tony Hatch walks in escorted by the director, Gareth Morgan, and the actress who will play the leading role. She is accompanied by a small brown dog.

Mr. Hatch is wearing an elegant cashmere overcoat, a tailored suit, and a neat, sober tie. He looks exactly the way he does on television, freshly scrubbed, not a hair out of place, and affecting a slight prissiness that is redeemed by a sardonic smile.

Mr. Morgan, in his anorak and aran sweater, has the barrel chest and demeanor of a Welsh prop forward, a proud bullet of a head and a thrusting jaw. With his wild red hair and the lilting song of the valleys in his rumbling baritone he is all Celtic fire. *Joseph's Technicolor Dreamcoat* was his triumph, and here he is a general presenting his troops to a visiting head of state. The young actress who will play Mary has a straggle of dark curls escaping from beneath a long gypsy headscarf, and the darkest eyes I have ever seen. Her brown dog seems to be half a corgi attached to the oversize head of a springer spaniel. He begins snuffling around the band's equipment.

We are only cursorily introduced by the director to Mr. Hatch and then the actress, who graces each of us with the briefest of glances. I am the last to be introduced, although all she can see of me are two green eyes peering through the slit of the green hat, and then she takes herself into the corner of the hall to prepare. Her dog seems fascinated by the Hammond organ. Gerry unwisely aims a discreet kick at the animal's flank when he imagines the dog is taking an undue interest and about to lay some territorial claim on the polished walnut panel of his instrument. Fortunately I'm the only witness to this act of folly.

The first instrumental run-through of the song goes well, and Mr. Hatch doesn't look too unhappy. Mr. Morgan takes a seat at the back of the hall, lights up a cigarette, and starts blowing smoke rings into the air as he watches the girl he has cast as his leading lady with a cool scrutiny. The little brown dog has by now successfully managed to cock his leg by the side of Gerry's precious Hammond and has left an unmistakable proprietary mark, but Gerry is thankfully too busy with his part to notice. Again I say nothing.

The leading lady is pacing in the far corner, quietly warming her vocal chords in the cold room. She is wearing a dark coat over a long bohemian skirt and green plastic shoes. Two large gypsy earrings frame the exotic features of her face, but it is the eyes that draw me like magnets. There is a fierce obsidian intensity about them that is as unsettling as it is compelling.

Mr. Hatch, now satisfied that we can play the tune, indicates to the actress that she should come to the microphone in the center of the hall. While this is not an audition, there is still a charge of tension in the room—seven males and one female, everyone watching, waiting. Like a diver about to leap from some great height, she breathes deeply and a mist forms around her in the chill of the room.

The song begins and her singing, at first understandably tentative, grows in assurance with every phrase, and by the final notes of the rising coda there is a nodding agreement among us that this may well work; the awkward mood in the cold room has been transformed, and we are all buoyed with a confidence that perhaps this show could be a hit and carry us along in the wake of its success. Of course I have no idea at the time, but this woman will soon play a part in altering my world beyond all recognition.

The rehearsals continue, and at least from the band's point of view, they seem to go well, although *Rock Nativity* as a whole doesn't have the innocent charm of its predecessor, *Joseph*. It all feels a little too ponderous and top-heavy, pastiche pretending to opera. The supporting cast seem unsure exactly where to pitch their performances. In the previous production they were at ease with the unpretentious spirit of the music; now they aren't at all sure how se-

riously to take it, and more important, neither does the director. Inflated with more than a little hubris by his previous successes and the
presiding eminence of Mr. Hatch (not to mention that the play concerns one of the central tenets of the Christian religion, that of the
virgin birth), Mr. Morgan's production teeters between solemnity
and hilarious parody. At least that's how it seems from my subterranean perspective beneath the stage. The full dress rehearsal before
a sold-out opening night is traditionally expected to be chaotic, in
order (so the superstition goes) that the performance to follow can
be flawless, but here there seems to be a level of panic, of confusion
and sheer incompetence that everyone knows is way off the scale for
a normal run-through.

Part of the problem is the set. It is a massive pyramidal steel structure of precipitous platforms at different levels connected by staircases, ladders, and a series of ramps, I suppose to represent the
Judeo-Christian hierarchy of deities, angels, and lowly mortals, with
musicians occupying the lowest realm of hell beneath the main
stage. Since some of the actors have to transmute between these different levels of being, as well as different levels of height and vertigo,
the staircases and ramps are dangerously congested with compli-
cated choreography and explanatory songs.

In one number the actors will begin singing and dancing on the
raked lip of the stage in front of the stalls. By the second chorus they
will have split into four separate groups, mounting the ladders and
staircases, crisscrossing the upper levels of the pyramid, weaving
chaotically through each other in an effort to make their way across
to the opposite side of the structure and all the while trying to keep
up with a score as convoluted as the set. That no one falls and injures
themselves is a miracle in itself, but the chaos is far from pleasing on
the eye. We in the band are largely invisible in the dark bowels of the

stage set, and merrily provide a brooding accompaniment to what will surely be a biblical disaster, in every sense.

Each musical number seems more inept than the last, and from my vantage point in the dark I can see the director in the second row of the stalls, alternately with his head in his hands or staring hopelessly and helplessly at the stage, his creation in ruins. His normally proud face has grown redder and redder with mounting apoplectic rage, until he finally explodes in a fearful bellow that silences the music and shakes the theater to the high rafters.

"RELAAAX! CAN'T ANY OF YOU JUST FUCKING RELAAAAAX?"

Needless to say, the director's beseeching has the opposite result, reducing already tentative actors into terror-stricken wrecks. The leading lady still shines like the star in the East, but the rest of the population of Bethlehem, including the three wise men and the angel Gabriel, seem to be laboring in a sandstorm of confused aims, inflated egos, and hopeless misdirection. No one will sleep easily tonight, and I also have a nagging personal worry that I still haven't dealt with Sister Ruth over the matinee issue.

Next day as I drive north through the morning traffic, I resolve to broach the subject with the headmistress. I shall be direct and fearless, explaining that while I want to do the best job I can at the school, my true vocation is to be a musician, and if she would just let me have Wednesday afternoons off I would try and make up for it in other ways. Perhaps organizing the carol service or directing the Christmas play. I begin rehearsing my pitch in the privacy of the car.

"Sister Ruth," I will say grandly, "I feel after my long experience in the provincial theater" (pause for effect, perhaps taking a deep breath, as if about to dive heroically into a cold pool, or offer oneself selflessly on a sacrificial altar), "that it wouldn't be inappropriate if I were put in charge of the Christmas play this year" (and considering the debacle that I've been privy to over the past weeks, I can't imagine that I would do a worse job). "After all, I do have some very talented performers in my class."

By nine-fifteen I am taking the morning register. The usual people are missing, but also one of my budding extroverts, Kevin Anderson. Kevin is a delightful lad, charming and funny, and what he lacks in normal academic skills he more than makes up for with his singing and his jokes, which occasionally err toward the blue end of the spectrum, but are delivered with preternatural comic timing.

At the break the school secretary comes in to the crowded staff room and tells me there is a phone call for me in the office.

"Helloo?" It is a high-pitched yodel on the other end of the line. "It's aboot oor Kevin, 'ees not feeling very well, ah think 'ees gorra bad coold, so am ganna keep 'im off school the day, okay?"

There is something suspiciously unconvincing about this phone call.

"Who is calling, please?" I ask, as politely as I can.

"Er . . . It's me, Mam!"

"Kevin, if you don't come in to school right now, you're going to be in big trouble, do you hear?"

"Yes sor." His voice has miraculously returned to its normal pitch.

"By the way, Kevin, where is your mam?"

"She's at work, sor, at the factree."

"Okay, Kev, come back right now and I won't say anything, deal?"

"Yes sor!"

I'm sure if Kevin had used the word *bilious* in his performance, I would have let him get away with it.

After lunch I have a brain wave. I will suggest to the good Sister that next Wednesday we should take the top two forms to the theater to see the matinee of the nativity play, stressing of course the religious aspects of the production as well as the cultural. While they are watching, I shall be able to perform my tasks in the orchestra at the same time. And when she sees what a success it all is, she too will be swept up in the magic of the theater and I shall then be able to convince her to give me some time off for the subsequent Wednesday matinees.

By the end of the run I have managed to play every single matinee by the ruse of escorting the entire school week by week and class by class to the theater, and cutting deals with the head as well as the rest of the staff.

The reviews for the first night of *Rock Nativity,* while not the ecstatic notices that *Joseph* had received, are nonetheless respectable. We seem to have averted disaster by the skin of the donkey's arse.

I am also feeling rather pleased with myself in that during the first-night party in the theater bar I have worked up enough courage to approach our leading lady. She is deep in conversation with Mr. Hatch's famous wife, Jackie Trent, and feeling too out of my depth to have anything interesting to say to either of them I decide on the strategy of engaging enthusiastically with the brown dog. The dog seems to see through me right away and glares at me with a studied indifference, and it is a while before his owner notices me.

"Och, don't mind him," she says with an unmistakable trace of Northern Irish in her voice. "He's just an old curmudgeon, an obstreperous wee git."

"What's his name?" I ask, keeping to my pretense as an expert dog fluffer.

"His proper name is 'Buttons,' " she replies. "But everyone calls him 'Turdy,' for obvious reasons."

I look down at the sad-eyed brown dog with the oversize head. "That's nice," I say, not sure at all how to take this conversation any further.

Ms. Trent by now has moved on, leaving the two of us alone with the dog, and for the first time the actress grants me a look of cool appraisal.

"You have lovely eyes," she says, handing me her empty champagne glass. "Would you buy me a drink?"

I have no idea whether I've been dismissed or if she really wants another drink, and I'm half-expecting her to be gone when I return with the champagne, but she's still there, looking cool and relaxed with her attendant dog. I offer her the thin fluted wineglass, and while she thanks me graciously, her lips display a subtle irony that is difficult to decipher.

We both sip our champagne silently and watch the social commerce in the room.

"Where's the guitarist?" she asks me out of the blue.

"John?" I say, playing for time. "Why?"

"No reason," she says calmly.

"He must have gone home to his wife," I say, after a pause and with as much innocence as I can muster.

"What a shame," she says, equally deadpan.

Her name is Frances Tomelty and from the program notes I have learned that she is the daughter of the famous Belfast actor Joseph Tomelty, and before coming to Newcastle she had starred in plays at London's Royal Court and the Shaw Theatre, as well as acted in films and television drama. She is a real actress and I suppose at first I'm starstruck, because night after night from the darkness of the band's cave I will stare up at her through the superstructure of the stage set, where she stands illuminated in a single shaft of light.

We will fall in love and within eighteen months this woman will become my wife, but as the play progressed and I became increasingly infatuated with her I began to wonder if our relationship had the remotest chance of surviving when she returned to London. This unlikely fantasy seemed to have become interwoven with the equally unlikely fantasy of becoming a recording artist, but I did begin to take the idea of the big city three hundred miles south more and more seriously.

My life at this point seems to have many different strands to it, like an improvised musical composition with the weaving and independent lines of a chaotic fugue. The ground bass of the fugue is my progress as a musician, slow but steady like a pulse; the line above it is the more complex progress of the band and the interrelationships that both weld us together and threaten to separate us. Then there is the central triad of my teaching job, my work with the Phoenix Jazzmen and the Newcastle Big Band, and the wilder flights of fancy that are my dreams of fame and fortune. These in turn are increasingly woven with the airy romantic descant introduced by Frances. Sooner or later the strains and tensions between all these disparate elements will begin to tell, and then I am going to have to make some radical, life-changing decisions. At the time, I don't have the emotional maturity to know whether I am falling in love with an idea rather than a person, and even if the distinction had been pointed out to me, I wouldn't have recognized it.

The play ends and Frances returns to London. We say our goodbyes, and I resolve to drive the three hundred miles south on the first weekend I have free.

Last Exit resume their residency at the Gosforth Hotel and Gerry and I get back to writing songs. I will write two songs in this period that will have a longer life than most, "The Bed's Too Big Without

You" and "I Burn for You." Gerry of course gives me a few of his cynical, knowing looks when I debut these songs for him, and while it wouldn't take a genius to identify the source of their inspiration, I half deny it, telling him "they're just songs" and that no conclusions should be drawn.

We don't have the easiest relationship at this time. I'm clearly defensive and he may be frustrated by my growing ascendancy, or that I'm becoming more and more prolific as a songwriter, or he may feel that my relationship with Frances is just a distraction from the band. He would deny all of these interpretations if he was challenged, and tell me that he didn't give a fuck, but we are close like brothers and we share the same dreams, so there are few secrets between us. Whatever the truth, both the new songs get a better-than-average-response from the audience at the Gosforth, and Gerry, who is as honest as anyone I've ever known, will allow them a grudging respect as well as a place in the band's repertoire.

As the songs become more complex, handling my duties as the band's bass player as well as singer presents an interesting problem. Playing the bass and singing is not as natural as strumming on a guitar and singing. There is a certain amount of neural and muscular independence required, something like riding a bike and juggling at the same time. While I certainly put in the required hours trying to perfect this combination of skills, I also begin to rationalize the bass parts so that I have more freedom to sing, leaving gaps that I would normally have filled. In doing this, I begin to develop the genesis of a style, a spare and economic bass signature that I would later justify as part of a deliberate "less is more" ethos, but it really comes out of the necessity of having to deal with my own limitations.

Last Exit now have a couple of roadies, Jim and Paul. They're not real roadies, of course, but two student punters from the audience

with a van and some electronic expertise, who don't charge us anything and are happy just to be along for the ride. It has certainly
made life easier for Gerry and myself, and paradoxically the frail ship
of our dreams feels more and more buoyant with every extra soul
who steps aboard, every extra face in the crowd, every extra pound in
the night's takings, and every extra gig offer. "Hell," we say to each
other. "Pretty soon John and Ronnie will start believing and then
we'll really be going somewhere."

It is the spring of 1975 and I am twenty-three years old. In the
months that follow I will begin to commute back and forth to London to see Frances. These are long, five-hour drives on the motorway, sometimes in the middle of the night after a Friday gig, or
sometimes driving straight to the school on Monday mornings,
bleary-eyed and unshaven. The head is beginning to notice that I'm
looking more and more exhausted, but the fact is I am blissfully
happy, probably for the first time in my life. The world seems to be
opening up for me on many different levels and Frances seems to be
the key to all of it. I will follow her to Edinburgh Playhouse, where
she plays Bianca in *The Taming of the Shrew,* and when she walks onstage I desperately want to nudge the total strangers sitting next to
me in the dark stalls and tell them that she's my girlfriend. A month
later she's playing an heiress in *The Voysey Inheritance,* and then I'll
follow her to Sheffield's Crucible Theatre, where she will play one of
the leads in *Kennedy's Children.*

On her returns to Newcastle, Frances watches my performances
with the band and afterward gives me notes on how they can be improved, how to hold the audience's attention, how to increase my
concentration and focus and instill absolute belief into what I'm doing. Gerry may quietly disapprove of these "theatrical" pretentions,
but in his pragmatic way he also believes that the band will ulti-

mately benefit if the lead singer can become a better showman. Frances begins to breathe the embers of my ambition into life, until my courage as a performer begins to look like something close to arrogance and my tentative vocal experiments begin to resonate with certainty. Whether or not I am justified is moot, but I begin to see myself as a favored nation within the democracy of the band.

6

AS LAST EXIT WE WILL MAKE OUR FIRST RECORDINGS AT
Impulse Studios in Wallsend, coincidentally above Mr. Braidford's
music shop in the old Gaumont Cinema, where I'd bought my first
guitar. The studio is the brainchild of local entrepreneur Dave
Wood, who had been influential in the early career moves of Lindisfarne, the only local band to succeed on a national level since the
Animals. The studio is primitive but efficient, and will make a name
for itself much later with the relative success of various heavy metal
outfits.

Old Mr. Braidford is long dead and the shop is boarded up and
terribly sad. I remember what a magical place it was for me as a
child, but now the doorway is a mess of old newspapers, and peering
through the wooden boards is to gaze into an empty tomb. The
whole town seems to be suffering a slow, painful death. Orders for
the tankers that had kept the shipyard and the town alive have
gradually dried up. The industry has been undercut by the heavily
subsidized Korean and Japanese consortiums, and there have been
massive layoffs of hundreds of skilled workers. A few repair jobs are
barely enough to keep a fraction of the workforce in employment.

There are no more steel leviathans blotting out the sun at the end of the terraced streets. An industry that had taken centuries to build up has been allowed to die almost overnight, and the collective skills and shipbuilding crafts of the town have been thrown onto a scrap heap of terminal unemployment. The bustling High Street of my childhood is now a deserted thoroughfare of empty shops. The economic downturn has affected my father's business as well as everyone else's and accomplished what the German bombers failed to do. Wallsend has had the beating heart ripped from it, it seems like a ghost town now, and the graffiti on the wooden boards of Braidford's music shop seem like an epitaph to another era. The old Gaumont Cinema had closed down many years before, and had for a brief period become a club called the Manhole where bands played. The club enjoyed a dangerous reputation for amphetamines and gang fights. The Ritz was now a bingo hall. The irony of beginning my recording career in the Gaumont, haunted as it was by the ghosts of old Mr. Braidford with his cleft palate, was not lost on me as I carried my bass up the stone steps.

There is nothing in those early Last Exit tapes to indicate anything but the floundering of an inexperienced group working without the help of a producer. There is no evidence of the raw, visceral power of the unschooled or the primitive punk charm of the musically inept. The tapes contain only the uninspiring bromides of competence and mimicry. If we had any potential as a band at all, it was well hidden among the acetates and the magnetic tape. We hadn't captured any of the excitement that we could generate as a live band. The recording art is learned slowly, and we were intimidated by its novelty into the prim good behavior that the wise elders of the band thought proper. I was bitterly disappointed but I kept my own counsel, not wanting to rock the boat too much. Gerry and

I would take more of a leading role in subsequent recordings, and we progressively got closer to the sound of the band at its best.

Our live show is getting better and better, and soon we will be rewarded for our improvement. Andy Hudson manages to get us a spot at the San Sebastian Jazz Festival on the Basque coast of Spain. The Big Band had played there successfully two years before and Andy had kept in touch with the organizers. The festival would take place over a week and begin toward the end of July. This is exciting news for us, our first date abroad. Our new roadies, Paul and Jim, are excited too. Now they can take their own fantasy a stage further. They estimate that it will take three days and nights to get the van and our equipment across the Spanish border. We don't have anything as sophisticated as an export carnet, so the band gear will have to be loosely disguised as camping equipment. Paul and Jim will have to suspend their macho roles while going through customs. I suggest they wear knotted handkerchiefs on their heads and learn the words to the holiday anthem "Viva España." This suggestion does not go down well, particularly as I'm going to have to miss this journey and travel to San Sebastian by air. The three days of travel coincide with the last three days of the school term, and as I've already gotten away with murder in the amount of time I've taken off school with all the theater work, I don't want to push the good Sister any further. The others of course think that I'm being grand, and even though I'm paying the fare out of my own pocket, there is an atmosphere. Gerry will rough it in the van with the roadies and the "camping equipment," and Ronnie and John will drive down in Ronnie's car.

My first year as a schoolmaster has turned out to be a relative success. I haven't been fired; I've managed to sustain my career as a working musician, developed as a performer, and kept the Last Exit dream afloat. I've arranged to meet Frances in London after the festival so I can spend the rest of the summer with her. As the plane takes off from Newcastle Airport on the way to Spain I imagine that my career too is on its way. Tyneside recedes beneath its covering of clouds as we head toward the sun. Viva España!

While my itinerary via London and Paris has been relatively painless, the journey south for my compadres has turned out to be a hellish odyssey of breakdowns, non–air-conditioned traffic jams, and absurd mishaps worthy of Don Quixote. When we finally meet up, I find myself even more persona non grata than I was already. A night of Cuba Libres and sangria lubricates me back into the fold, though, and after the sagas of the last three days have been recounted, we drunkenly help each other mount the four-story climb to the two attic rooms at the top of the pensione as if we were summitting the Pyrenees. There are three of us to a room, and I don't get much sleep: one, because I'm exhilarated, and two, because of a horrendous symphony of snoring punctuated by farts. When the Spanish sun pours through the window, I am visited by *la madre* of a hangover, but though I know we're still only tilting at windmills, I'm very happy to be here.

The big acts in the festival are Ella Fitzgerald and Dizzy Gillespie. They will play at the weekend in the huge velodrome on the outskirts of town. We will perform along with several other little bands from all over Europe in the town square in the old city, a picturesque jumble of alleyways, street cafés, and bars. There is a buzz of anticipation in the streets. We will complete a brief sound check that night along with all the other bands and then it's back to the serious business of reveling.

The citizens of San Sebastian take their music very seriously, and all the bands that play in the town square play to a packed, attentive audience. There is a bright sliver of a moon making its way over the rooftops as we launch into our opening number, Horace Silver's "The Tokyo Blues," which is Gerry's chance to shine on the electric piano, reminding all of us what an asset he is to the band. He is still our leader and all of us begin to relax when he shows himself in such form. Ronnie is all slick and flash, and John starts wailing and rocking like the blues giant he always was. With such a platform I have no choice but to give the performance of my life. After all those weeks upstairs at the Gosforth, straining my vocal chords into a flexible, resilient instrument that owes more to bloody-minded commitment than it does to any trace of finesse, I stare into the white nothingness of the spotlight and know that even if some people may find the result unlovely, it is my voice and the unique song of my life soaring on the night air all the way to the moon and back.

The Spanish papers next morning are very kind to us and there's a good shot of us on the front page. On the strength of this we are offered another week in nearby Bilbao. I am so thrilled that I attempt in my jubilation to pick up the promoter, who must weigh close to three hundred pounds. Seconds later I'm in excruciating pain. Something in my lower back has clicked into spasm.

I spend the four-hour drive to the Basque capital bracing myself against every bump in the road and cursing my own stupidity. Gerry is his usual sympathetic self, reminding me that we have a gig tonight in the city and we have to be as good as we were in San Sebastian. I try to concentrate on the rolling blue of the mountains in the distance as our little convoy heads west. Despite the pain, part of me just wants to keep going, driving from town to town, from gig to gig, never knowing what will happen next, and this seems the perfect antidote to the sedentary, settled life that could easily trap me if I let it.

It is probably the vision of this journey into the unknown that infects me with a wanderlust that will keep me on the road for twenty-five years.

By the time we have set up our equipment in the little club I can barely stand up straight. Strapping a Fender bass to my left shoulder almost causes me to double up in agony. I really don't want to let the band down, nor do I want to disappoint the promoter, who is putting us up in his large apartment. He is a large man, as I said, and feels partially responsible for my predicament. He owns the club in Bilbao, as well as a bookshop, and is something of a political figure. There is a dark political undercurrent throughout the region at this time, and we are made aware of this without understanding the historical and cultural complexities of the problem. The locals talk about the civil war and bombing of Guernica as if it were yesterday, and Franco's civil guard are perceived to be almost an occupying force by many of the population. The horrendous violence of later years is yet to erupt and there is an uneasy feeling when politics are discussed, but we are treated with the utmost courtesy and hospitality.

The promoter's wife, realizing I'm in a lot of pain, offers me two Valium. The band must play in one hour, but I'm desperate for relief, and one hour later, when I walk on the stage I'm indeed feeling much better—until I open my mouth to sing. The audience looks stunned at first and then somewhat bemused, as if the English band they've come to watch is introducing some strange new art form. I find to my horror that I have absolutely no control over the pitch of any note I sing. My voice involuntarily soars and swoops and dives like a demented police siren, turning the melodies into a roller-coaster ride of ludicrous glissandos and atonal cacophony. Some of the discerning members of the audience have their hands over their ears, others are laughing, while some earnest types seem to be taking it seriously. I turn to the band, but their dark expressions indicate that they are neither amused nor remotely sympathetic. "It's the drugs," I mouth hopelessly between verses. We manage to get to the end of the disastrous song and Ronnie will take over the singing for the rest of the evening. I am horribly embarrassed and skulk off to bed as soon as our somewhat truncated show is finished.

Some days later, as part of a Basque festival, there is a big open-air show near the beach, where we will regain our previous form despite playing through a massive thunder and lightning storm under a hastily constructed and totally useless stage covering. The heavens open after the first three numbers, accompanied by the most spectacular lightning forking and splitting the sky in a huge arc over the surrounding hills. We all get absolutely soaked to our skins, as does the audience, who seem to enjoy the community spirit of this shared catastrophe like crazed dancers in a monsoon. We have no choice but to carry on playing, for to abandon the show would seem, in the context of all this wildness, ungracious and cowardly, although I am well aware of how dangerous wet electronic equipment is when the gods decide that you will be the perfect conduit to ground a million volts. I had been electrocuted onstage a couple of years before, backing a singing comic in a nightclub, and counted myself lucky to be alive. I have an abiding memory of the audience laughing as I was thrown onto the floor, thinking it was all part of the act. It wasn't.

Since that incident I've come to consider singing as a form of prayer, and tonight I find myself singing to the sky with a pleading intensity and focus that eventually seems to placate the gods, and by the end of the show the storm abates into the rumbling distance. We have been spared, but our gear sits on the stage forlornly dripping under acres of useless tarpaulin. Now, for the first time, it actually looks like camping equipment, drowned under a sea of woes. We can't afford to replace it and we just pray that it will dry out by the time it gets back to England.

The Spanish campaign over, proudly suntanned, worldly, seasoned, and full of stories both glorious and ignominious, I join Frances in London for the rest of the summer. These weeks in London will utterly galvanize me; it is as if the air itself is charged with energy. Sitting in the back of black cabs, I will stick my head out the window like a dog to take in more of this rarefied air, as if it will infect me with success. Frances thinks I'm an idiot, but I even love the stagnant air of the Underground as we wait for the train to take us to the West End, the tunnels lined with movie posters and buskers, beggars—so many people, so many stories. I drink it all in.

This time in the city will convince me beyond any doubt that the future for the band lies here, as does any realistic notion of my relationship with Frances being sustained. The two ideas have become inextricably linked, each fueling the other like two elements in an alchemical experiment, and London will be the magical alembic where our dreams will be joined and made real. In a dizzying whirlwind of love and novelty and excitement, Frances and I see everything there is to see, plays, musicals, classical concerts, art galleries, rock gigs in pubs and clubs, and I return to Newcastle with a determination to transplant the band as quickly as possible from the safety of our little pond in the north to the opportunities of the bigger pond in the south. We resume our residency at the Gosforth Hotel, and I begin my second year as a teacher, but now I have a goal. And I know the rest of my life will be shaped exclusively by the success or failure of this goal.

Much of our equipment was indeed destroyed in the Spanish

rain, so we begin to apportion some of our nightly fees to replacing it. We manage to raise the down payment on a new solid-state PA system and some new mikes. There is some debate as to whether I should be wholly responsible for this as well as my bass duties, as I've taken over most of the singing, but I'm growing in confidence and I lobby aggressively that this should not be the case, and seeing how determined I am, the others acquiesce.

We also need to capture the energy of the band on tape, so that we can hawk the material in London, so we can get gigs in London, so we can secure a record deal in London. All of the projections for the band's future will be focused exclusively on the city whose name will become like a mantra on my lips. Gerry understands and supports my logic in this, but John and Ronnie grow silently skeptical. I can sense their resistance even when nothing is said. They have mortgages and a settled lifestyle, and I can at least acknowledge the reasons for their reticence, but if they imagine the big world is going to present itself in all of its glory at their doorsteps without them having to lift a finger, then their fantasy is more ludicrous than mine. We are a damned good band, but no one is going to notice us here, and I am now in no mood to be complacent, because not only do I have a goal but somewhere a clock is ticking.

The local media are beginning to take notice. We are interviewed on BBC Radio Newcastle, and that winter, Phil Sutcliffe, who writes reviews for *Sounds,* a London music paper, will include us in a review of Osibisa, who we support one night at the Polytechnic. I remember my excitement at seeing our name honorably mentioned at the end of his article, and thinking, "There we are at last, a tiny microcosm in the body of the music business." There is a definite spring in my step as I walk from the newsagents back to the school for afternoon classes. Phil will prove a very influential character in the subsequent story of my life.

As I walk through the school gates I notice an unfamiliar car in the car park and a disheveled-looking man smoking and fidgeting nervously at the door of the school as if he's afraid to enter. It's my father. He looks like he hasn't slept for days, or if he has, it's been under a hedge or the back of his car. The curtains of the staff room are twitching. I don't want the staff to see my dad in this state. There's a half hour before class starts and I quickly usher him upstairs into my room, where he takes one of the small classroom chairs and lights up another cigarette. His eyes are red and he looks pitiably sad. He wants me to put him up for a while, until he can "sort himself out." It is clear that the détente between him and my mother has broken down, and that he is seriously thinking of seeking a divorce. I believe he has come to ask my permission, although he doesn't quite say so.

"Why now?" I ask. "What happened?"

He stares out the window looking miserably uncomfortable, as if he's unwilling to say any more, but then blurts it out as if he's spitting bile from his lungs: "I found some letters addressed to your mother."

There is so much unsaid between my father and me, years and years of mutual denial and obfuscation, of welcoming the blinkered darkness rather than negotiating with the truth. To begin at the beginning would be a long road all too painful and torturous to take. It seems as if it's easier for him to pretend that my mother's liaison is something new to both of us, as if he doesn't want to admit that we've been living in the belly of a lie all these years.

He is desperately trying to maintain his pride as a man and a father and a husband, and to acknowledge that his children have suffered too is beyond even his courage.

I acquiesce to his unvoiced pleading, as if I've learned to understand his silences as easily as a language, but I don't ask him what is in the letters. I will not carry the charade any further than this. I offer my own silence as we watch the passing cars on the main road. He needs my help and support, but what is also clear from his anguish is that he still loves my mother, and that the rack over which he's been stretched for so many years is finally about to break him. I hug him to my chest and try to tidy up his hair as if he is my child and I give him the keys to the flat. I watch him from my window, remembering the proud, courageous man that he was, and as he climbs like an invalid into his car and drives out of the school grounds, lonely and lost and shell-shocked, I wonder how on earth I can help him.

The novelty of entertaining my father as the new lodger turns out to be more fun than I would have expected. We go to the pub together and after a few drinks he starts to laugh a little, tell me stories about the old days.

"Did you know you were conceived in the Lake District?"

"No, Dad, I didn't," I reply, a little uneasily.

"Oh yes," he continues. "Audrey and me used to drive over to Keswick for weekends, you know? Before we were married."

He's not actually winking at me, but the inference is clear nonetheless. I have no feelings either way about which side of the blanket I was conceived on, but I'm aware that my dad needs to take me to a place where he shared romance and adventure with my mother. In fact all his stories seem to circle around my mother, like birds circling a tower, the central tragedy of his life, that he'd loved her but that she'd loved someone else. I could have pointed out that if he'd loved her more, or at least shown it, then things may have turned out differently, but even then I seem to know that life and love are too complex to be contained by simple formulae, and I allow him his nostalgia.

He will return home after a few days, hopefully refreshed, to resume the uneasy truce that has sustained throughout most of the cold war. I imagine his silences continuing and my mother's frustration growing by the day, locked as they are in their melancholy dance to the scraping of a broken fiddle, sad and chronically out of tune.

My own relationship with my mother vacillates between anger and devotion in a wild arc that I feel powerless to control. Part of me wants to comfort her, while the zealot in me wants to shake her. It is this unresolved and largely unconscious anger toward her that I suppose will color and distort all of the relationships with the women in my life. My mother was the first mistress of my imagination and for that reason I am utterly devoted to her, but in my young mind she has also betrayed me. The archetype of the supposedly "fallen woman" conflated with that of the artistic muse is a complex, unconscious drama that will both inspire my work and more than often doom to failure whatever emotional commitments or promises I imagine I can keep.

My mother has still kept in touch with Deborah, who, she tells me, is working as a trainee assistant in a mental home. What my mother will keep from me in the months and years that follow is that Deborah will soon be hospitalized herself, suffering from severe clinical depression.

When I bring Frances home for the first time, I'm pleased that my mother is a little intimidated by her. And one of the reasons I'm attracted to Frances is that she and my mother couldn't be more different. My father, of course, adores Frances, but Audrey, while clearly impressed, is a little put out. Frances does not seem the type to be taken under one's wing. She is not Deborah. She is very much a woman, and Audrey sees her role once again diminished. Frances has also just secured the lead in a TV series, which qualifies her, at least in our house, for some sort of godlike status. There is, of course, some danger in introducing a higher being to my charmingly mortal though dysfunctional parents, but I don't really have any choice. Reinventing myself is tough enough without having to reinvent my parents, but Frances knows how to work a small room as well as a big one and she charms them into the agreeable good behavior expected of a supporting cast. I just don't know how long this play will run. If I am going to build a lasting relationship with Frances it can't be founded on the building codes bequeathed to me by my parents, because beneath the apparently pleasant surfaces of the family island there exists a massive, dangerous fault line that threatens constantly to shake the whole enterprise to the bottom of the sea.

At the time, I believed that I could escape the legacy of my family by force of will, or by the forward momentum of my ambitions, and Frances would be key to this transformation. I certainly didn't want to imagine that what had been seeded in me by my parents couldn't be left behind.

The year 1975 will end on both a good and bad note. Phil Sutcliffe will choose us as one of the bands likely to make it in the coming year. PICKED TO CLICK IN 76 runs the headline, and there among a dozen other hopefuls is our name: Last Exit. The bad news is that John Hedley, my boyhood hero and mentor, has left the band to take a job at Sunderland Empire. The fact that he's playing in the pit band for *Puss in Boots* only adds absurdity to this bitterly disappointing development.

Here we are, picked out of untold thousands to succeed by an important national magazine and our lead guitarist has joined a pantomime. Unbelievable. I can't blame John. The money is too good and Last Exit hardly provides a living wage for a man with a mortgage and car payments to meet. Still, I'm devastated and fearful that the bubble has burst and the dream that we'd so carefully maintained over the past year seems to be over.

It is Gerry who pulls me out of my despondency. Where I am heartbroken and utterly at a loss, he is furious, and determined that this setback, far from being fatal to our enterprise, is actually an opportunity. We have our residency at the Gosforth, and tonight we shall play as a trio. "And we'll succeed if it fucking kills us."

I have played many memorable gigs in my career as a musician, but often the most memorable shows were performed in conditions that were less than perfect, or even adverse, conditions where you felt you had to play for your life, or you had to improvise around some unexpected limitation.

Playing as a trio with Last Exit would prepare me for my subsequent role in the Police. By playing as a trio I would learn the value of space and clarity between musical frequencies, which larger bands can't help but fill. Being limited to just three instruments helps this learning process, where each has more work to do and more responsibility. It also helps to remember those who have gone before you, trios like Hendrix's and Cream. Because to do that is to be reminded of the principle, the central act of faith in the catechism of small bands, that "less is more."

Playing as a trio that night was a dogged and bloody-minded triumph that certainly thrilled the audience, and it may have taught me that to survive in this business longer than five minutes I would need to be tough, resilient, and adaptive.

We will remain as a trio for a couple of months, but the guitar at this time is the prime inspiration for my songwriting and many of those parts don't transpose well to the piano.

I have no desire to play the guitar parts myself, as I don't want to give up my role as the bass player, and so we decide after some serious deliberation to recruit a new member.

Not wanting to beg John to return after his theater run, Gerry and I set about finding a replacement. We settle on Terry Ellis, a well-respected jazz guitarist ten years older than Gerry and me but more than able to cope with our aspirations to become not only a successful act but a serious musical outfit, able to play in any style. While Terry certainly fits that bill, his inclusion in the band definitely draws us closer to the adult jazz market and away from rock and roll. Where John had been a wild man who could play jazz if he wanted to, Terry is quiet and studious and only indulgent of rock and roll. He reawakens my own interest in the classical guitar. I have hopes that the band will adapt to the delicacy of his style and that he will adapt to ours, and that together our music will become a hybrid of youthful passion and cool sophistication. And the dream will continue.

Frances's TV series has ended, and while still looking for another acting job she effectively becomes our manager, turning her efforts into a whirlwind of activity on our behalf. She calls every major record company in London and arranges meetings with their A and R departments. Armed with a new and improved Last Exit tape, she uses her engaging charm and considerable presence to get through the doors of Island Records, Chrysalis, Pye, Charisma, Virgin, EMI, A&M, Arista, Decca, as well as publishing companies and booking agents, while also sending tapes to pubs and clubs around the metropolis that have live music. It is a mammoth task, which she does alone and unpaid, even as she is still going for meetings and auditions on her own behalf. When I speak with her from Newcastle on the phone, she seems galvanized and resolute and enjoying the challenge. Why would a successful young actress devote herself to a band that lives three hundred miles away?

Part of the answer must be that she believes we can make it, and if we don't make it, or at least try to make it in London, then the relationship she and I have will be unlikely to survive the commuting distance between the two cities. And part must be that she loves me, and if it should go any further she doesn't want to be stuck with a failed Geordie musician with a chip on his shoulder. Part of it must also be the joy of role-playing. Frances certainly isn't the normal supplicant type that record companies are used to seeing cringe at the door, and if someone as impressive as she is believes in us, then we, the band, must have something to recommend us, even if the tapes don't set the room alight. Some of the companies do become interested enough (probably more in her than us) to offer to send a representative to see us in Newcastle, or to see us if we play in London, or at the very least would be interested in hearing more demo tapes. Dave Dee, ex-policeman and formerly the singer with Dave Dee, Dozy, Beaky, Mick & Tich, famous for such sixties' classic hits as "Bend It" and "Zabadak," was now an A and R man with Atlantic Records. He was interested enough in our tape to ask if he could hear more of our work.

Frances telephoned us with his address at Atlantic Records, telling us to send a cassette of our latest songs, and that she would then organize a further meeting. Gerry and I excitedly send off a cassette to London and a few days later receive an unexpected reply.

*Dear lads,*

*The next time that you want me to listen to your music, please make sure you include the actual cassette along with the case, it's difficult to judge the musical merits of an empty box.*

> *Best Wishes*
> *Dave Dee*

Gerry and I are too embarrassed to send another tape.

One of the agencies Frances sends a tape to is the Sherry/Copeland agency. The latter name will come to play a large part in the rest of my life, but on this occasion we get no response.

It is early evening and I am standing in the public phone box in Heaton Hall Road. I've just put the phone down after speaking with Frances, who is in London. I am staring at my image in the tiny square mirror above the receiver. I suddenly look older than my twenty-four years. She has just told me that in seven months from now I'm going to become a father, and if ever there was a time in my life to assess the reality of my feelings, then this was it. But I am too stunned and confused to be able to do so. I am still staring into the mirror, wondering how I should feel? In hindsight one of the most wonderful events of my life has been foretold, the birth of my first child, a miracle gifted to his mother and I, and yet at the time how could I have foreseen this? A smattering of rain has started to fall outside, but as I walk back to the house, nothing seems real anymore, my life, my ambition, the bricks on the wall, the slates on the roof, or the rain on the pavement. I am watching myself from a great distance, and I have nothing within me that I can recognize as an emotion.

I will drive to London as often as I can on weekends when there are no gigs, trying to sketch in the lines and colors of our possible future and then drive the three hundred miles north and manage to get back for the school bell at nine on Monday morning. I am torn between my dreams of escape and an impending reality that threatens either to entrap me or vault me into another unknown universe. But there is a stubborn streak of fatalism in me, a feeling that the die has been cast and that I will deal with whatever fate has in store for me. Frances, against her better judgment, eventually agrees to marry me, and now I have to make this work, I can't lose courage now.

While a couple of record company reps do come and see us in Newcastle, whatever lures or bait we dangle in front of them in the way of songs, virtuosity, passion, and commitment, we don't really get a bite. They sniff around us cursorily but nothing more. There is something else in the wind as well. Our push to be recognized in the big city will coincide with a sea change in the musical taste of the nation. This is a polemical and violent reaction to the moribund corporate pop music that has dominated most of the seventies, and is led by anarchic bands like the Sex Pistols, the Damned, and Eddie & the Hot Rods. These groups play aggressive, basic rock and roll, derivative of three-chord American thrash bands like the New York Dolls, the Stooges, and the Ramones. Last Exit, having just signed a quiet, "arty" jazz guitarist, are as far removed from this new movement as a party of country bumpkins hopelessly trying to make a belated splash in town while wearing last year's clothes. While I'd trained myself out of an affinity with such music by always playing with older, more sophisticated musicians, the anger and the energy emanating from these groups is something I feel in my bones. The aggression in this music may be little more than pantomime faux, but it is nonetheless effective in challenging the complacency that has up until this point hung like a shroud over the music business.

In this new climate it is difficult to get very much interest in our music, which the record companies seem to consider too sophisticated for the current taste. They are polite and appreciative, but it is clear that we are not what they are looking for. The only company to show a genuine interest is Virgin Publishing, part of Richard Branson's burgeoning empire. Virgin's publishing director, a petite blonde named Carol Wilson, loves "I Burn for You," the delicate waltz I had written for Frances that has proved so popular with the audience at the Gosforth Hotel. The song is tender and romantic and may as well be a madrigal played on a lute, so distant is it from the current fashion for raucous anthems of disaffection. Despite this, Carol still wants us to come to London and record some songs with a view to signing us to a publishing deal, hopefully as a first step to securing the band a recording deal.

Needless to say we are over the moon. An expenses-paid trip to London, recording in a big studio, and just the simple compliment of being taken seriously by one more person in the big city is enough to set our heads spinning. The recording date is to take place four days before my wedding, as if in fateful confirmation of the twin symbiotic and romantic dreams that I had been nurturing for over a year now.

As it turns out, Pathway Studios in Islington, North London, is hardly the futurist palace of technology that we had imagined as we drove south on the M1 in the rented van. In fact it is not much better than the studio in Wallsend. Pathway is a tiny room somewhat smaller than the circumference it takes to swing a cat, with an even tinier control room. Sad scraps of soundproof paneling hang loosely from the walls and a filthy, threadbare carpet is patterned with food stains and cigarette burns. We feel right at home immediately, and set to work laying down about ten tracks in an afternoon. We just play through the songs as if we are performing a live show, using none of the multitracking facilities to layer the sound. The music is raw and honest, but lacks any studio luster, density, or real power. The engineer looks a little bemused that we have managed to tackle so many songs in the limited time available, but in our proud, and I suppose provincial, way we want to demonstrate just how versatile we are. If we had been more experienced, we would have realized that versatility is not something the record industry values at all. What they are looking for is something singular and fresh. We don't yet understand that versatility is a premium for nightclub bands and journeyman musicians, not pop acts.

The next day is one of mixed fortune. Carol, despite the sketchy nature of the demos, can hear the value in the songs, and she offers us a publishing deal. It is a fifty-fifty deal, wherein the publisher takes half of whatever royalties the songs generate. For example, when a record is sold, the royalty earned is split down the middle between the artist and the songwriter. The publisher then takes half the writer's share. As we don't have a recording deal at the time it all seems academic to us. We just want someone to help us out, and if it means signing away fifty percent of an improbable future, then so be it. We are told this is a standard contract, and as none of us has ever seen a publishing contract before, we look suitably grateful, hoping this is a significant step toward realizing our dream.

Carol takes us all to lunch to celebrate at a little restaurant in Notting Hill, just around the corner from the Virgin offices in Portobello Road. She tells us that she will take the demos across to the record company after lunch, and we all feel confident that with the publishing wing of the company supporting us, then perhaps the recording wing will at least take us seriously, if not sign us up there and then. What we are naively hoping for is a big enough recording advance to allow us to move our whole operation to London, find affordable places to live, buy a van and some better equipment, and begin a new life dedicated solely to creating music. Only the record company can provide this; for their 50 percent share, the publishing arm is offering us free studio time at Pathway, but nothing else.

We return to the offices later in the afternoon, where Carol gives us the bad news. The record company has in fact turned us down. We are not the kind of thing they are looking for. Carol seems genuinely disappointed, but we are all pretty sanguine about it, as if we had half-expected it. Suddenly this had all seemed like too much to hope for. Carol promises that should we sign the publishing contract, she will continue to work on our behalf, and try to get us more gigs in London and encourage other record companies to listen to our demos. She also tells us to have our lawyer look at the contract before we sign it. On the long road back to Newcastle, we clutch the publishing contract as if it were some kind of trophy. As the countryside flashes behind us like the fleeting promise of our grandiose hopes, Gerry starts to laugh quietly.

"What's so funny?" I ask.

"I'm laughing that Carol would think we'd have such a thing as a fucking lawyer. I can't even afford a pot to piss in, never mind a fucking lawyer. Who does she fucking think we are?"

I nod in solemn acknowledgment of Gerry's ever-superior grasp of reality.

"I have a lawyer," Ronnie pipes up rather pompously from the back of the van. Ronnie is now into his third Carlsberg Special. "I shall take the contract to him first thing Monday morning and have it looked over properly."

"Shite!" says Gerry. "It's just more money down the drain. Gizza beer, will ya?"

"It's not shite," replies Ronnie sullenly, "it's just good business sense, something neither of you two have. What do you think, Terry?"

Terry, the other wise elder, is asleep like a child, his face pressed flat against the van window.

I've been driving for four hours now. We are approaching the end of the M1, about to commence the last hundred miles to Newcastle, when Terry wakes up.

"What do you think, Terry?"

"About what?"

"About the fucking contract."

"I don't know, what do you think, Sting?"

"Well, I was just imagining that in six years' time, say, after we've sold millions of records all over the known world, that fifty-fifty deal will translate into millions and millions of pounds for Virgin Publishing, unearned, mind you, apart from a few donated hours in Pathway Studios. And we'll have to sue Richard Branson in the high court, at great personal expense, in order to regain our most valuable copyrights."

"Fuck off, Sting," says Gerry, exasperated.

The argument will continue for much of the remaining journey, but we all end up agreeing that beggars can't be choosers, no one else is going to look at us, and we're lucky to have someone like Carol rooting for us in London. We agree to let Ronnie take the precious contract to his lawyer on the Monday following my wedding.

What Ronnie doesn't tell us is that his lawyer has never seen a music business contract in his life, and while perfectly adept at the efficient conveyancing of deeds for house purchases, he has as much experience arguing the points and percentages on a publishing deal as he has of the arcane legal complexities of canon law. When Ronnie brings the aforesaid contract to the attention of his legal genius, the latter looks at it curiously, shrugs, and claims that it looks okay to him. Now, aglow in the comfort and security of the best legal advice that twenty quid can buy, and fully satisfied that we are not being ripped off, we duly sign the fifty-fifty contract, and the rest will be court history.

On the night before the wedding, we are having a small gathering in the lounge of the old Grand Hotel on the seafront. Frances's family have booked rooms for the weekend: Joe Tomelty and his wife, Lena, and a few actor friends who have trained it up from London. Joe is seated in a big leather chair by the open fire. He is very much the old stager, leaning on his walking cane like a prop, ruddy-faced and cheerful, grinning widely under the shock of his white mane and with the same piercing dark eyes as his daughter. Lena is more reserved, a little shy even, and not in the least theatrical.

My own parents are on their best behavior, although they do seem ridiculously young, like juvenile actors playing older roles, and it strikes me that they've always seemed that way.

They are, of course, of a younger generation to Frances's parents, but their posed approximation of stability seems sadly transparent to me.

My handsome brother, Phil, is watching all of this with the sardonic detachment of an Elizabethan rake at a pantomime, amused but hardly entertained. Does he doubt that I can make this work? He says nothing, nurses his beer and toasts me silently with one raised eyebrow and half a grin.

My best man will be Keith Gallagher. We have been drinking buddies for over ten years now. When he left school at fifteen he became an apprentice at Parson's, the huge engineering works in Byker, working himself up from the shop floor through night school to a degree in mechanical engineering. He is truly a self-made man and has long been my champion and arch-encourager of whatever musical talent I might possess. Keith has always believed in me, especially when nobody else did, and that is why he is my best man. As I'm the first person in our peer group to get married, he has put his faith in me again as some sort of pioneer.

Gerry and the band are there, and some of the guys from the Phoenix and the Big Band. We huddle around the piano and I sing a few songs for my bride-to-be, then I return alone to my parents' house stone-cold sober.

St. Paul's is a simple parish church overlooking the banks of the river Tyne as it flows resolutely into the powerful and contradictory swells of the North Sea. Below the church stands the Collingwood Monument, dedicated to our local hero, the great Admiral Collingwood, who was Nelson's second-in-command at the battle of Trafalgar. It is a fine, blustery, northern day with a mild southwesterly breeze blowing and the sky is an enormous dome of translucent blue. I can almost hear Nelson's most famous admonition as Keith and I walk purposefully into the old churchyard: that England expects every man to do his duty; and so we will.

It is not a grand wedding, but the church looks pretty, decked out with spring flowers and shafts of midmorning sunlight filtering through the stained glass. I'm wearing a blue corduroy suit and a tie, and I'm nervously happy. Keith has the ring I bought in Portobello Market last weekend. I know it is secreted safely on his person because I made him check his pockets in the car, but somehow he looks even more nervous than I do, as if it were he entering this strange ritual and not me.

Gerry is playing the old organ at the back of the church, some two-part inventions by J. S. Bach that he's kindly and diligently been perfecting for a week or so. His feet are pedaling furiously to keep the bellows full, and like the proud musician he is, there's a look of intense determination on his face that he won't make any mistakes.

The church is a third full. Frances's family and friends are on one side, mine on the other. As Keith and I walk down the aisle I see Buttons the dog at the end of the second row wearing an oversize blue velvet bow around his neck, looking utterly miserable, as if someone has stolen his bone. I give him what I think is a reassuring pat on the head, but he growls at me with quiet menace and is shushed by Lena.

My mother is already crying, though she smiles at me brokenly, her face swollen and shining with tears. My father just stares at the crucifix above the altar. My grandmother looks thrilled to be wearing her new hat, and old Tom just looks as if he'd rather be somewhere else. He's made an effort, though; his hair is neatly parted and battened to his brow.

While Keith and I wait, I resolve that, just by sheer force of will, marriage for Frances and me will not turn out as it did for my parents. Gerry plows doggedly into another prelude, but it is dramatically foreshortened as the bride and her father appear at the doorway. Our errant organist improvises a stately march as they enter. Frances is wearing a simple white shift of cotton with delicate flowers in her dark hair, and her eyes are fixed on mine. Now everyone else has turned as well. My mother's weeping enters a second stage of intensity. Lena gives her a thoughtful look across the aisle. Joe Tomelty is walking stoutly at his daughter's side, beaming at everyone on either side of the aisle.

The priest keeps the ceremony light, and apart from Keith's momentarily fumbling with the ring, it goes smoothly. Frances speaks her vows with an actor's assurance and I try to follow suit. It is done now. As we make our way down the aisle as husband and wife, Gerry can contain himself no longer and breaks into "The Tokyo Blues," discomforting the devout among the celebrants but amusing the hell out of me.

We hold a small reception in a restaurant across the road and Joe makes a succinct, charming speech in his stage Irish: "They told me that if I should ever be making a public speech like this one, that I should stand up, speak up, and then shut up!" and with that, he promptly sits down again.

After a few embarrassed speeches and awkward best wishes from people unused to speaking in public, it is time to leave. Frances, the dog, and I climb into the car with everyone waving to us from the pavement as if we were setting off on an Atlantic voyage. We are actually driving sixty miles north to Bamburgh Castle. One night in a small hotel is all that we can manage in the way of a honeymoon, but our room overlooks the magnificent castle on its ancient volcanic crag between the flat gray sea and the sand dunes. It was built by the Saxon king Ida and is where Roman Polanski filmed *The Tragedy of Macbeth,* only a few miles south of the holy island of Lindisfarne. A fortress on a cliff top is a dramatic symbol of strength and resilience, as well as a violent history, and perhaps not the most romantic location to represent the beginning of a marriage, but it is an image that will stay with me, its ambiguity becoming clearer as the years pass. Bamburgh is also the birthplace of Grace Darling, another maritime hero, who risked her life in a small boat, rowing out in an appalling storm to rescue the surviving crew of a sailing ship that had foundered on the Longstone rocks south of the Farne Islands. The incident became a nineteenth-century cause célèbre and the young Grace the personification of female heroism. The tiny rowboat is still there in the museum and looks too frail to have survived the elemental sea and the storm at its worst. This image too will stay with me.

It feels different being married, as if we have suddenly become strangers again, shy with each other, a little afraid and tentative, where in the church in front of our families we had played our roles with such surety. We will spend the afternoon walking around the ancient churchyard, marveling at the ancient weathered gravestones among the lilac trees, calculating the lifetimes of the dead. Some lives had been cut tragically short, others lived well into old age, then there were couples who had died in the same year, one after the other, as if life was no longer worth living alone. Life seems so random, so temporary. We both realize that we are no longer playing games, and that marriage is a frightening commitment, and that we will have to be careful with each other. A cloud briefly obscures the sun, just as a chill northeasterly breeze picks up and shakes the blossoms from the lilac trees, and drives us inside.

## 7

I AM NOW RESOLUTE THAT THIS WILL BE MY FINAL TERM AS A schoolteacher, and the fact that we will be expecting our first child by the end of the year makes me even more determined to make the move to London. Would people less driven than Frances and I have reacted differently to the news of a child? Wouldn't the normal reaction of a young couple have been toward safety and security, and having a roof over our heads? The pregnancy instead provokes the opposite reaction, a spur to movement, almost a call to arms, and whereas in the past the responsibility of fatherhood had terrified me, there now seemed a rightness in the timing that forces us to put our trust in fate, and summon our courage.

But we also know that the old clock is ticking and we will have to make the break this year or we will be stuck here forever.

In the meantime, the band are offered yet another bible-based rock musical at the University Theatre. This one is prophetically called *Hellfire,* which will soon become edited in the band's shorthand to *Hell.* The subject matter is the perennial struggle between good and evil. There are the good angels and the bad angels. The good angels wear costumes of feathery, fluffy chic, showing lots of leg and winged ankles, while the bad angels wear a sort of celestial biker chic, all chains and leather, again showing lots of leg and big black boots. The bad angels are charismatically led by one gay actor playing Lucifer, writhing around the stage like a pole dancer at every opportunity, trying I suppose to tempt the good guys into his version of what looks to me like a gay disco. However, the fact that the good angels are also led by a charismatic gay actor, writhing only slightly less lasciviously than his satanic counterpart, in his own version of heaven, seems to defeat any reasonable logic or the chance of any traditional moral purpose. God will be played by a six-foot-tall gay Nigerian named Chris, who sits above the action singing the words "I am, I am" in ominous tritones, often sadly flat. Why all this pseudoreligious claptrap needs to get in the way of a perfectly workable good disco/bad disco story, à la *Flashdance,* I shall never know. Meanwhile, we are contracted for a six-week run, and while *Rock Nativity* may have proved itself to be no work of genius, we will remember it as if it were Verdi's finest, compared to this fiasco.

After a week of rehearsals I realize, like a whore on her second night, that I am doing it solely for the money. My father had always warned me not to end up down the pit—of course he was talking about the coal mine, not the orchestra pit, or the pit of hell, although there are parallels. The money, of course, is not to be sniffed at. Once again sixty pounds a week added to the pittance I get as a teacher adds up to a decent wage, and with a child on the way, putting some money in the bank would seem prudent. Particularly as I shall be resigning very soon from the only steady job I have.

Frances has given up her flat in London and moved into bachelor chaos with Gerry and me, but the place is now looking much better from having a woman's presence. I've painted our bedroom all white with a blue floor, Frances has bought new bed linens and curtains, the flat has a newly scrubbed look, and we have started to replace the furniture that we had foolishly burned last winter when we ran out of coal. We do have one embarrassing encounter with the landlady, who miraculously finds us home one Sunday morning for the first time in two years, as our lunchtime gig has been canceled. In fact it's the first time I've seen the landlady since Megan and I pretended we were a married couple and got the place, having always left the rent upstairs with Jim and Stef.

The landlady, who really does look like Mrs. Thatcher, the current leader of Her Majesty's Opposition, is curious to see the property after so long, and thank God the place looks better than it did a few months ago. After inspection, she seems satisfied, and I am just about to get her out the front door, when Frances walks in from the newsagents and introduces herself as my wife. The landlady is confused, to say the least. Frances looks nothing like Megan, in fact they couldn't look more different. Frances maintains a disarming smile, while the landlady looks from her to me with mounting puzzlement.

"She dyed her hair," I offer by way of some explanation.

Now it is Frances's turn to look puzzled. "No, I di—"

"See you next month then, Mrs. Thatch—er, see you then?" I hurry her across the step and manage to close the door before she can object and this incident gets out of hand. Frances is still looking at me strangely as through the new curtains I sight the landlady stopping in the path and turning, as if she's considering coming back in.

*Please, no . . .*

Thankfully, she changes her mind and turns to get into her car, still shaking her head and now looking, perplexed, at the front door. And then she is gone.

Gerry, who up until that point has been sleeping in, and doesn't even officially live here, emerges in one of his dressing gowns with a scarf around his head. He looks like Marley's ghost.

"Who was that?"

"Mrs. Thatcher."

"Shite, I forgot."

"So did I."

Frances is still smiling, but it is also clear from her expression that she is looking for some sort of an explanation.

Gerry and I reply, in practiced unison, "Don't ask!"

We shall continue to be consumed by the torments of *Hellfire* until mid-June, but not until we have fallen out with the cast, who seem to think it's our fault that they can't keep in time with the music and have taken to stamping their feet, winged or booted, on the stage above our heads to demonstrate that we are playing out of time and not them. As we are being conducted by a musical director with a white stick and a metronome, there is nothing much we can do. Now that the cast have stopped speaking to us, and I've fallen out of love with the theater, this is indeed the last time I'll work in the pit.

We resume our residency at the Gosforth on Wednesdays, with a new Monday night slot at the Newton Park Hotel. Andy Hudson has been something of a guardian angel and has gotten us some dates in the Newcastle Festival, the biggest of which is a support spot with Alan Price at the City Hall. Some honchos from London have promised to come and watch us strut our stuff. With Carol Wilson's help, Frances has continued to rustle up interest among the record companies.

To be a local support act is akin to entering an old pre-democratic subspecies of humanity that was thought to have died out with slavery. As a new member of this subspecies, your self-image is reduced to that of one belonging to a lower caste, a caste of untouchables, lowlifes, invisible men, and ciphers of minute significance. For the privilege of walking onto the big stage, however, there are few performers who haven't suffered this humiliation at some point in their careers, willing to trade the denigration of their fragile egos for the vague promise of the spotlight and a few minutes of attention.

The harsh facts, though, are these: No one has paid to see you, and the devotion of those who have paid is generally exclusive to the star of the show. This singular devotion, while flattering to the star, will preclude any chance that they will be interested in watching or listening to the local support act. More likely they will be in the bar quaffing lager while you're bleating your heartfelt songs to a cavernous and empty room.

As you now belong to the subspecies, you will rarely be ushered into the presence of the star, or even those close to him, but you will invariably have to deal with the roadies in his entourage in order for you to get your equipment on and off the stage as efficiently as possible. The roadies, generally "nasty, brutish, and short," to quote Hobbes, know that they too are members of a lower caste, but not quite as low as yours, and this differential allows them to exercise that uniquely human characteristic of making your life even more of a misery than is theirs. I have seen equipment thrown carelessly from the stage and swept aside like so much refuse littering a street before a royal parade. I have heard words that I'd hitherto thought to be only apocryphal—"Get that shit out of here"—as the amplifier I've sweated and saved for is unceremoniously booted into the wings so that the Star's pristine, hi-tech equipment can be gracefully wheeled into place. However, not unlike lowly officials in the medieval church selling indulgences, it is in the granting of sound checks where these serfs can exercise their truly malicious power.

To walk onstage without having first checked your equipment is about as advisable as jumping out of a plane without having first checked your parachute. It needs to work. The sound levels need to be balanced and you need to be able to hear yourself, as well as the other members of the band. This takes a little time.

The star's equipment will have arrived at some point in the afternoon. The roadies will be ostentatiously tinkering with whatever seems to be the latest piece of technical wizardry to have arrived from the future. They will continue tinkering and posing with these scientific miracles until the Star deigns to arrive, to perform his or her sound check. The Star is invariably late, if he or she bothers to turn up at all, and the Hobbesian serfs will keep up the pretense of tinkering until minutes before the doors are supposed to open, leaving you little time to ascertain that your antediluvian technology is at least working. These are not the best circumstances in which to prepare for an important showcase intended to impress record companies.

In this case the star of the show, Alan Price, the keyboard alumnus of the Animals, has arrived and has commenced his sound check. He is dressed in an impeccable linen suit, cool and cosmopolitan and utterly unapproachable. He is, of course, a local man, raised in Jarrow, but hasn't lived in the area for years. (If you can recall, it was his seat I inherited at the tax office.) Mr. Price is an excellent musician and he puts his band through its paces, changing a few arrangements, checking the monitors and the mikes, rehearsing a new number. We are waiting in the wings, patiently seated on our equipment, but time is marching on toward the opening of the doors. He runs through the new number once more and now there seems to be a problem with his keyboard, which precipitates more tinkering until the band can begin again. Everyone is, of course, oblivious to our needs for the evening as the clock gains inevitably upon the hour. When they begin the number yet one more time, Gerry and I begin to shuffle on our careworn speaker cabinets, staring anxiously at our watches. The Hobbesian serfs are looking at us with a smug "can't be helped" expression—"The master's at work, he can't be disturbed"—when I am witness to a sight I shall never forget.

Frances, who is up for the week from London, and has been seated in the hall watching Mr. Price rehearse, is now leaving her seat and striding purposefully with her long legs and high heels toward the stage. She is still not visibly pregnant, and is looking officiously at her watch as she mounts the stairs, a look that signals clearly that if the star's minions so much as think of impeding her progress they will be making a terrible mistake. Gerry and I can't believe what we are seeing, nor can the roadies. We are all openmouthed. She is certainly impressive, sophisticated, elegant, and not to be messed with. As she approaches the piano at the center of the stage, I watch as her face assumes an impermeable mask of confident charm, and when Mr. Price eventually looks up I can see that he is at first shocked and then not a little intrigued.

"What the fuck's she doing?" asks Gerry under his breath.

I'm unable to answer, so fearful am I. Mr. Price is famously cantankerous. Even now he is trying to convince the muscles in his face to glower, but he can't quite manage it, so powerful is Frances's presence. She speaks to him quietly, out of earshot, and now pointing with authority at her watch and gesturing toward us at the side of the stage. Mr. Price is suddenly transformed from a glowering martinet into a compliant, eager schoolboy. He closes the piano lid and tells the band to quit the stage so that the support act can have a sound check. The sullen roadies cover their precious equipment in black drapes while Gerry and I gleefully carry the Hammond on-stage. We are almost dancing as we place it proudly in front of Mr. Price's piano. Frances has now returned to her seat, and I mouth a grateful "Thank you, I love you" from the stage.

We play, as expected, to a virtually empty hall, but there are some record company types from Island Records, Virgin, and A&M sitting with Frances in the Royal Circle. We play extremely well and I ignore the empty seats and sing straight at the center of the spotlight, imagining a throng of seventy thousand, which is okay until the end of a number, when all that can be heard are a smattering of almost derisory hand claps.

We leave the stage feeling pleased that we have done our best, while the hall fills up for the main act. A few minutes later Frances arrives backstage with the record company people.

We receive measured congratulations on our performance—enough, anyway, to make us feel that we haven't failed.

"You're definitely getting better," says one. "Oh yes, definitely better," says another. "Yup," says the third.

Then there is an awkward silence, which continues a little too long, but nobody feels like breaking it. Everyone starts taking undue interest in things like shoelaces and posters on the wall, until the man from Island says, "Except"—we wait expectantly—"except you didn't really get the audience going, did you?"

"You were the fucking audience!" says Gerry.

"Yes," he replies absently, "I suppose we were."

There are only a few more weeks left at school when I tell the good Sister I'm leaving. She is a bit taken aback when I hand in my resignation, even though matters had become somewhat fraught earlier in the term when the awful *Hellfire* matinees had clashed with my teaching commitments. She had indulged me over this, much to the irritation of the other staff, and perhaps she expected some form of loyalty from me in return. It had always struck me that there was something playfully childlike in her character, and that part of the tension between her and the staff, who were all married with children, was these fundamental differences of personality and life experience. She was far happier in the company of children, and I suppose to a large extent I fitted that description. I'd tried to explain to her over most of the last two years that I couldn't see teaching as my life's vocation and that it was music that was my passion, but she could never understand how music could be anything more than a hobby. She had been indulging my fantasies because she liked me, or because my eccentricities amused her, or made her feel less isolated. When she finally realizes that I'm serious about giving up my job, despite the fact that there is a baby on the way, she will play her final card. Shaking her head sadly, with the exasperation of someone who can't make head nor tale of an argument, she offers this:

"But you'll lose your pension."

I look out the window across the playing fields at the vans and lorries heading south on the motorway and I'm silent for a while.

"I'm sorry, Sister, it's what I want to do."

I spend a great afternoon with the kids and at four drive back into Newcastle with all the windows open and singing at the top of my voice. My elevated mood is further enhanced by the news Ronnie gives us later that night at the band rehearsal. He's managed to secure the band a job on a P&O cruise ship for the summer, and this will put some money in the coffers for the last big push toward London at the end of the year.

# 8

THE S.S. *ORIANA* WILL SET SAIL FROM SOUTHAMPTON ON THE seventeenth of July, which is fortuitously the day after I finish school, and we will be entertaining the passengers as the Ronnie Pearson Trio, and not as Last Exit. This, of course, is no career move. We will be playing covers, cocktail music, tea dances, and Old Time Night, which I suppose is the geriatric ballroom dancing that I've become so familiar with in my odd apprenticeship. The money, however, is exceptional, and Frances can see perfectly well that though we shall miss each other a great deal, since she is no longer working, her man will have to go to sea and bring home the family bacon. Because of the pregnancy she has gone from being a strict vegetarian to a rabid carnivore, so the bacon will come in handy. I am beginning to absorb the fact that we really are going to have a child, and it's hard to keep anxiety for the future at bay. We plan to meet up in London when the job is over.

Ronnie has worked on these cruises many times, all over the world, and he warns us that we'll have to be smartly attired and polite to the passengers. Gerry and I are wondering why he's directing this warning at us. However, as we are now temporarily members of the Ronnie Pearson Trio and not Last Exit, we promise to maintain his high standards.

"No, Cap'n, ye can keelhaul us or make us walk the plank, to be sure, but we won't let thee down," we cackle, touching our forelocks and crouching in mock deference.

Ronnie is singularly unimpressed by our Long John Silver impersonations and tells us that this is a serious job, for serious money.

"Aye-aye, Cap'n."

So we pass our medicals and secure seaman's cards, and become official members of the British Merchant Navy.

The *Oriana* was built in 1957. She is forty-two thousand tons, eight hundred feet long, and can accommodate over two thousand passengers. Her superstructure is painted a creamy off-white. She has sixteen floors, seventeen public rooms, eleven passenger decks, swimming pools, and a tennis court. She has over nine hundred crew members, including us.

I am very excited to be walking up the gangplank with my guitar case; if only my dad could see me now, he'd be proud of me at last.

The ship is like an enormous floating city delineated by class, the upper decks used solely by the first-class passengers and the bridge officers; the lower decks, by second-class passengers, deckhands, maintenance staff, cooks, and cleaners; and below them the denizens of the immense engine room.

I have a small cabin in the bowels of the ship, with a single berth, no porthole, and plain metallic walls. There is a small man from the island of Goa in Southern India, named Michael, who will clean my room and do my washing. He tells me that P&O have a deal with the people of Goa, and that he's saving up to buy a guesthouse back home, but that he and the other Goans aren't ever allowed abovedecks during the voyage. The entertainment staff, however, are able to move freely around the ship between the decks. Sometimes we'll play dinner music for the captain's guests and then finish off the evening farther down the ship, entertaining the second-class passengers.

Ronnie will be doing most of the singing, which is fine by me, as I don't know a lot of cover material. I'm perfectly happy just to play the bass, although Ron does get irate when I mess up on one of his songs and accuses me of not taking the job seriously enough. I do take his point, but he is starting to sound like Captain Bligh.

We play about three times a day in different locations on the ship, carrying our own gear from the restaurants to the lounges, the ballrooms and the nightclubs. Between these spots I spend my time reading on some quiet part of the deck, whenever I can find one. I've decided to tackle Melville's *Moby-Dick,* as it is suitably nautical and dense enough to last the whole voyage. I'll read a paragraph and then gaze dreamily off the bow as the gray of the English Channel turns to the blue of the Bay of Biscay.

It is in this bay that we experience our first storm. The sea has been choppy all day, but by the evening we are in a full and dramatic ocean swell, the ship rolling from side to side and then pitching forward erratically. Luckily, I've never been prone to seasickness, but we are unfortunate enough to be playing our set in the ballroom at the stern of the boat, right above the propellors, where the pitching and rolling seems to be the worst. Ronnie's drum kit is set up on a small carpet, and as we play, it proceeds to roll backward and forward over the smooth wooden floor with the motion of the ship, and from side to side. As I'm just standing, I can sway with the rocking ship, and Gerry's piano is tied down, but poor Ronnie can hardly control his drum kit as it careens around the stage. Whenever he reaches for the mike to sing, it is either swinging away from him or heading back toward him at speed and threatening to hit him full in the face, which is understandably turning from an embarrassed red to a bilious green. The fact that he can play at all in these circumstances is a tribute to his skill as a drummer, as well as a sailor. I'm just not sure how long any of us can keep this up. Every so often I'm sure I can hear the propellers below us ride above the surface of the ocean with a sickening angry roar. The last few intrepid souls attempting the fox-trot have since given up, and the dance floor is now empty.

The ship's purser is peering at us from the corner of the room, a look of surly amusement on his face. He walks across the ballroom floor, seemingly unfazed by the horrendous pitching of the ship. It is uncanny. He is walking as if he were on dry land, and stands in front of us as relaxed as if he were standing in the middle of Oxford Street. It is this, as well as his rather smarmy grin, that starts me feeling a bit queasy.

"All right, you can stop now, nobody's listening."

He is just about to turn on his heel when he begins to stare at my feet.

"What are you wearing on your feet?"

I look down stupidly. "Tennis shoes, sir."

His mouth assumes a malicious sneer that wouldn't have looked out of place on Captain Ahab sighting his white nemesis, but seems oddly disproportionate on the ship's purser in the face of a pair of tennis shoes.

"And why are we wearing those?" he asks, checking at the same time that the others are wearing their regulation black pumps.

"They're more comfortable, sir."

"I don't give a stuff how comfortable they are. If I see you wearing them again onstage, you'll be off the ship at Gibraltar."

"Yes sir."

He exits across the dance floor in the same eerie way he crossed it. Now Ronnie is glowering at me.

"I told you, you're not taking this job seriously enough. Now he's got it in for us."

The ship continues to roll for the rest of the evening and I spend a fitful night in my cabin, dreaming about the *Pequod* and the white tennis shoes.

The storm has abated by morning and I take a brisk walk around the main deck. I like being at sea. I like the perpetual forward motion, the idea that a journey might never come to an end. The air is getting warmer as we head south, and I think of Frances back in England. She's given up a lot to marry someone like me. I think about the baby growing inside her, and I wonder what it will be like. I wonder what kind of father I'll be. I don't want to have the same relationship with my son as I had with my father, but he was trapped—yes, that's the key. If I never allow myself to be trapped like him, then everything will turn out differently. But then I begin to wonder if I'm crazy. I just have to keep moving, that's all, like this ship.

I'm awoken from my reveries by the sight of Gerry heading toward me. He looks worried. "Ronnie's really pissed off with you," he says, tugging anxiously at his cigarette.

"I know he is," I reply.

"The purser just asked to see him in his office, we've been taken out of the ballroom tonight. He wants us to play in the crew's mess."

"Yeah, so?"

"Ronnie seems to think that it's some kind of punishment."

"Why?"

"Dunno."

That night, with the western coast of Spain twinkling on the port side, we carry our gear down to the lower and lower decks, and then farther down as the staircases narrow, where there is no natural light, past fearsome bulkhead doors at the end of long steel corridors, until we finally emerge into the noisy, suffocating hell of the engine room. We are suspended on a swaying gantry above six massive turbines, built by Parson's of Newcastle, with the combined power of eighty thousand horses. There is something ridiculously incongruous about carrying a piano through a ship's engine room, the images and the technologies simply don't gel. We are strangers in an alien land. The stokers below us stare up with expressionless, sweat-stained faces as we struggle ludicrously with the upright piano on the narrow and precarious bridge. On the other side is where the crew's quarters are situated, and their mess is a dingy common room with a tiny stage at the far end. There is a card school of Goans at one table, a couple of guys playing dice, a darts game. Everyone stops to stare as we fall into the room with the piano. There are a few seconds of silence and some tension, and then on cue they resume their games as if we didn't exist.

"Nice," says Gerry, managing some irony while looking around in the gloom of a bare lightbulb strung from the low iron ceiling.

"We've played far worse clubs in Sunderland," I remind him.

We deposit the piano then make the return trip for the drums, back through the engine room, through the bulkheads and the long corridors, staircase after staircase until we reach the bracing air of the upper decks.

By now, the crew's mess has undergone something of a transformation. The bare lightbulb has been replaced by a mirrored disco ball, and while the room is still dingy, a few scattered lamps glowing red and blue give the place something of a festive air, like a grotto.

The Goans are still playing cards as we tune up, not interested in us at all, but the rest of the crew are beginning to arrive. They arrange themselves around the edges of the room nursing drinks, and I notice there are quite a few women among them. At least I think they're women, the room is so dark.

We start with a little instrumental, to break the ice, a jazz waltz called "Way Down East" by Larry Adler. It's Gerry's feature and I've always liked it. The music coaxes a few couples to the dance floor in front of the stage. It is only now that I realize the women I'd been so pleased to see earlier all have tattoos, and enormous biceps, and muscular thighs sprouting incongruously from Chinese dresses with dragon motifs, slit to the groin, and stockinged legs teetering on enormous stilettos. There are blondes and brunettes, the odd redhead in full makeup, false eyelashes, extravagant earrings, and full red lips.

Ronnie looks as if he has been expecting this all along and displays a kind of smug stoicism as he delicately applies the brushes to his snare drum like a pompous chef whisking an egg. He's still pissed off with me. He thinks it's my fault we're down here and not entertaining the captain's table in the first-class restaurant.

I'd gotten used to the lighthearted camp of the theater, enjoying the outrageous humor, the fun and genuine gaiety of the actors, but this is something different, something darker. Despite the feminine clothes and the makeup, these types look seriously tough. You wouldn't want to cross any of them for fear of having your arms and legs broken. There is a couple in front of the stage who are beginning to worry me a little. He is dressed as an old-fashioned matelot, with a blue-and-white striped sweater, tight bell bottom trousers, and a white neckerchief. There is a lurid, painful-looking scar running from his nose, under his cheekbone, and all the way to his earlobe. "She" is in a red satin Suzy Wong outfit, an auburn wig, nail varnish, black stockings, and red high-heeled shoes. They are slow dancing in front of me, and each time "she" turns, she pouts at me lasciviously with languid half-closed eyes and a flaring of her nostrils as if she's trying to catch my scent. When her boyfriend turns he glares at me darkly from beneath a single black eyebrow, his scar glowing livid in a continuous line from the thin malice of his lips. They continue to turn, alternately offering me seduction and destruction, like a spinning Janus. One part of me thinks this may be a regular psychodrama they indulge in to get each other off, another part of me is preparing for a fight, when from the corner of my eye I recognize the purser and his greasy smile, obviously enjoying the spectacle from the back of the room. The rest of the band seem oblivious to my predicament. I ask Ronnie if I can sing the next number, he says yes, and we begin "Friend of Mine" by Bill Withers.

I'm singing because I've learned from experience that when I sing I become fearless, as if there is something in the act of giving voice to a song that makes me feel invincible. I also have a Fender bass in my hands, and should there be a fight, it is as good a weapon as it is an instrument. However, the uptempo song and the warm sentiment of the lyric seem to change the mood in the room. Everyone starts rocking, the moody lovers in the front seem to be having a good time at last. The Goans are still playing cards, but we definitely have the makings of a great Last Exit gig. The purser skulks back to the upper decks, and we have the best band night of the entire voyage.

Soon we are in the Mediterranean, heading due east past Gibraltar and the Pillars of Hercules, past the Balearic Islands, the south of Sicily, and then the Greek islands. I sit on my quiet corner of the deck looking out at the fabled isles as if they're floating in a trick of the falling light between the golden sea and the sky. I imagine Odysseus searching for his home, and his wife Penelope fighting off suitors and waiting patiently with her only son, Telemachus, but my reverie is suddenly broken by a loud announcement on the P.A. that there will be bingo in the second-class lounge at 7 P.M. prompt, followed by the Mysterious Madame Calypso, a female contortionist, and a one-eyed python.

Having had such a success in the crew's mess as Last Exit, we are feeling a little more confident about giving it another go. The night before we dock at the Turkish port of Izmir, we are due to play in the large ballroom at the stern of the ship. There will be a mixed crowd there and enough young people for us to risk running our true colors up the mast. Ronnie can see the logic here and agrees to the change of plan.

The band's playing is fresh, muscular, and unshackled. It's not that we are playing with any more volume, it just seems that way. The crowd goes from bored indifference to genuine excitement, particularly among the younger crowd at the front of the stage and spreading out toward the back of the room. I feel in fine voice, having spent most of the voyage singing backup for Ronnie, with the result that I'm even more strident than usual. I'm beginning to feel invincible again, a quality I've heard described so many times as arrogance but is simply the joy of singing, and tonight I'm having a ball.

We play for forty minutes to much applause, but during the break the purser pays us another visit, bristling because I'm still wearing the hated tennis shoes. He gestures over to a group of dowagers at a large table under the crystal chandelier.

"You, Mr. Tennis Shoes, you will stop singing now," he whispers menacingly. "You're upsetting some of the lady passengers over there." And with this he transports the most obsequious, slimy grin across the ballroom to the flustered maiden aunts who are fanning themselves beneath the chandelier and nodding their assent.

We resume our former guise as a lounge act. The younger elements of the audience disappear and I quietly resolve that the next time I sing on a ship, I'll own the fucking thing.

# 9

"ODYSSEUS" RETURNS AT THE END OF THE SUMMER AND "Penelope," waiting on the Southampton dockside with a hired van, is now visibly with child. It has been one of the hottest English summers on record, and carrying all that extra weight can't have been comfortable, but she looks splendid and so happy to see me. We drive back to London to stay with her friend Pippa in Battersea, and the next day we leave for Newcastle, this time determined that when we return to London in the new year, it will be for good, although how we are going to survive financially, I do not know.

During our final season in Newcastle we have lots of gigs, our residencies are thriving, and we're playing colleges and universities as far away as Sheffield and Leeds. Carol Wilson has even booked us some showcases in London, at the Nashville Rooms in West Kensington, at the London School of Economics, and at Dingwalls in Camden. Although we still have a little left from the ship to keep us solvent, we don't make much money. The harsh reality is that I no longer have a salary or an institutional safety net, and Frances can't work at all.

I begin to keep a diary in earnest for the first time in my life, attempting perhaps to elevate my anxieties to the level of drama or poetry and render them less frightening by fashioning them for the page, as if they were just a story to be told in the security of the future. But I feel like a raw recruit on the eve of a battle, and while the prose may at times be purple, I am not shamed by its intent.

*The long autumn is over, and there is a cold Baltic chill in the air this evening, our child has turned around in his mother's belly and I hear the wind in the telephone wires above the house and the first brittle songs of winter.*

*Our son seems determined to be born into a world that is unfinished. There will be no convincing of him that now is not the time.*

*And yet, not three streets away, and only a week ago a boy was kicked to death by a gang of skinheads. I suppose they would have chosen their victim randomly, and after the scant pretense of some imagined slight, offended by his aloneness, by the insult of his difference to them, they would have thrown him to the ground and are now each struggling to land a blow to his head as if it was a football, afraid to murder alone, afraid to stop, afraid to think, and unable to hear his cries for the desperate singing in their own heads. "I belong, I belong, I belong," they sing with every blow that falls, removing an eye and half of his teeth in a gushing spray of blood and snot, and driving his septum like a stake up into the frontal lobe of his brain and stamping his collar bone like a broken twig, again and again and again, until maybe a door opens or a car appears on the street and then they are running, running, running like a pack of dogs. The slower ones desperate to catch up in their clownish boots, sweeping in wide arcs around the corners, and past this very house and across the bridge of the train station, and then slowing down to*

*a nonchalant pace, regaining their breath and their insolence,
and skulking home in ones and twos, as the life drains from
their victim and the ambulance arrives too late. It makes me
weep.*

*Yet still my boy has aimed himself at the world, poised like an
artillery shell waiting for his moment, whether we are prepared
or not.*

Inside the Newton Park Hotel there are only a few punters in isolated
corners of the room. Mondays are always like this, but tonight I am
distracted and anxious. I can't get inside of the music and singing fails
to bring me the usual courage. The contractions began early this afternoon, gently at first and then strong and stronger. I've left Frances
at the General Hospital on the West Road. She seems calm and confident and is happy to let me go do my job, but I know that she has
an actor's habit of appearing unruffled regardless of whatever turmoil
there might be beneath the surface. While she assures me she will be
fine, I feel uncomfortable. The ward Sister confirms to me that nothing will happen before midnight, and herds me out of the room like
an unnecessary hindrance. After the show the others kindly relieve
me of my transport duties so I can drive straight back to the hospital.
I am terrified and excited and as usual I can't help myself projecting
into the future, to protect myself, as I've always done in times of
stress, where this ordeal will just be a story, and everything will have
worked out fine. I try to imagine how Frances must feel, her body in-
vaded by this other being. Is she certain this is what she wants? Is she
afraid? Or has instinct taken over? Are there chemical imperatives
that impose the necessary calm and the stoic acceptance of the in-
evitable, as if in giving birth there is a kind of death, a giving up of the
ego? But I'm just a man and I can only speculate as to where such
courage comes from; I shall never know.

I know the route to the hospital well enough to get there blindfolded. I used to take this road to school every morning for seven years, and now look at me, I'm going to be a father.

The Sister keeps me in the waiting room for a while; she seems to be used to treating men as barely tolerable nuisances, like children. I see screens being removed from around Frances's bed and then I'm marched in. Nothing has happened, except that the contractions seem to have stopped, but Frances appears to be in fine shape. She tells me that I look exhausted, and I feel slightly ashamed that she's going through this ordeal and I'm the one who looks terrible. She smiles and tells me to go home, get some sleep, and come back first thing in the morning. The Sister confirms that nothing will happen until tomorrow. I skulk out of the ward, feeling useless, overwhelmed, and in awe of women.

When I get back the gear is safely stacked in the hall, and Gerry is sipping thoughtfully at a can of beer in one of the armchairs by the fire. He offers me a spare one and I give him the latest report from the hospital. We sit silently with our own thoughts, watching the fire. I suppose because Frances and I are leaving for London in two months, Gerry is reasonably sanguine about the growing population in the house. At first it was just him and me and the equipment, then came Frances and the dog, and now a baby. I'm sure he is as grateful as I am about the feminine touches around the house, but it's going to get pretty congested around here soon and we are going to have to make compromises. But none of these thoughts are voiced, we just sit sipping our beers in the firelight, as we always used to.

He and I are a strange pair. We are close but not too close; good friends but hardly inseparable. We have been thrown together by our ambition, by a passion to make music, and by expediency, but there has always been a subtle level of tension between us. I know that there are things about me that annoy the hell out of him, just as there are things about him that piss me off. We are different, that's all: we think differently, we react differently. My dreamy optimism about the future will often fall foul of his blunt, down-to-earth honesty. Our agendas may dovetail much of the time but they are beginning to unravel.

I began in this relationship as a kind of apprentice, and now the dynamic is changing. He is without a doubt a better musician than I am or ever will be, and will tell me, only half jokingly, that if he could only sing he'd fire me. But he does have a growing if grudging respect for the songs I am beginning to write, and that I'm finding a voice to express them, and this both delights and frustrates him. I enjoy the competitive edge between us, but maybe that's only because I seem to be winning. Would I feel the same if things were the other way around? I doubt it. Still, whatever problems we have, there remains a bond of respect and mutual need between us, and we'll all be living in London soon, and we're going to make it, and nothing else will matter.

When I wake up next morning, I know there's something wrong. The light in the room is wrong. I feel wrong. I never sleep in; my father and his milk round cured me of that forever. When the sun rises so do I. It is unthinkable that I would have slept in, but there is still something wrong. The noise in the street is wrong. This is not how the street sounds at seven in the morning. My eyes are now wide in terror, thinking the unthinkable. I turn my head slowly to find my wristwatch on the bedside table. I blink at it disbelievingly, shaking it in my hand, blinking at it again. It is five to one. My first thought is that is must be one in the morning, and then slowly dawning logic presents the certainty, and full horror, of my predicament. I have slept for twelve hours, probably for the first time in my life, and I have almost certainly missed the birth of our child.

I leap from the bed and burst into Gerry's room. It is empty. I rush back, get dressed, and run upstairs to knock on Jim and Stef's door to use their phone (we still don't have one). There is no answer. Of course, they're working. I race to the phone box at the end of the street and feverishly call the hospital. My fingers can barely find the holes on the old-fashioned dial. The phone rings for an eternity. Finally I get through:

"General Hospital, can I help you?"

"Yes, the Maternity Ward, please."

"Putting you through."

Another eternity.

"Maternity Ward." It is the Sister, the one who thinks all men are useless pests.

I take a deep breath. "It's me."

"And who might you be?" I can tell that she knows exactly who it is, she just wants to play me like a fish on a hook.

"It's Frances's husband."

"Ah!" This now gives her full permission to torture me like an angler exhausting a heavy catch. There is a long silence as she lets out more line.

"And where might you have been, young man, while your wife has been laboring so?"

I can't take any more of this. "Sister, please, do we have the baby, are they okay?"

"Yes!" I can feel the tug of the hook in my stupid mouth.

"Is it em—?"

She does not allow me to finish my sentence, or take any initiative in this struggle at all. She answers abruptly, "You have a very healthy wife and son, and it's no thanks to you. Where were you?"

I ignore her question. "And Frances is okay?"

"She's fine!"

"Can I come and see them?"

"Visiting isn't till five-thirty, you know that."

"Please, Sister!"

Now that she has landed me breathless and humiliated, she can afford some of her largesse. "Get over here right now!"

I race across town to the hospital, double park, and rush down the corridor, bursting through the double swinging doors of the maternity ward like a saloon gunfighter, where I am greeted by a sight that is both joyous and also leaves me slightly chagrined. My brother is in the center of the room, holding the baby, grinning in his usual infuriating manner as if he's got one over me, firstly because I'm half a day late and secondly because my son looks exactly like him. I am in no mood for his innuendos, lighthearted or otherwise.

Thank God, Frances looks pleased to see me. My brother relinquishes the baby and we have a family moment.

"I'm so sorry. I don't know what happened. I slept in, and I never sleep in."

"Never mind. Look at your son, he has beautiful eyes."

"Yeah, he's beautiful," says my brother from across the room, "just like me!"

In the years since then I have tried to work out why a man who is never late for anything, and who rarely lies in bed after sunup, would sleep in and miss one of the most important events of his life, the birth of his first child. I should have slept in the corridor. I shouldn't have listened when they told me nothing would happen and I should leave. The baby was born only a few hours later, at 1:30 A.M. If only we'd had a telephone.

Perhaps I was truly overwhelmed, and way out of my emotional depth, and the child within me withdrew into sleep and wouldn't come out until it was too late. Frances may have forgiven me but I never quite forgave myself.

We bring him home the next night, to the freshly painted room, where I sit and stare at him cocooned in his cot, snug and warm while his mother sleeps. I marvel at the flawless perfection of his fingernails, the lines in the palms of his hands, like details in a work of art, the exquisite ridge between the flaky translucent skin of his lips and the softer wetness of his open mouth. But I am haunted by the image of the dead boy on the street and I try to push it out of my head as I watch my son, but it keeps returning and returning. He too must have looked this way once.

There are delicate blue veins on his closed eyelids, and I listen to the soft air in his nostrils and the drum of his heart beating and watch the faint rise and fall of his chest. I wonder how I should protect him, and I imagine the pack of boys who ran like baying dogs across the bridge must have all looked like this once too, vulnerable and perfect. There is some rain on the window and I close the curtains on the dark street.

My mother, of course, thinks that it's already Christmas, the new baby held close to her face. My father rolls his eyes to the ceiling as she starts cooing gibberish at the drowsy child lolling like a drunk in her arms. He is, of course, "dead chuffed," he just expresses it differently, and being a grandfather for the first time takes a little getting used to.

"I don't think I'm old enough to be a grandfather, am I?"

"No, Dad!"

I'm exactly the same age as he was when he became a dad, and we are watching each other like two men in a hall of mirrors.

He sees his younger self when he looks at me, just as I see an older version of myself when I look at him, graying at the temples, his hairline receding to a tonsure at the back of his head—though he is still a very fit man, his job has kept him trim and athletic where vanity alone would have failed him. He doesn't seem to mind that we've named our son Joe, after Frances's father. Ernest, after all, seems far too Edwardian, although the little girl born next bed but one in the maternity ward is blessed with the ponderous, and I would suspect, difficult-to-live-up-to designation of Ms. Chastity Fawcett.

Everyone loves Joe, and his arrival allows all of us to climb out of our trenches and indulge in a rare family hug with the baby as our tribal totem, a conduit receiving and transmitting the affection we would normally find so hard to express or accept. Perhaps Joe also arrived as a talisman, a harbinger of change, because shortly after his birth a meeting occurs that will eventually alter the direction of our lives.

Last Exit is picking up a momentum that augurs well for our move to London. Gerry and I are feeling more and more optimistic. Two days after Joe is born we begin a whole week of gigs. In addition to our two residencies, we play in Redcar, supporting Jon Hiseman's Colosseum and acquitting ourselves well, then play an extremely successful gig at Newcastle University, the Polytechnic Ball on Friday, then St. Mary's College on the following Sunday. Toward the end of the St. Mary's gig, which is in the college refectory, our only ally in the music press, Phil Sutcliffe, turns up and stands watching from the back of the room with someone that I don't recognize. After we've finished our last few numbers and a couple of encores they come over to talk and I meet the stranger, a tall American named Stewart Copeland, drummer with the well-known London band Curved Air. He has long brown hair and a handsome chiseled face with a prominent jaw and a confident demeanor. Phil has just been reviewing Curved Air at the Mayfair Ballroom and asked Stewart if he was interested in seeing the hot local band.

Phil goes to pay his respects to the rest of the band, leaving the American with me. I can't help feeling that he's sizing me up. He says that he was very impressed by what he saw tonight and if I should be in London anytime soon to give him a call. I'm flattered but notice that he doesn't pay the same compliment to the other members of the band. I put his number in my pocket, then he and Phil disappear into the night. As we pack up, the band ask me who the tall guy was and I tell them, but I don't mention the phone number he gave me. I don't really know why, I just have a selfish instinct that I shouldn't.

When we get back Frances is feeding the baby and after Gerry has crawled off to bed I tell her about the tall American and I show her the phone number. She tells me it's a Mayfair number, and must be a pretty swanky address. I write it carefully in my diary as if it's a mysterious cipher to be decoded.

The following week, my best man, Keith, will marry Pat, his childhood sweetheart, and now it is my turn to be his best man. With typical foresight he has organized his stag night two days before the wedding and, apart from the location—the Ford Arms in Byker—I have only one memory of the evening: playing the piano blind, from a supine position on the floor, with my nose pressed to the pedals and my arms stretched above me. I'm told it was rather a successful effort, but then no one else in the room was sober either, and I have never managed the feat since.

### Diary entry, Sunday, December 12, 1976

*Disaster, Terry announced tonight that he's been offered nine weeks in* Dick Whittington * *at Sunderland Empire. What is it with these fucking guitarists and their pantomimes, we are cursed, first John, now Terry. Well we survived without a guitarist when John went off, but how will this effect our move to London?* Dick Whittington *will run til February, and if that wasn't tragic it would be funny, "Twelve o'clock and still no sign of Dick."*

*I want to strangle our guitarist but Gerry does point out after our initial disappointment that if Terry has some money in his pocket then he'll be more likely to make the move to London. I tell him that this Dick Whittington is leaving for London on the first of the year, Terry or no Terry.*

Last Exit will play their final gigs in Newcastle in January of 1977, in the bar of the University Theatre. It is a bittersweet triumph, the culmination of two years of creative effort, rehearsing, arranging, songwriting, arguing, falling out, making up, saving on food and clothes so that we could buy equipment, and then the backbreaking

---

*Dick Whittington is a pantomime farce based upon the life of London's celebrated lord mayor of the fifteenth century. Legend paints Whittington as a poor orphan who comes to London because he believes the streets are paved with gold. His black cat is his only possession, and he works as a scullion in the home of a rich merchant. Distressed by ill treatment, he runs away but is called back to London by the sound of Bow bells, telling him to "turn again." Which he does, eventually becoming the wealthiest man in the city, and then its lord mayor.

The real Whittington was no orphan, but a very successful businessman and a great benefactor of the city of London. He died in 1423 and left his vast fortune to charitable and public purposes.

In the play, he is traditionally played by a female actor in thigh-high boots, while all the older female roles are played by male actors in drag. I have no idea why.

labor of humping it in and out of vans, up and down stairways, hoisting it onto stages, setting it up, breaking it down, repairing it when it didn't work, driving all over the north of England, sleepless nights back and forward time and again to London for no money, and all for two hours of playing and singing and trying to convince people that we had a chance, that we could be contenders, asking people to be part of the dream that we could make it. We realize that tonight is the end of an era for us, we have taken this dream as far as it can go in this environment, and either we go on to greater things or we die. It is early evening; the theater bar is empty as we set up our equipment against the back wall beneath large black-and-white stills of the current production. David Rudkin's *Sons of Light* is playing in the main house.

There is some tension among us, although unspoken as we busy ourselves with wires and plugs, string changes and the tuning of drum heads. It is Terry's night off from the pantomime, and although he has another six weeks of the run to complete before he is free, the understanding is that when it is over he will come to London along with Ronnie so that we can take our adventure to the next stage. The uneasiness that Gerry and I share is that neither of us can quite believe that this will ever happen, as if our elders are merely humoring us in our fantasies, but unwilling to shoot us down in flames, hoping perhaps that we'll come to our senses, realize that we are onto a good thing here, plump for security, and forget our dreams of moving away to make it.

And so, although Gerry and I have come tonight to bid farewell to our friends and supporters, Ronnie and Terry are hoping that we'll be convinced to stay. Once the gear is set up, the four of us sit in the corner of the bar nursing our beers and our private dreams as a crowd gradually assembles around us. There is a palpable air of expectancy; it is going to be a big night regardless of what happens at the end of it. Everyone turns up, and as the room fills to capacity it becomes impossible to greet everyone. I catch sight of my brother at the far end of the bar giving me one of his sardonic, silent toasts, ever supportive but always tempered with a gentle mockery. My brother loves me—of that I have no doubt, he doesn't need to verbalize it, never has, and probably never will—but the fact that he is here tonight means more to me than a thousand words.

It is time to take the stage. I test the microphone, tapping it nervously to bring the room to order. "Ladies and gentlemen," I begin tentatively and perhaps a little formally, but nonetheless needing to make some kind of clarifying statement. "Tonight is a special night for us, and sadly it's probably our last gig here for a long time. We're off to London tomorrow, to see if we can make a go of it in the smoke." There are a few derisory cheers, encouraging whistles, and not a few glasses raised in our honor. I can't help but notice that Ron and Terry are staring blankly at the walls.

We begin our set. "The Tokyo Blues" as usual gets the room moving, and after a few numbers the applause builds and builds and you just know that it's going to be a great night. Perhaps for Ron and Terry, the better we go down the more likely it is that we'll be convinced to stay put, but for Gerry and me the mood in the room seems to be willing us on to greater things, telling us we can do it, as if the fans too have a stake in our journey south. It really is the most heartening feeling to be supported in your madness this way, and I'm absolutely determined that I will neither let these people or myself down.

We leave a cheering, stamping crowd, ebullient and raucous, yelling and yelling for more and unwilling to let us leave the stage. The two opposing parties in the band could each claim victory in this ambiguity, but discretion seems to be the sensible course.

"Great gig!" says Ron as he unscrews the nuts at the top of his cymbal stands.

"Great gig, Ron." I nod in agreement, but nothing else is said.

The next day the local television station offers us a spot on the evening news to say good-bye to the area. We play my suitably ironic song, "Don't Give Up Your Daytime Job." This is our first TV performance and I'm so nervous I forget the second verse, so I sing the first one twice, and recover nicely for the third.

When it's over I say good-bye to the band, and that I'll see them as soon as they can make it down. Gerry gives me one of his direct gazes, while Ron and Terry shuffle awkwardly, but I'm already halfway to London in my head and nothing can stop me now.

It is nighttime on the M1 south. In the car are Frances, myself, little Joe asleep in his carry-cot, and the dog. We have a couple of bags of clothes, two guitars, and a wicker rocking chair belonging to Frances, and this is all we have. We have no jobs, we have no house, we have hardly any money, but we are elated because this is what we have been planning for a year. I feel as if my real life is only now beginning and that everything before has been a kind of random apprenticeship for this moment. Every mile that passes takes me farther from the past, the confusion and isolation of my childhood, the emotional cul-de-sacs, the distractions and false starts, so that now as we head south, I can remake myself in this new world. I have this growing suspicion, though, that the band have no intention of following me. They will watch how I fare in the metropolis, certainly, but apart from Gerry I can't see them slumming it, or taking a risk with their lives, uprooting themselves like this, and I don't blame them. They've worked hard to achieve their security and they don't have the guardian spirit and ally that I have in Frances. I ask myself what making it really means. I know I want to make my living solely as a musician, but I also want to be recognized as someone unique, defined by my voice, by my abilities as a songwriter, to have the world know my songs and my melodies just as they had known and acknowledged the songs of the Beatles. I want to do this on my own terms, I want to be singular, and if that means being marginalized, then so be it. I will become stronger, and even if no one else knows who I am, I shall know myself.

My wife is asleep on my shoulder, the baby oblivious to the adventure and the dog no doubt wondering where in the hell we are going now, as the night falls around us and the commuter traffic disappears from the motorway.

# 10

PIPPA MARKHAM IS FRANCES'S CLOSEST FRIEND. THEY HAD
been young actors together and now she has begun a new career
as an agent. Pippa has kindly offered us her living room floor on
Prince of Wales Drive in Battersea, a series of mansion blocks running along the south of the park. She lives on the top floor at the
back of the building and so doesn't have a view of the park, in fact
she has no view at all, but the two-room flat is pleasant and tastefully
decorated. We are grateful to be able to have a roof over our heads,
taking over the sitting room until we can find a place of our own to
rent.

The morning after our arrival I wake early, as usual, and after the
baby has been fed I take him for a walk in his pram in bright January sunshine. There are seagulls wheeling in high arcs above our
heads as we cross over the bridge to Chelsea, and their cries remind
me of home. Joe is asleep, but I talk to him nonetheless. No one else
seems to be up this early on a Sunday morning as we slowly make
our way along Cheyne Walk.

There are beautiful Georgian houses set back from the road with
what must be magnificent views of the Thames and Battersea Park
beyond.

"Don't worry, son, we'll be okay, we'll live in a house like that one day and we'll be safe and happy."

But my son isn't listening, he's sleeping soundly and I'm just talking to myself, although I am curious to know how it feels to look out onto the river from the dark-paneled libraries and the art-filled drawing rooms. Are these people any happier than I am? Are their lives perfect and untroubled? I doubt it and I am neither envious nor sad, but I can't help wondering where we are going to end up living.

The flat-hunting service in Kensington will cost fifteen pounds. Every morning at nine we call them and they give us a list of properties for rent in our price range (our price range being the lowest). It is exhausting and dispiriting work, trying to find somewhere to live when you don't have much money and have a baby to feed. You spend hours driving across London only to find that the flat has already been let or that you would have to share your Dickensian accommodations with a family of rodents, and all the cars in the street are vandalized wrecks.

I am stuck in early evening traffic on Park Lane, returning to Battersea from another abortive search, this time in north London. I have the phone number that the American drummer gave me a month ago, and knowing that I'm in Mayfair, decide to turn left onto a side street and work up the courage to give him a call. There's an empty phone box on the corner of Green Street, as well as a parking space, and I find the number scrawled in my diary in the light of a streetlamp. The phone rings and rings and I am anxious that he won't remember me, or that he may be away on tour, but finally a sleepy female voice answers. I ask if Stewart is in, she asks me to hold on. It's probably only a minute but seems far longer before she finally returns. "Who is it?" I tell her my name is Sting.

"Sting?" she says, I suppose incredulous that someone could have such a name.

"Yes, Sting, that's my name."

She tells me to hang on. Another long minute passes and then I hear what sounds like heavy footsteps hurtling down a flight of stairs probably three or four at a time.

It's Stewart. "Hi, how are ya?" says the breathless voice on the other end.

"It's Sting, the bass player from Newcastle," I tell him, still not sure if he has a clue who I am.

"Where are ya? Are you in London?"

"Well, actually, I'm in Mayfair," I admit, a little embarrassed; it would have been much cooler to call from Pippa's flat instead of sounding like some homeless person on the street.

"Whereabouts?"

"I'm in a phone box on, er . . . Green Street."

"No kidding, that's where we are. Number 26, top floor. Come up."

Now I am truly embarrassed. It will seem like I've been stalking him.

"Okay, then," I say, looking up at the grand Georgian terraces towering darkly above the phosphorous light of the street lamp.

This all now seems like a terrible idea. I should just get back home to Frances and the baby. This is just another wild-goose chase. I'm wasting my time, and this guy is just being polite. Anyway, the band will be traveling down from Newcastle for a gig here in London next week, and this seems like I'm trawling for another one. I look down the dark street at the traffic heading south on Park Lane and wonder if I'm doing the right thing. Something steadies my nerves, as I make my way across the street toward the grand houses on the other side, trying to make out the door numbers in the gloom.

Number 26 is an impressive eighteenth-century house with a

pillared portico. I peer into the entrance hall through the stained-glass panels of the front door, and press what I imagine to be the top-floor bell. The door buzzes and then mysteriously opens. I walk in and begin to mount the imposing, richly carpeted staircase to the fourth floor where the door is ajar, and I hear the sounds of dissonant music.

As I enter the dimly lit apartment I see a bearded man with long dark hair, sitting cross-legged and playing a Perspex bass connected to a tiny portable amplifier. I ascertain immediately that he is not very good and the sound is closer to the annoying buzz of an insect at a window than the normally sonorous tones of the instrument. He is seated in the center of what looks like some sort of eastern shrine and is totally oblivious of my presence, his eyes way back in his head, either in a meditative trance or stoned out of his gourd.

I begin to take in the rest of the room. There are many artifacts that seem to be Middle Eastern in origin, a hubbly-bubbly pipe, or narghile, Islamic tapestries, engraved brass plates, Arab swords and daggers, silk rugs and harem cushions. There is a faint smell of incense and patchouli oil. Through an open door in a room off to the side I see a strikingly pretty woman with long red hair. Her full lips seem to be held in a permanent and seductive pout as she distractedly plays a small guitar and hums softly to herself, as if she too is in an enclosed world of her own. She must be the source of the female voice on the phone but she also looks oddly familiar.

Whatever she's playing has nothing whatever to do with the bass parts being played in the other room or the unrelated clatter of a drum kit emanating from the floor above. It is more than a little disconcerting.

Just then another female figure emerges from what I assume to be a kitchen. She is huge, with long dark hair and muscular legs atop shiny high heels. She has enormous hands and they are pressed tightly to her ears as she brushes past me, almost knocking me back down the stairs. She is clearly unhappy with everyone in the flat and turns to glower at me menacingly, as I'm the only one taking any notice of her. My reflexive apology is rebuffed as she slams a bedroom door behind her. This is some strange place.

The red-haired girl gives me a languid smile through sleepy, half-closed eyes, which I take as permission to mount the stairs. I am intrigued by the physical surroundings and appalled by the cacophony, which is getting louder and louder. I enter the upstairs room, lit by a bare lightbulb suspended from the ceiling and full of what I assume to be furniture draped in ghostly white sheets. There are cardboard boxes blocking the windows, I suppose as makeshift soundproofing. The tall American is playing an enormous drum kit in the corner of the room. He smiles with the grim resolve of someone firing a machine gun as his long athletic arms thrash at the splashing ride cymbals and the snare drum cracks like an uncoiled whip. The hi-hat rocks from side to side on its metal fittings, while his right foot throbs like a road drill and shakes the entire room. If this is a percussive exhibition designed solely to impress me, then it works. Stewart Copeland has an easy animal grace as a drummer, and where Ronnie was all finesse and fussy technique, Stewart is an object lesson in sheer power. He plays for another sixteen bars before he launches himself across the tom-toms to greet me.

"Hi! How long have you been in town?" he asks, offering his large right hand and shaking mine vigorously.

"A couple of days," I reply, trying to sound casual while recovering from the shaking I've been given.

"Grab that bass over there, let's play."

"Won't that disturb the people downstairs?" I ask.

"Nah, that's my brother Ian and Sonja. They won't mind."

I realize now that the redheaded girl downstairs is Sonja Kristina, the singer of Curved Air, the beautiful ingenue who fronted the seminal art rock band of the early seventies. I'd seen them supporting the Who years before. Electric violins and guitars playing psychedelic pop, folk rock and bombastic slabs of Vivaldi tagged on, I supposed, to demonstrate that the band had all been to music college. But Sonja was a real beauty, otherworldy and unattainable, and I make a mental note to check her out on the way downstairs.

"And your brother's a bass player?" I ask, wanting to know as much about the terrain here as I can before embarking on any journey.

Stewart catches my drift immediately. "Oh no, no, he's an agent, but he likes to play for fun." Then he adds confidentially, "He got back from Vietnam pretty weirded out. He's only just come out of his shell."

I nod politely, remembering the psychonaut downstairs and wondering how he must have been when he was in his shell.

I pick up the bass, unsure if this is a jam session or an audition, or perhaps both.

"And what about the other lady?" My curiosity is getting the better of me.

"That's George. Don't ask," says my new friend, rolling his eyes. "What shall we do?"

"What you were playing when I came in sounded pretty good to me," I reply as I plug in the bass and tune it up.

He starts at a blistering pace, so I just settle myself behind the engine and wonder where this ride will take me. Off we go, riffing and pumping with his machine gun intensity, the bass weaving like a python through a jungle of rhythm and splashing cymbals.

Even at this very early moment of our relationship, it is clear that there is something going on, some chemistry, some understanding, some recognition, a rapport and a tension between the amphetamine pulse of his kick drum and the shifting, rolling ground of the bass. It is like two dancers finding a sudden and unexpected harmony in the glide of their steps, or the sexual rhythms of natural lovers, or the synchronized strokes of a rowing team in the flow of a fast river. Such rapport is not common, and I realize very quickly that this guy is the most exciting drummer I've ever worked with, almost too exciting. I also realize that tempos will be abandoned as easily as loose baggage on that runaway train, and whatever music I shall manage to make with this whirlwind, it will not be gentle or easy, it will be a wild ride to hell and back.

We play for over an hour and finish the session flushed and embarrassed like spent lovers, exhausted, exhilarated, and neither of us quite sure what to do next. He talks to me about Hendrix and Cream and how he has always had a hankering to play in a three-piece band. How the interplay between a trio and the added responsibility for each musician is a challenge he relishes. That less is more. That real art thrives in conditions of limitation, demanding improvisation, innovation, and creative problem-solving. He talks in the same scattershot way as he plays the drums, telling me how he's been galvanized by the punk scene, how these unschooled musicians have thrown out finesse and technique for the sake of raw undiluted energy, that he wants to be part of it, and that it will sweep everything aside like a tidal wave. I do not point out to him that his current band is the style antithesis of this movement, a band that personifies arch-hippiedom, and that the beautiful Sonja Kristina with her long red hair is the poster girl for the old regime. And he in turn politely doesn't mention that the band I'm in is a bunch of provincial "musos" so far off the style scale so as not to register at all.

If there is something disingenuous about the two of us forming a punk band (for this is the unspoken subtext for everything that we have discussed so far), there is also something deliciously subversive about it. Flying a flag of convenience while the doors of the fortress that is the music business have been torn open would suit my purpose and method as much as it would his. Stewart wants to call the band the Police. I hate the name, but I say nothing. He plays me a couple of songs he has written, recorded roughly on a home tape recorder, tailored musically and lyrically to fit the new dispensation, and while they seem generic and vacuous, what excites me is his energy, his brash Yankee spirit of "can-do." He shows me a feature about himself in *Sounds*. There is a picture of him behind his enormous kit and below it a letter ostensibly from a fan asking, "Who is this brilliant new drummer with Curved Air and what equipment does he use?" There follows a CV and the specs on his Tama kit.

"Do you know who wrote that letter?" he asks me rhetorically, and before I can even shrug he answers himself, smiling like a big greedy cat. "I did. It got my picture in the paper. It'll also get me a free kit from Tama."

I am both appalled and fascinated by this blatant and unashamed self-promotion, but it has clearly worked, I couldn't argue with that. I was witnessing for the first time what I would later come to recognize, when I got to know the rest of the Copeland clan, as a family trait. Those boys could promote, and I as much as anyone would profit from their efforts. By coincidence, Stewart's letter ran in the same issue of *Sounds* in which Phil Sutcliffe had written about Last Exit. That article is called "Making It" and takes up three pages in the middle of the paper. It is well written and well meaning, but the headline is clearly ironic in that the story outlines the impossible odds stacked against even good provincial bands trying to gain a foothold in the music industry. Next to the explosive Semtex of Stewart's self-promotion we looked like sodden fireworks after a damp bonfire night.

So here is a conundrum for me. An amazing drummer, whose dynamism is in no way limited to his musical abilities, but with an artistic agenda that I can only half subscribe to, compared with allegiance to a band who I'm not even sure is committed to coming to London and whose chances of making it seem increasingly nonexistent.

But I don't want to sing tuneless, disaffected rants. I sing tender love songs. This is what I'm good at. But I also realize that there's an opportunity in the chaos, and that I am perfectly able to morph, adapting what I do to suit the current climate without necessarily compromising the integrity of my songs. I can establish some sort of position, some kind of defensible space, and when the dust has settled, run my true colors up the mast.

Whether this medium-term strategy is identical to Stewart's, I don't yet know, but I'm willing to suppress my misgivings and attach myself to this new and dynamic energy, and see where it takes us. But before any of this can work, we will need another player, and Stewart will need to get a haircut, and quickly.

I return to my wife and baby in Battersea, my head spinning with ideas about music, loyalty, integrity, money, and more important, somewhere for us to live.

The next night Frances and I drive up to Southgate in north London to an address that the flat-hunting agency has given us. Southgate is a long way from the center of town, but by now we are getting a little desperate. Joe is asleep in the back and we've left the dog with Pip in Battersea in case they don't accept animals. It is a freezing cold night with icy rain and sleet clinging to the windscreen and hapless pedestrians being soaked by the wash of passing buses in the glare of brake lights and shop windows.

The flat is above a row of shops and the entrance is around the back. We find a parking space, and with the baby in his carry-cot we make our way slowly across the treacherous ice and up the stairs in the darkness. As Frances rings the bell apprehensively we are nervous and cold and our month-old baby looks so vulnerable. The door opens and we are flooded in a warm light, a haven from the icy wind and rain. We are wearing our best clothes and fixed smiles. I look for somewhere to put the baby.

The woman who ushers us in, who has been a tenant here for five years, is named Freddy. She has short black hair, slacks, and a man's shirt. She seems to take to us immediately, especially Frances, and after a few cups of hot tea and a couple of shortcake biscuits, shows us around the flat. After Pip's tiny living room the two-story maisonette seems enormous. There are five pleasant, spacious rooms looking out onto the High Street, and for sixteen quid a week, it is the nicest place we have seen. There would be room for Gerry if he wanted it, and the baby looks very comfortable.

Freddy asks what it is we do. She's intrigued that Frances is an actress, but Carol Wilson has instructed me not to tell her I'm a musician, so I say that I'm a copyright executive for Virgin Music with a giddying bogus salary of five thousand pounds a year. This subterfuge seems to have worked successfully for other musicians trying to put a roof over their heads, and indeed Freddy says she will recommend us to the landlord tomorrow, and if we can send our salary details and a reference she can't foresee any problems.

We emerge from the warmth into the foul weather of the night, relieved that we'll have a place of our own, and fairly confident that we'll manage to scrape the weekly rent from somewhere.

I do have to visit the social security office, though, and sign on the dole. Walking to the Lisson Grove dole on Wednesday afternoons will put me into the blackest of depressions. I hate signing on, queuing up in long straggling lines with hundreds of others like me, able-bodied but marginalized individuals made to feel utterly useless by an impersonal and dehumanizing bureaucracy. But like most of these others in the noisy hall, I really have no choice. We have a baby to feed, we have to find the money to pay the rent. There is no other way but to put myself through the system, ferrying coded forms from office to office to be stamped and filed. In my quest to become unique, I've become a statistic.

My papers have yet to arrive from Newcastle, and this makes me anxious that the undeclared pittance I get from the odd gig with Last Exit may have emerged as a piece of evidence against me. I stand in the queue every week expecting to be hauled into the office and given the third degree about my unemployment. The queue in front of me stretches like a winding snake from the grubby glass doors to a series of grilled windows, and beyond these windows, designed as if to protect someone from contamination, is a row of sallow, over-worked civil servants, just as bored and indifferent to the situation as those on this side. In front of me a man is reading the *Daily Mirror.* The headline I can see reads, MOTHER OF NINE JAILED FOR SOCIAL SECURITY FIDDLE. As if she didn't need it. I eventually get to the window, hand in my dole card, sign my name, and a giro check for £18.50 will be posted to whatever address I have given. I say thank you but I get no response from the man on the other side. At least I don't have to go through this for another week.

Even at these low points, I still have no doubt that I've done the right thing in coming to London. I can give no rational reason why it feels right to have done this, except I know that London is where the prize is. I know that at the center of this labyrinth, this multi-dimensional, socioeconomic, psychocultural, and artistic puzzle is the glittering, singular trophy of success. It may be elusive, but it is so powerful in its gravitational pull as to render everything else insignificant. Success and happiness have to be the same thing, don't they?

William Blake said that "a man who persists in his folly will become wise," but at this time I am blindly unaware, even at such a remove, that I have become addicted to the notion that everything will be solved in the afterglow of success, and I am being drawn inexorably toward its center, deeper and deeper. How dangerous this addiction is, I do not yet know.

Last Exit's long-scheduled London gigs are upon us. I haven't seen the boys for a month and I miss them, though there isn't much I can tell them about my adventures that will make them happy. The flat in Southgate has fallen through at the last minute. We think the landlord must have smelled a rat over my bogus employment at Virgin Music and had the locks changed after Freddy had sent us the keys. It is a long drive to Southgate, the car repacked with all of our possessions and our hopes, only to find a locked door, our vain knocking echoing hollowly in an empty flat with a key that doesn't work. We feel humiliated, defeated, and angry and the only positive outcome of this is that I will write a song that evening. An angry rant of a song called "Landlord," which Stewart will hear and praise paternally.

"That's my boy! Keep them coming like that."

So we are outstaying our welcome on Pip's floor. She's been so kind but we can't live here forever. I'm on the dole and haven't done a day's work since I got here, but when the band arrives I try to present a cheerful front, pretending that all is going as planned. We are parked outside the Red Cow pub in Hammersmith.

"How's it going, Sting?"

"Oh, great!"

"Found somewhere to live yet?"

"Still looking."

Ronnie and Terry give each other a subtle look that is not meant to be unkind, but it nonetheless hurts.

Gerry comes out of the pub, cigarette in hand, with a look that would curdle butter. "The fuckin' gig's been canceled."

Next night in Bristol, after a four-hour drive, we discover we've been double booked. This is not going well. How am I supposed to attract this lot down here when there is nothing but doom and gloom? However, the next night at the Nashville Rooms in West Kensington we triumph, blowing the headliners off the stand and restoring our flagging spirits. We are a good band, and while a couple of record company types turn up they offer us no more than a patronizing pat on the back.

The boys head back to the north in the van and I'm on my own again, holding the baby. I think they're beginning to feel sorry for me, as if I've lost my marbles. I wave them off as cheerfully as I can, but only Gerry looks back.

Stewart's swanky Mayfair address that so impressed me has turned out to be a squat. He and Ian and Sonja have only been there a few months. The flat is actually owned by an American lady named Marcia McDonald, who is Muhammad Ali's publicist. She had lent the flat to a friend who then refused to leave. This is George, the large lady who almost knocked me down the stairs when I first arrived. On the advice of Miles Copeland, Sr., Stewart and Ian's father and a friend of the owner, the Copeland brothers had been brought in as subsquatters to make life as uncomfortable as possible for George (who preferred to be known as Georgina), so that Marcia could regain possession of her flat. If this sounds like a ridiculously convoluted CIA plot, it is probably because Miles Copeland, Sr., the head of the clan, was one of the founding members of that byzantine organization.

What I had witnessed on that first evening was the Copeland offspring carrying on the family business, practicing an extended campaign of psychological warfare and attrition involving wild all-night parties and hideously cacophonous jam sessions. Georgina would leave soon afterward, so there was some method in their apparent madness, but now the Copelands were forced to accept the realization that they had successfully plotted themselves out of a wonderful place to live, meaning that their days in the luxurious squat were now numbered.

One morning during those last days, Stewart called to say he'd found a guitarist and to ask if I could come round to hear him. I tell him I'll have to bring the baby, as Frances has an audition. So that afternoon I haul Joe and his carry-cot up the four flights of stairs and into the rehearsal room. Stewart is seated at the drums wearing sunglasses and a leather jacket. As the room is sunless and adequately heated, I am slightly puzzled as to why he's wearing this getup, until I see that in the other corner, framed perfectly by the white sheet draped over a chest of drawers, sits another man in impermeable wraparound sunglasses, a black tank top, and sprayed-on leather trousers. They are both wearing, as far as I can see beneath the sunglasses, expressions of abject seriousness, the way I imagine terrorists would look when they're posing for the camera after planning some outrage. This must be the new look, for there is a distinct smell of attitude in the room, and the sight of me in the doorway in my dungarees and holding a baby doesn't exactly harmonize with the terrorist chic among the drapes.

"This is Henry," says Stewart, maintaining his grim demeanor, I'm sure at the expense of his natural ebullience.

"Hello, Henry."

"Henry's from Corsica. He doesn't speak much English."

I can just see, in my mind's eye, a far more comfortable Henry at large in the picturesque nineteenth-century garb of a mountain brigand, with a cutlass and flintlock pistols, lying in wait in the hills above Bastia to rob and waylay hapless travelers.

Henry Padovani is the new guitarist, and it becomes apparent as we play that he hasn't been hired for his virtuosity. He only knows a few chords, but boy does he look cool in those leather pants. Stewart has taught him the two songs that he's written—"Nothing Achieving" and "Fall Out"—for a record Stewart wants to produce himself. Henry doesn't play them badly, but when we start jamming he's a little short on ideas. After my initial suspicions about him have dissolved, however, Henry turns out to be a rather delightful human being, polite, friendly, and desperately eager to learn, as well as having an amusing and rudimentary grasp of the English language. He stops playing at one point, seeming to have a problem with his guitar, and asks me, "Please to give me a rope?"

"A rope? What do you want a rope for?"

"*Oui, c'est ça,* a rope." He grabs a spare lead from my guitar case, indicating that this is the rope he needs, and from that day on we will call all guitar leads "ropes."

Joe, who has slept through all of this din undisturbed, has now woken up to be fed. Henry endears himself to me by offering to help heat up the milk, and we have a baby break until the bottle is finished. I place my little boy back in his carry-cot, and as we commence the unholy row once more, he falls immediately to sleep again. You would almost imagine that even if we were playing Brahms' Lullaby instead of some thrash metal vamp, he couldn't look more content.

The new guitarist is getting the hang of it now, and when we fizzle to a halt after one of our more successful musical harangues, he enthusiastically offers, "There was some really moments, yes?"

We nod sagely. "Yup, some really moments." Henceforth all of our inspired musical moments will be designated as "really moments."

And so the Police are born, with a few isolated "really moments," a baby's bottle, a couple of power chords, and a pair of leather pants.

# 11

WEEKS OF FLAT HUNTING HAVE WORN US BOTH DOWN, AND Frances and I have nothing to show for our efforts but sore feet, bruised egos, and a massive petrol bill from driving fruitlessly around most of greater London. I'm beginning to feel that the task is hopeless, when the gods seem to smile on us with some Olympian largesse. An actress friend of Frances's is doing a season up in Edinburgh. Her name is Miranda, and she rents a room on the top floor of a house in Bayswater. Aware of our predicament, she will let us stay there for a couple of months.

We drive across Hyde Park to find an elegant terraced house in Bark Place off the Bayswater Road. It is extremely posh, and I can't quite believe that we are even walking through the front door, never mind staying here. The house had belonged to a Lord and Lady Dunnet (whoever they were), but the current mistress is an opera soprano named Penny. The house has large spacious rooms on four floors, filled with sculptures and paintings, although our room at the top is the smallest. The main room downstairs has a grand piano (happily in tune) and French windows that open out onto a small garden with an enormous beech tree. Our bedroom window looks out onto the topmost branches of this splendid tree, and it doesn't take much imagination to think yourself in a tree house. This is probably the greenest place I've ever lived up until now.

Bayswater is as central as it is possible to be in London, a minute's walk from Hyde Park and the shops and restaurants on Queensway, the main thoroughfare, which seems to be bustling twenty-four hours a day. It is, in short, a perfect location for a couple looking for work and excitement and cosmopolitan glamour. Greeks, Russians, Turks, Italians, Indians, and Pakistanis all have overlapping enclaves here in a melting pot of immigrant energy and colorful street life. There is a casino, an all-night supermarket, and reportedly a high-class brothel or two. This is definitely where it's at. We feel outrageously fortunate to find ourselves in such a situation, if only temporarily. Since we only live from week to week now, a couple of months here seems like an eternity. But we can't afford to tread water for too long. Something has to happen, and thank God, Stewart has a plan.

We are going to record his two songs, "Nothing Achieving" and "Fall Out," on which I will sing and play the bass and Stewart will play the drums and most of the guitar parts because he's better than Henry. Then we are going to get the record pressed at the RCA factory in Durham and hand deliver it to record stores ourselves. Such passion and ingenuity is truly inspiring, and a telling contrast to the lily-livered procrastination that is my only abiding impression of the established record industry of the time. Stewart's energy is a breath of fresh air, and I'm transported by it even if the music isn't exactly my cup of tea.

We have a photo session on the roof of the Copeland squat in Mayfair on a bitterly cold and gray February afternoon. Stewart and Henry are looking either louche or cretinous in their sunglasses, depending on your point of view, while I'm looking sulky and wishing we could get this over with as quickly as possible.

It is around this time that I first meet Miles Copeland, the man who would become our manager, Svengali, mentor, and agent provocateur. Miles Axe Copeland III is the eldest of the Copeland brothers. Intimidating, intelligent, opinionated, and utterly serious, Miles had a reputation even then for being sharp, arrogant, and ruthless. I liked him immediately even though it was a year before he could remember my name, or have much to do with my career. He was busy elsewhere. In order to understand Miles, or indeed any of the Copeland siblings, it is essential to know a little about the father, Miles senior (mastermind of psychological warfare in the Mayfair squat).

Miles senior, one of the founding fathers of the CIA, had served as an operative in the crucial territories of Lebanon, Syria, and Egypt for its wartime genesis, the OSS. He had by his own admission brought down governments, sanctioned political assassinations, and acted as puppeteer to various bogus and corrupt regimes all over the Middle East. He had retired from the service to become a Washington lobbyist and writer of books on the covert, complex world of the intelligence community. Kim Philby, the British traitor and Soviet spy, had been a family friend and neighbor in the pleasant Beirut suburb he shared with the Copelands. Stewart always implied that Philby was a surveillance target of his father's long before he defected to Russia, but my favorite Miles senior story is this one.

After the Dead Sea Scrolls were found in a cave near Qumran in 1947, they were sent to the CIA office in Damascus. Miles senior and his fellow spies couldn't make much sense of them in the tiny, dimly lit office, so they took the first of the scrolls at hand up onto the roof, to get a better look. They had just unrolled the mysterious 2,000-year-old document from end to end on the flat, scorching concrete when a strong wind picked up and blew the fragile parchment into the air and across the rooftops of Damascus, where it fragmented into a million pieces, never to be seen again. Miles senior and the CIA boys retired downstairs in some disarray. The precious scrolls were then entrusted to the more circumspect and cautious hands of trained archeologists. I often wonder what was written on that scroll.

Miles senior had reared and educated his eldest child to become a businessman, preferably an oilman, and Miles the younger would have done so had he not caught the rock-and-roll bug while managing a local band in Beirut in which his little brother Stewart happened to be the drummer. After the family moved to London, Miles enjoyed varying degrees of success as well as failure managing acts such as Wishbone Ash, Caravan, and the Climax Blues Band.

As the eldest scion of an evidently dynastic family, MAC III was driven to create an empire comprising management, touring agencies, publishing and record companies, all grandly cross-collateralized and therefore all vulnerable to the hubris that invariably takes over most empires. It was on Miles's Illegal label that Stewart's two songs were to be recorded.

Ever optimistic, Miles had overstretched his resources and taken a spectacular fall in the world of business and was just beginning to stage a comeback when I first met him. He now had modest offices in Dryden Chambers off Oxford Street, where he presided over a burgeoning city-state of minor punk bands like Chelsea and Cortinas as well as a more musically accomplished band from Deptford called Squeeze. He also provided an office to punk's official chronicler, Mark P., the editor of *Sniffing Glue*, who was hatching plans to become a performer. Miles had no real interest in Stewart's own revanchist scheme to re-create himself as a punk, when what he considered to be the real thing, Chelsea and the Cortinas and Mark P., were already on his books.

"Listen to me, Stewart," he would shout in his nasal drawl just loud enough to be within earshot in the corridor outside his office. "Gene October is the real deal. He can't sing for shit but he's got that street thing. He's a real punk. You got this guy in the band, whatsisname, Smig? He's a goddamn jazz singer."

"His name's Sting," Stewart would reply huffily.

"Yeah, yeah!" Miles would say, waving his younger brother away.

Once Miles had heard our single he got a little more excited, although not excited enough to offer to manage us as yet, but Stewart was allowed to use the phones at Dryden Chambers to further his cause, albeit as a poor relation.

Ian, the middle brother, agent, amateur bass player, and Vietnam veteran, had become over those first few months my favorite Copeland. Less fanatically driven than the other two to succeed, he had the easygoing, relaxed philosophy of a man who'd been under fire and survived, as if the violence that he'd witnessed and taken part in during his service in the U.S. infantry had given him a broader perspective on the important things of life. Very little seemed to faze him; his agreeable humor became a constant that could be relied on as a counter to the often hysterical rantings of his siblings. He would call me Leroy, just as he called everyone else Leroy. For the sake of consistency he even called himself Leroy. I would seek out the pleasure of his company more often than the others and listen to his self-deprecating, humorous, and often terrifying stories of his Vietnam experience.

"Shit, Leroy, I was a radio operator in the infantry just before Tet. First time we were ordered out on patrol, the entire platoon had just dropped acid. We were shitting ourselves. I think we just went around the perimeter of the camp until it was time to go back in. Fuck knows what would have happened if we'd been attacked.

"Bravest thing I ever did was to go AWOL one night to visit a

Vietnamese whorehouse with my buddy Leroy. The Viet Cong used the same place, and we had to slip out the back door when they arrived at the front. Those girls said nothing though; money is money."

Despite his modesty Ian had left Vietnam as a sergeant with a Bronze Star and four campaign medals and would have gone back for a second tour if he hadn't been framed in a bungled drug bust while on leave in London. If the charges against him had stuck, he would then have been court-martialed by the U.S. Army and most likely incarcerated for a long time. As it was, he was proved innocent, and the delays in the trial made certain that he would not make his second tour of that ravaged country. This probably saved his life.

Ian would eventually become my agent. Many years later I would perform in what had been Saigon and is now Ho Chi Minh City, and Ian would join me to revisit the scenes of so much death and destruction and his coming-of-age.

My fate for the next twenty-five years would become inextricably linked to these three brothers, so much so that they would become yet another dysfunctional surrogate for my own family, with the usual blessings and a few perennial curses.

I don't think we have a snowball's chance in hell but there is an apartment being advertised in the *Evening Standard* as "Own your own for thirty pounds a week," with the address just around the corner from where we are staying in Leinster Square in Bayswater. In its centrality and glamour, Bayswater has become an essential ingredient in our vague and rather hopeful recipe for success. We make the call and go to see the unfinished flats the following night.

An entire block has been taken over by a housing association and is being refurbished for owner occupation within a few months. There are six basements available, each with a large living room, a bedroom, and a kitchen. It is a nice fantasy but I can't believe they will accept us, and what would we use for furniture? Apart from the wicker armchair we brought down from Newcastle, we have nothing.

I stand in the empty basement without windows or doors, and only a concrete floor, but in my mind's eye I can see how wonderful it would look with carpets and curtains, with an armchair and a sofa, an open fireplace and a few books. Also, the idea of living below the level of the street excites me greatly, as if it were a dugout or a cave from which we could plan our invasion of the city yet feel protected and safe in our own space. Frances tells me that most of the prospective homeowners seem to be actors. In other words, they are no more respectable than we are. We put in an application, and wait.

Meanwhile, the news from Last Exit is not good. It is now plainly evident that Ronnie and Terry have no intention of moving to London. I wonder if Gerry too is prevaricating, and write an impassioned letter pledging my allegiance to the band, but qualifying that my allegiance is to the band that decided they would come to London and try to make it, not the band that stayed at home. Only Gerry responds. He will come down and stay with some friends in south London and see how he fares. It is then I admit I've been working with Stewart and that I'm a semireluctant front man in a punk band. I can hear the unspoken disgust in the static on the line from Newcastle, but he's coming down anyway. It seems as if Last Exit have finally lived up to their name.

Back at the Police headquarters in Green Street things are getting a little fraught. The Copelands are trying to fend off the bailiffs, and it looks as if the swanky address is slipping from their grasp, but we will continue to rehearse there until the last moment. Henry by this time is driving Stewart and me around the bend. We spend hours trying to teach him parts that are beyond him. Sweet as he is, he is no substitute for a real musician, and I don't feel that we have enough time to wait for him to become one. In fact, at this moment in time the idea of the Police making it is just as fanciful as it was for Last Exit. If anything, it is more fanciful. At least Last Exit could play.

It is Miles who will come to our rescue, in what I will come to recognize as his own inimitable fashion. There is always another agenda with Miles, and it is usually about cutting costs.

After the explosion of new British bands transformed the scene here, Miles, ever the empire builder, decided to import a slew of bands from New York. Bands like Johnny Thunder and the Heartbreakers, Wayne County and the Electric Chairs, and Cherry Vanilla. Cherry Vanilla had been a part of the Andy Warhol scene in the late sixties, and later she became David Bowie's publicist. She arrived in England with bright copper hair, an Italian-American guitarist named Louis, a camp Puerto Rican pianist named Zecca, and a manager named Max. Max was soft-spoken for a manager, with fluffy gray hair and professorial spectacles, refined, quietly gay, and utterly devoted to Cherry. Cherry and Louis were an item although she was a decade older. They had left their drummer and bass player back in New York after Miles had told them that there was a perfectly adequate rhythm section already here, i.e., Stewart and myself. The money saved on airfares and hotel rooms was crucial for Miles.

Stewart will agree to become the drummer for Cherry Vanilla (volunteering my services on bass), providing the Police can be the support act. This arrangement seems mutually agreeable to everyone. Stewart and I will be perfectly happy to play two sets a night, we can pool gear and travel costs, and we might even make a bit of money.

An intensive period of rehearsal begins. We spend all day learning Cherry's set while trying to drag Henry through ours until the early hours of the morning. We are overworked and exhausted, but thrilled to be working. Louis and Zecca are fine musicians, well schooled and utterly professional. Cherry, who—to quote one of her own songs—says she's from Manhattan but comes from Queens, is full of delightful contradictions. When you meet her she seems like a shy Catholic girl fresh out of the convent, while her stage act is an outrageous burlesque of bumps and grinds and saucy lyrics delivered in the kind of lascivious Mae West drawl that wouldn't seem out of place on a predatory hooker. Her stage costume is a pair of tight black slacks stretched over a shapely derriere and a tank top with the words *Lick Me* written above her ample bosom in luminous rhine-stones. I feel a little superfluous, but not too unhappy to be shunted into the background, very much the way I used to feel when I had to accompany strippers in the clubs up north.

The opening number of Cherry's set is actually a swing-four jazz tune with a walking bass line, and that is guaranteed to confuse if not outrage the militant punks at the Roxy. I am intrigued, and for the first time since I've moved to London I feel as if I'm playing real music, even if it's only in a burlesque show masquerading as some kind of "new wave" sensation.

The Police now have about ten songs, all, apart from "Landlord," penned by Stewart, as I haven't felt confident or enthusiastic enough to contribute much more, but these ten supercharged ditties are played at such a furious pace that the whole set lasts only ten min-utes, and that's with an encore. But it is ten exhausting minutes with me caterwauling at the top of my range over Henry's approximations of the chords and the undigested panic of Stewart's drumming. He is a superb drummer and quite capable of driving a small power station with his energy, but he just needs to relax more. Every song is a hell-bent race for the coda, and he plays as if he wants to propel the drums not only to the front of the bandstand but out into the audience all the way to the back of the club. I'm plagued by persistent doubts that the whole thing is just not musical enough, but Stewart has no such qualms. For him it's all about excitement, and of course I will hang on to his coattails for as long as I can, for there is in reality no other game in town for me.

In my anxiety about the future, I've taken to praying. Whatever my doubts were as a child, I'd maintained a belief in this tenuous personal lifeline to the spiritual realm, having faith that when the chips were down I'd be forgiven and welcomed back into the fold as if my religious conundrums had been understood and allowed for. So whenever I wake up in the middle of the night and start to recite the rosary, I am comforted. Five decades of the rosary adds up to fifty Hail Marys, and although with repetition the words become meaningless, they begin to work like a soothing mantra for an anxious mind fraught with worries about our prospects as a family.

Since I was a child I've found it easier to conjure up the female deity in my imagination, one that the church was wise enough not to proscribe in the patriarchal, misogynistic purge that all but eradicated the worship of the goddess. Mary the Star of the Sea became my icon as a child, floating above the ocean in her blue veil, her head ringed by stars and tilted gently to one side, her eyes modestly downcast as if in thought. Her smile was delicate, Venusian, and held the promise of infinite patience and compassion. She was a being who could intercede for me in the court of heaven. My favorite childhood hymn had ended:

> *Virgin, most pure star of the sea,*
> *Pray for the wanderer, pray for me.*

In later life I would have a problem with the virgin birth, wondering, I hope not blasphemously, why having created the miraculous and sacred mechanism of sex, God would see fit to bypass it in order to send Christ into the world untainted by his own invention. It just seems like one miracle too many.

Nonetheless, I'm now praying on a nightly basis for no more than that God or the Goddess will keep us safe. Asking for a place of our own to live would have struck me as being too venal to be taken seriously in the celestial realms.

However, some sort of miracle does take place, because the housing association accepts our application to join the partnership, effectively giving us ownership of the basement flat at 28 Leinster Square. Frances and I are dancing for joy and I'm silently thanking the Virgin for her help. Now all we need is some money to pay the deposit, eleven hundred pounds, plus the first month's payment. Frances's father lends us five hundred, and my dad says he can lend us two hundred, but we have a couple of months before the flat will be ready, so we'll just have to earn some money and start saving.

# 12

OUR FIRST GIG WITH CHERRY VANILLA TAKES PLACE IN Newport, Wales, at a shabby little nightclub called Alexander's next to a railway line. There is a vicious March wind blowing newspapers down the narrow alley between the club and the embankment, as a coal train clanks noisily overhead. Inside, the club is cold, damp, and dingy, and there is a pungent smell of stale smoke and the sickly hop-infused stink of last week's beer.

Stewart and I have driven cross-country with Chris, our roadie, in a Ford Transit van. We set up the gear and PA on a tiny stage covered in angry cigarette burns and sticky underfoot with spilled drinks and old sweat. We will play scores of these clubs up and down the country, with dressing rooms no bigger than toilets, covered in the self-aggrandizing graffiti and puerile obscenities of our fellow musicians, resentful that they've been lured into this circus of seedy glamour by the vague promise of the big time just a little farther down the road.

The rest of the band arrive as we finish the setup, and while the American visitors don't seem all that impressed by the decor, they do not complain unduly. I get the impression that this is exactly the kind of place they play back home. They arrange themselves in the dressing room while I dismantle my amplifier, which seems to be broken again. I remove each of the valves in turn, shake them gently next to my ear to make sure they're okay, and then replace them so they are snug in their sockets. The ritual, for it is no more scientific than that, seems to work and the valves begin to glow a reassuring red. The club begins to fill up and the colored lights above the stage make a brave show at a kind of gaiety, veiling the squalor in the same kindly red glow as the valves in my amplifier. Everything's going to be fine tonight.

The Police set begins at ten to eleven and is finished on the stroke of the hour. It blisters along at such a pace—no gaps between the songs, defying the audience to be critical or appreciative, as if we don't give a fuck either way, and then we're off before they know what's hit them. When we burst into the dressing room we're all laughing as if we've just pulled off a successful bank raid. Louis and Zecca are duly impressed, Louis particularly with my singing.

"Hey!" he tells me, "you're gonna be a big star someday."

"Oh yeah, sure," I say, but there is a small part of me that wants to believe him, no matter how unlikely it seems.

There is a half-hour break and Henry decamps to the bar at the back of the club while Stewart and I take the stage again, this time with Cherry's band. Cherry really is dynamite and she goes down a bomb, the audience rabid for every bump and grind, lusty innuendo, and knowing wink. We may make a few first-night mistakes but we perform well enough for them to be forgotten in a warm sea of approval. It's not a bad start. After a few congratulatory beers in the emptying club, we dismantle the equipment, load it back into the van, and are on the road by two A.M. I get home at seven in the morning, having dropped everyone else off at their digs. I have my wages for the evening in my pocket. Six pounds and fifty pence.

We will continue in this way, playing clubs up and down the country, for much the same kind of money, staying in flea-pit hotels when it's too far to drive home, sustained by the lousy coffee and fast food in motorway service stations. Sometimes we go down well, and all the effort seems worthwhile, and sometimes we don't.

One night after a particularly awful gig for both the Police and Cherry Vanilla, I find myself alone in the truck, listening to an old Last Exit tape. It is by no means brilliant but I get terribly nostalgic and I miss Gerry and the old boys and I wonder if I haven't made a terrible mistake. My voice is shot, exhausted with overuse. I'm playing music I don't really like with people I have very little in common with, and I find it hard to figure out exactly what it is I'm doing here.

Frances and I have been married for a year now, and it's been very tough for her: the constant insecurity of our living situation, continually going up for auditions in plays, musicals, and TV, as well as looking after the baby. She would, of course, regain the momentum of her career playing major roles in seasons at the Royal Shakespeare Company and the National Theatre up to the present day, but those early years we spent together would be difficult and fraught with anxiety.

Still, even if it is only an article of faith that those who take risks with their lives are somehow protected, then that will have to be enough to sustain us until our luck changes. In fact, a few days later, Frances is offered a part in a BBC drama called *The Survivors*. It is a series based on the exploits of a group of survivors after a nuclear attack, and while this is not exactly the kind of work she has been waiting for, it is work nonetheless and we are both happy that it will put some money into our dwindling bank account.

Shortly after this my grandmother Agnes called to tell me that my father is ill and keeps having blackouts. I ring him up but he says his mother, as usual, is just being overly dramatic and that there's nothing to worry about.

"Are you sure, Dad?"

"Yes, I'm sure."

My father has never been sick in his life, but Agnes wouldn't have called if something wasn't truly the matter. I know that getting my father to a doctor if he doesn't want to go would be nigh impossible. I resolve to see for myself as soon as I can.

By the beginning of May we have moved into our basement in Leinster Square. We have one bedroom, which we share with the baby, a kitchen, a bathroom, and an enormous living room, as yet uncarpeted, and a bare window through which we can see a small stairwell below a set of wrought-iron railings and the disembodied legs of passersby on the pavement above. Our first month's rent will be paid, and most of the second payment is in the bank. I am extremely proud and determined that it will stay ours.

By the early summer Cherry will have lost her voice and fallen ill, and a projected European tour will have to be canceled. We will be reunited with her again later, but meanwhile, in another of Miles's cost-cutting exercises, we find ourselves supporting Wayne County and the Electric Chairs on a low-budget three-week tour of Holland and Belgium.

Wayne County is a singer from a small town in the Bible Belt of the U.S.A. Self-exiled by his strangeness, he had transposed himself to the bohemian freedoms of Manhattan. At the time I made his acquaintance he was still of indeterminate sexuality, and though he would soon call himself Jane and become to all intents and purposes a woman, in 1977 Wayne hadn't quite made the complete transition. He wears baggy clothes over his tiny frame, a floppy hat, and full makeup. He is a shy, sensitive, complex individual and I like him very much, although with songs like "If You Don't Wanna Fuck Me, Fuck Off" he clearly isn't from quite the same romantic tradition as I am when it comes to songwriting, but he is a fascinating performer.

He and the guitarist are a discreet if incongruous item, Greg being well over six feet tall, an ex–Golden Gloves boxing champion, with the mental age of a child of seven. He is extremely lovable but, when Wayne is not looking, given to drinking excessive amounts of alcohol, whereupon he can become violent. Wayne will accept no such nonsense from him, though, and frequently assumes the role of the shrewish wife, henpecking him mercilessly until he sobers up and calms down, smiling vacantly like a scolded dog. The manager, Peter Crowley, whom I privately dub "Aleister" (Aleister Crowley, the celebrated twentieth-century satanist and occult philosopher, wrote *Diary of a Drug Fiend*), looks like an aging Jet from an amateur production of *West Side Story*. He has a large head and a ludicrous greaser's pompadour that hangs pendulously between his eyebrows like a limp penis. The exaggerated padding in the shoulders of his leather biker's jacket creates the visual impression that his spindly legs have been cruelly foreshortened, like a bad photograph taken from an unflattering perspective. He can't seem to speak without sneering, as if he's suffering from some muscular disorder of the mouth, and the sound that emerges is little more than an incessant nasal whine. He gripes constantly about English weather, English food, English roads, English cars, English driving, even when we get to Holland. I begin to wonder if he isn't suffering from Tourette's syndrome, so violent are his outbursts.

At customs I catch sight of his U.S. passport over his shoulder and notice to my great surprise that Mr. Crowley, with his studded jacket and a silver dagger hanging from his ear, is an Episcopalian bishop. I'm not sure whether he really is a bishop, but this group is so weird nothing would surprise me. The drummer, who wears thin summer clothes, is a silver-haired Hungarian refugee named Chris Dust. He is attempting to claim political asylum in England and is not supposed to leave the country while his claim is being processed. I ask him why he is now boarding a ferry bound for Ostend.

"I need the gig, man. Got to eat. Got to buy some clothes for the winter"—indicating his careworn Hawaiian shirt.

The bass player is a thoroughly nice English boy named Adrian, although he goes by the name of Val Halla. He has an enormous simian jaw and blue-black dyed hair that makes him look like a fugitive from a band of Muppets in a bad wig.

With Stewart, myself, and the Corsican pirate making up the motley number, it is something of a freak show driving up the ramp of the ferry in Dover. The boat leaves at ten past midnight in heavy seas and torrential rain. It is a reasonable crossing and I manage to catch an hour's sleep. We reach Ostend at 4 A.M. It is dark and still raining. We have a carnet to export our equipment, but as we've failed to have it signed by a British customs officer, it isn't worth the paper it's printed on and the Belgian customs man wants nothing to do with it. He tells us that we will have to wait here until 8 o'clock and take it up with his boss, then storms back into his warm office and slams the door. Henry is at the wheel, the rain has now stopped, and the gates of the customs yard are invitingly open. Beyond them lies the open road, and we estimate that we could be in Holland by eight o'clock. We look from the office door to the open gate and the road beyond, and with a last complicit glance at each other we just drive into the night. We almost run out of petrol before we reach the border, but by dawn we are in the Netherlands, and safe from Belgian officialdom.

Peter Crowley—or Aleister, as I now openly call him—offers to take over the driving duties. As we are all pretty exhausted by now, we agree, but this is a bad mistake. Not only is he thoroughly unpleasant, he is also one of the worst drivers I've ever had the misfortune to travel with. He insists on driving like a wiseguy—too fast and with only one of his ostentatiously ringed hands on the wheel. He likes to drive even the shortest distances with his foot to the floor and then brake suddenly behind stationary vehicles. I've tried reasoning with him to no avail, and I'm losing my patience. Poor Henry is a nervous wreck behind his wraparound shades.

At a set of traffic lights, a car on the inside is straddling the white line and is transgressing maybe an inch at the most into our lane. I watch as Aleister narrows his eyes, mouths the word *motherfucker* through gritted teeth, and guns the engine so that we hit the offending nearside wing at speed and with a loud bang.

"What the fuck?" I shout.

"The asshole was in our freakin' lane," he shouts back.

"No, he was not. You deliberately hit him."

The asshole in question has gotten out of his car to inspect the damage. The poor man looks bewildered and a little intimidated, and then even more so when he sees the freak show in the van.

Aleister winds down the window as if to offer an explanation. "You're a freakin' asshole," he shouts. And then we're off on the green light, foot pressed hard to the floor in first gear.

"Crowley, you're the one who's the fuckin' asshole," I tell him, as he crashes the gear box into second, forgetting to use the clutch. "And you can't fucking drive."

He slams on the brakes, I suppose in an attempt to put me through the windscreen, but he only succeeds in dislodging Henry's amp, which flies to the front of the van like a guided missile. I'm close to tearing this guy's head off.

"Saying I can't drive," he whines, "is like saying Keith Moon can't play the drums."

I am utterly dumbstruck. What kind of cruel karma is working here to have trapped me in this van with this lunatic? When I've recovered my composure I convince Aleister that he will no longer be driving the van unless he wants to return to the U.S. in a body bag.

Our first gig is in Groningen, in what looks like a village hall. The PA system, which has been rented by the promoter, is being driven down from Amsterdam. It doesn't arrive until seven-thirty, so there is no time for any sound check. We go on anyhow, and halfway through the first number, the sound, such as it is, starts to go off and on, off and on. Then comes the deafening howl of feedback, bass end rumble, and high-frequency squeals, which have the audience covering their ears. I've had a trying day and uncharacteristically throw a tantrum, threatening the hapless Dutch sound crew with dismemberment unless they sort out the sound. Stewart plays throughout my tirade even more frenetically than usual and the audience, made up of stoned hippies seated cross-legged on the floor (who believe this new punk rock is somehow associated with violence), think my behavior is all part of the act, which infuriates me even more. I launch myself from the admittedly low stage, trying to shake the audience awake at least, kicking them, knocking them, rolling onto their backs. They thankfully start to fight back and I retire to the comparative safety of the stage.

The sound out front seems to have sorted itself out, whereupon we have a genuine if slightly delayed rock-and-roll experience. We are now going down a storm, the entire audience on its feet, when

Stewart, who is playing like a man possessed, snaps the metal rod of his bass drum pedal in half, closely followed by the collapse of the rest of his kit. Hi-hats, tom-toms, and cymbals roll all over the stage. The set dwindles to a pathetic halt, and in a stunned and embarrassed silence we exit the stage. It is only when we close the door of the dressing room behind us that we hear the ovation. Cheering, whistling, stamping. I think they must be out of their minds. We were rubbish. And anyway, we can't do an encore because the drums are in pieces. Our set has by now expanded to fifteen minutes from its original ten, and now it's Wayne's turn. Being as the audience have been prompted to react in the correct manner, Wayne too goes down a storm.

At the end of the night we each get a twenty-guilder note, then drive to a small hotel in the town's red-light district. Sad, middle-aged women sit in the windows reading paperback romances or knitting baby clothes in the red glow of cheap lampshades. My room is tiny, and while it has a bird's-eye view of the ladies across the street it has no hot water, no heat, and damp sheets. As I go to sleep in my clothes I wonder how Frances and the baby are.

The next few days will find us playing similar gigs in Eindhoven, Rotterdam, Nijmegen, Maasbree, and finally Amsterdam. My last-ing image of the Wayne County tour is of the Paradiso Club, a con-verted church in the center of Amsterdam. The stage is located where the old altar must have been, below a luminous stained-glass window that soars heavenward into the darkness of the high gothic ceiling. There is a strobe light strafing the audience, which is sparse and disparate, and scattered around the floor of the building in var-ious states of well-being. Some are asleep, smiling beatifically, others are huddled in corners under filthy sleeping bags. Some are dancing crazily like whirling dervishes, spinning out of control into their neighbors, who will push them away and send them reeling wildly in another direction. One of them hits the floor with his head, lying still for a few seconds, and then he's up again spinning and spinning. The sound from the stage is hellish. There is a surreal, nightmare quality about this scene, presided over by Wayne, screaming with demented fury "The Last Time," by the Rolling Stones, while Greg, dangerously drunk, is holding his only guitar by the neck and raising it high above his head and smashing it repeatedly against the front of the stage.

It is only the end of the tour but it seems like the end of the world.

The next day on the ferry from Zeebrugge back to England, Greg is nursing the mother of all hangovers. He is sitting on the upper deck of the rocking boat, his head in his hands, flanked by Wayne and Aleister.

"What are ya? Yarra freakin' idiot."

"Where we gonna find the dough for a new guitar? Huh? Tell me that. Ya freakin' moron."

"Ya spent every nickel we made on booze. Now look at us."

Crowley spits theatrically into the wind and it dribbles down his leather jacket. "He's a freakin' moron."

Greg suddenly makes a bolt for the rail and spews a yellow stream of his bilious demons over the side of the boat and into the English Channel.

"Freakin' moron," grumbles Aleister, as if in final judgment of the hapless Greg.

"Leave him alone," says Wayne, watching the pathetic figure hunched over the railing. As he goes over to comfort him, I realize Wayne loves him, and that Greg will be cared for as he's been cared for many times before. Aleister walks off in disgust, but not before fixing me with one of his evil unspoken curses.

Chris, the drummer, is on the other side of the boat watching the coast of England loom out of the mist. It is freezing, but he is still wearing the pathetic summer clothes that he's worn every day and every night onstage. As the port of Folkestone gets closer and closer he looks more and more anxious and fidgety.

"How're you doing, Chris?"

"I'm okay. Just hoping they let me back in."

"What if they don't?"

"I don't know. If they send me back to Hungary I'll go to prison."

He tries to light a cigarette but fails in the wind, and leaves the cigarette hanging, like a French movie star. "Maybe I should jump the ship and swim."

"I don't think you should do that, Chris. I'm sure it'll be fine."

He shrugs and disappears below and I realize how fortunate I am.

When we land in Folkestone the immigration authorities keep the Americans in the party for six hours, checking work permits, searching their bags and their clothes, and generally making life unpleasant. The rest of us wait in the car park. We will wait a further four hours for Chris until we are told that he is being sent back to Zeebrugge on the night ferry. Poor guy. There's nothing we can do, so we drive back to London in a black depression.

When I eventually get home to my wife and son, whom I hardly recognize because he's grown so much, she asks me if I know someone called Deborah. I have a bad feeling in the pit of my stomach.

"Yes, I do. Why?"

"Your mam called. She said that Deborah is dead."

That night I lie awake and I watch my wife and child as they sleep in our tiny bedroom at the back of the flat in Bayswater. I've tried to sleep, and I've tried praying, but it's no use, and I start to wonder at the terrifying strangeness of life. It's as if I can see it for the first time, like the workings of a vast machine suddenly revealed behind the opaque scrim of my meager understanding. How did I arrive here? My life until I met Frances seems to have been made up piecemeal, as if it were an aggregate of small choices and inconsequential decisions. And yet these small adjustments to the compass of my life have somehow led me to a momentous responsibility. I try to trace the pattern of my life back from this moment like an amnesiac attempting to remember how he could have arrived in such a place. I ponder that one small alteration, one tiny deviation in the course, would have set an entirely different set of wheels in motion in this complex machinery of fate. I'm a husband and a father, I live in a city far from my home, I am following a dream, and yet a girl I had loved, a girl that I easily could have married and led quite another life with, is now dead.

It is only a few days later that I will, for just a brief moment, imagine that I have seen a ghost.

The Housing Association to which we belong comprises almost the entire terrace on the eastern side of the leafy Bayswater Square, to the north of Hyde Park. There are six tall, white-painted houses of six floors split into thirty-six separate properties. All of the flats, apart from the six basements, look out across the street onto the verdant lawns of a private tree-filled garden in the center of the square.

Our flat, like all of the other basements in the square, is below the level of the pavement. We have a separate front door from the one that accesses the flats above, and unfortunately the only view we have from our windows is of a small yard with a stone staircase leading up to the street. We really don't mind, the flats upstairs were far more expensive than Frances and I could afford, and the subterranean life seemed appropriate to our needs as well as our clandestine ambitions.

But when some of the upstairs neighbors start lobbying to keep their rubbish in the little yards in front of the basements, in effect reducing our already nonexistent view to a collective refuse site, there are rumblings of sedition belowstairs. We may live below the ground but that's no reason for us to be treated like lower-class citizens.

When some of those who live upstairs begin unilaterally depositing their bags at our front door, I know that rebellion is our only hope. A meeting of the basement dwellers is called at number 32, and I am the first to arrive.

Descending the stone steps into the yard and peering through the window, I can see that the basement at number 32 is just like ours. I am met at the door by a tall sandy-haired man in his early thirties. His name is James, he is an actor, and he shares the flat with his girlfriend. They moved in a few weeks after us, but we have never met. James sits me down by the fireplace and asks if I would like a cup of tea. I tell him I'd love one and he makes his way to the kitchen at the back of the flat, leaving me in the sparsely furnished room. Looking round, I see that they are certainly no better off than we are, except that they do have a carpet. There is no glass yet in the doorframe leading to the kitchen corridor so I hear a muted conversation and the tinkling of female laughter. James returns. "Be here in a minute. The old girl's just brewing up.

"So," he continues in an actor's baritone, "what do you think we should do about this rubbish situation?"

"Well, you know, I've been thinking about it and . . . and . . . !"

I have stopped talking because a young woman has just walked through the empty doorframe from the kitchen holding a pot of tea and some china cups. She is a stunning blonde in tight blue jeans and a powder-blue sweater. Her eyes are a pale, pale green, and across her left cheek is a whitened strip of scar tissue that curls like the violent memory of an animal claw around the socket of her left eye. Strangely the scar in no way detracts from her beauty, because she looks to me like a kind of damaged angel. There is something else about her that has stunned me into silence. It is the shape of her mouth. I feel as if I am witnessing an apparition for she has the full lips and wide smile that are so like Deborah's as to be uncanny. For a brief moment this strange tableau of the beautiful girl with the pirate's scar and the ghostly smile seems to be frozen in time like a photograph and then burned into my memory.

It is James who breaks the spell between us, "Have you met Trudie?" he asks.

I would discover that Trudie Styler had run away from home as a teenager with a dream to become an actress. She had run, naively and instinctively to Stratford on Avon, the town of William Shakespeare's birth and the home of the Royal Shakespeare Company. She knew no one who lived there and was forced on her first night in the strange town to knock on doors asking for shelter. She was taken in by a theatrical family called the Churches who would give her a bed for the night and later a job as nanny to their children. With their encouragement she would successfully apply to study drama at the Old Vic Theatre School in Bristol. She would graduate and work as an actress in television and theatre, eventually starring in an RSC production at the Warehouse theatre in London. Between jobs she would work as an MC in an Arab night club where she was known as "Angel." The scar on her face was the result of a terrible accident when she was a small child: she'd been dragged down the street underneath a truck and escaped miraculously with her life, but needed over a hundred stitches in her face and head. No one had expected her to become a great beauty or a successful actress.

It would be three years before Trudie and I would become lovers, but our attraction to each other would not only be instant but blatantly obvious to everyone around us. There was open childlike innocence about it at first, a joy and spontaneity in each other's presence that was impossible to disguise, but as this infatuation became more and more intense I began to struggle with my true feelings. I did not want to re-enact my mother's tortured conflict between romance and familial love but I was falling for the girl next door and a chasm was opening up beneath me.

Stewart and I are becoming more and more joined at the hip. We seem to have a growing belief in each other and that we somehow share a common future. While not identical to the apprentice-mentor relationship I have had with Gerry, my relationship with Stewart is becoming increasingly important, and though this one isn't growing at the expense of the older one, there is a renewed tension in my dealings with my old friend.

During our Holland tour, Gerry had moved to London and gotten a job playing organ in a topless bar in Soho. He's making fifty pounds week (still a king's ransom to me) and staying with some friends in south London until he can find a place of his own. When we return, I invite him round for an impromptu session with Stewart, hoping they'll get on, and we have a good time jamming a few old Last Exit tunes and a few standards. When Gerry goes off to work I drop as many hints as I can to Stewart that he ought to add a keyboard player to his plan, to give us more versatility. But Stewart seems adamant that what he wants is a three-piece guitar trio, and any replacement for Henry would have to play guitar. History would prove him right.

I believe Gerry, on the other hand, is beginning to feel a little left out. While he is certainly not the kind of person to be jealous—I'm not sure he'd even want to be in these bands I'm playing with—he's the only one from Last Exit to have made the leap of faith to come to London, and I don't want him to feel like I've abandoned him. It is Gerry, however, who will be the one to take the first step away.

He calls me the next day to tell me he's been offered a tour as the musical director for Billy Ocean. I'm thrilled for him, but when he asks me if I want the bass seat I have to decline, even though it's a hundred pounds a week plus expenses. If I can make that amount in a month with the Police I'll be lucky, and while the money would obviously make us feel more secure, I'm not tempted in the least. Put it down to instinct. But this does mark a delineation of my partnership with Gerry, who will chart his own course from now on. I owe a great deal to him in many ways—he was my teacher, even though he would treat such a suggestion with contempt. We will remain friends up to the present time, and after many adventures of his own he will become a highly respected lecturer in a music college back home in Newcastle, and of course he's still gigging.

But now I have really thrown my lot in with Stewart, and peripherally with his Machiavellian brother, Miles.

Then commences a period that can only be categorized as marking time. Cherry has recovered her voice and Max wants us to play a month of dates with her, culminating at the Roundhouse in Chalk Farm with the Jam and the Stranglers. We play as far north as the Glasgow Apollo and as far south as Plymouth and Penzance and we go down well most nights, both with Cherry and as the Police, and although our set is getting longer and more accomplished, I feel we are treading water and that my creative energy is being lulled to sleep. It is interesting and probably only a coincidence that I will fall asleep at the wheel of the van, driving back from a gig in Stafford in the Midlands, and almost succeed in terminating all of our careers prematurely.

It is the early hours of the morning and the others are asleep in the back. We are all exhausted. I have been driving the truck for a couple of hours and Henry is trying to keep me company in the front seat although he keeps nodding off against the side window. The others are asleep in the back. The motorway is empty, and we are cruising in the middle lane doing about eighty.

Henry stirs himself and becomes aware that I'm inching the truck slowly into the outside lane. As there is no traffic around us he can't work out why I'm making such a maneuver, until he realizes with horror that I have my eyes closed. He screams at me, and I suddenly wake from a dream to see the road looming and the van heading for the central barrier. My own screams join with Henry's for what seems like an eternity, as I try to wrench myself fully awake and we go into a mind-bending skid away from the barrier but heading with the terrifying screech of tires toward the embankment on the other side. The words *opposite lock* burn themselves into my brain and I turn the hurtling wagon into the skid, finding to my immense relief after a tire-burning hundred yards that we seem to be under control. I slow the van down and pull over to the hard shoulder. Everyone is awake now.

"What the fuck...?"

"I'm sorry, everybody, I fell asleep, Henry saved all of our lives."

"Fuckeeng 'elle. *J'ai pensé un* really moment, yes?"

"Yes, Henry, that was a really moment."

But Henry's really moments as a member of the Police will be sadly numbered, for it is in the following period that Stewart and I will meet Andy Summers, a musician who will be hugely influential in our subsequent careers and the history of the Police.

\* \* \*

My publisher, Carol Wilson, has a boyfriend who is the former bass player of Gong, an Anglo-French, quintessential hippie band popular in the early seventies. (Steve Hillage, the guitarist, is probably the band's most famous alumni.) Carol's boyfriend is named Mike Howlett and he's a very good musician, his music being closer in feel and sophistication to the ideals Last Exit had aspired to. Mike is interested in forming a band with us called Strontium 90. I do point out to him that having two bass players in a band is not standard practice, but we have a few rehearsals together and work out a few tandem parts where we don't step on each other's toes. Stewart comes one afternoon for a session and agrees to give it a punt, neither of us having anything to lose. Again I bring up the possibility of Gerry's joining us, but Mike says he has another player in mind. So it will be in the small studio of Mike and Carol's pleasant terraced house in Acton that we first meet Andy Summers.

Andy has a youthful, intelligent face, framed with angelic golden locks. He is urbane, good-humored, something of a dilettante in things artistic, well dressed, and alert to any slights that may be directed toward him intentionally or otherwise. He possesses the kind of elegance that in a different age would have been described as dapper. I had seen him play once in the sixties at the Club A Go-Go with Zoot Money's band and more recently as part of Kevin Coyne's backup group. He had lived for a long time in the States and been a member of the New Animals with Eric Burdon, but he has been back in England for a year now with his American wife, Kate, to reestablish himself in the new British music scene.

I am on my best behavior.

When I get to know Andy better I will appreciate how well read he is. He has a large collection of books, with a leaning toward the esoteric, an encyclopedic knowledge of film, and is highly opinionated in all matters cultural. All of this might have made him a terrible bore but for his excellent and often absurd sense of humor. He can be the best company, and having been on the road most of his life has learned the survivor's knowledge—that to maintain a modicum of sanity when everyone else is losing theirs, you need to occasionally send yourself up. He does this with the same ease and grace that he displays as a guitarist. Stewart and I will dub him the "art monster," which he will accept as the greatest compliment.

Andy blows us all away. He is clearly a fine musician, a master of many musical styles and techniques, from classical to jazz and everything in between. This is the kind of musician I could write for, the kind of musician I could entrust with my songs, who could inspire me, who could realize the music in my head, and although I don't say anything because we are in Mike's studio, this is exactly the kind of musician that the Police need. I can tell that Stewart is impressed too.

We wait until the session is over and we are driving back into town before anything is said.

"I know what you're thinking."

"Really, Stewart? What am I thinking?"

"You're thinking that Andy is the guy we're looking for."

"Why, don't you think so?"

"Well, yes and no."

"I understand yes, but why no?"

"Well, he can certainly play, but . . ." He chooses his words carefully. "It's a question of image."

He knows I'm going to bristle here and go off on one of my rants about music versus fashion, but I bite my tongue and say nothing.

"Henry has the right image."

"Henry can't play."

"He can play."

"Stewart, you play better guitar than he does, and you're crap."

Stewart, ever the patient diplomat, tries a different approach. "Andy's a whole decade older than we are."

"Yes, he is, but strangely enough he looks younger than both of us."

"Then it's just a question of image."

"Stewart, believe me, I love Henry as much as you do. He saved all of our lives, for fuck's sake, but we're not going to get any farther than we have done unless the fucking music improves, and I don't want to be in Cherry's band for the rest of my life."

"No, Sting, nor do I."

Neither of us will address the very real possibility that Andy will have no interest in joining our wretched little band or that we already seem to be painting Mike out of the picture, as if he is an unwanted Trotsky in a retouched photograph of the politburo.

I'm not sure which one of us said it, but it is as if we both reach the same conclusion at the same instant:

"What about if we used them both? Henry and Andy?"

The lights change and we are off, heartlessly planning a revolution in our heads all the way home.

So for a while we will continue supporting Cherry Vanilla, as well as playing in her band, and also rehearsing with Mike. He seems to have Virgin Records interested, so we put together demos of two of his songs. One is "Electron Romance," a pseudo-scientific ditty with a textured, convoluted bass line, and the other, called "Not on the Planet," is a proto-ecological rant, with some fine slide guitar by Mr. Summers. The demos are fine, but Mike's voice and mine hardly blend, and while it is interesting to have two bass players, it is getting harder to justify the amount of work we have to do so as not to get in each other's way. I'm not really sure what my function is in this band, but Stewart is far more cynical.

"You're there to make up for his deficiencies. He can't sing. You can."

Whatever the case, we have a great time playing with Andy. I've introduced a couple of my own songs into the set, which he seems to enjoy playing, and there is now a tacit understanding in the air that perhaps the band we had envisaged may be more than a pipe dream.

The RCA pressing plant in County Durham is a shrine to Elvis Presley. His picture seems to be on every wall in every corridor in the place. The first Police single is scheduled to be released in May, so Stewart, Henry, and I stop at the plant to pick up the first pressings on our way to a gig at Newcastle Poly.

We are led into one of the listening rooms, and through a common glass window is another listening room with six ladies, all in advanced middle age, each wearing headphones and identical working smocks. They sit like religious devotees under their portrait of Elvis with the blank look of people in a trance, staring at nothing in particular, isolated in their private world. Two of them are knitting, one is crocheting, the other three are reading magazines. They are checking for crackles on the discs, one after the other, for hour after hour, day in day out. They could be listening to Puccini or Ziggy Stardust, they don't care. I feel like we've walked into some obscure suburb of hell, and I must force myself not to look at them.

Listening to our single, we discover a fault, and indeed a whole box of fifty is deficient. We are somewhat deflated but they produce a further box of fifty perfect singles, which we load into the back of the van and head north to Newcastle.

I haven't been home in five months. My mother is thrilled while Dad is amused. I peer closely at him and he looks healthy enough to me, which of course is reassuring. My parents are on their best behavior, entranced by Stewart's American glamour and Henry's Gallic charm. Stewart gets a great kick out of smoking a joint in my parents' house. Ernie of course can't resist having a toke, and after his second is telling us that it's not making the slightest difference to the way he feels, but pretty soon he gets the giggles and ends up lying almost horizontal on his favorite armchair and dozing off. I don't think I've ever seen him so relaxed.

The next night at Newcastle Poly is far from being the glorious homecoming I'd envisioned. We get blown off the stage by a local punk group called Penetration who are, to be honest, absolutely wonderful. The best punk band I've ever seen, and that is not just local pride. When we walk onstage all the Penetration fans have left, and we face a discreet smattering of disapproving Last Exit followers, a few polite music lovers, Keith Gallagher, my best man, Terry Ellis, my erstwhile guitarist, Phil Sutcliffe, the father of the whole enterprise, and my ever-loyal brother. We play well and are applauded politely. Cherry gets the same response. Keith will tell me that he thinks the Police are a one-man show. I assume he means me, but I don't press him for clarification. Terry has disappeared. Phil Sutcliffe is sphinxlike, and my brother, who now sports an awful mustache, thinks we're crap. We sell four records.

When "Fall Out" is finally released it gets reasonable reviews in the U.K. A French music weekly votes it single of the week (though how much that has to do with Henry being a French national is hard to ascertain) and Radio Clyde makes it record of the week. Mark P. of that august and by now almost respectable organ *Sniffing Glue* says it's rubbish. I suppose this was to be expected, despite us being stablemates at Miles's Dryden Chambers. We end up selling four thousand copies.

There are great plans afoot for a Gong festival in Paris at the end of May. As the group had enjoyed cult status in France, someone had suggested a massing of the clans wherein the various offshoots of the original band would play at the Hippodrome, a permanent circus in the north of Paris. Strontium 90 are, of course, invited to play and we all are energized by the idea. The band will be fairly low on the bill, but we are used to that, and the event will dovetail handily with a festival in Colmar the next day that the Police have been booked for, supporting Dr. Feelgood.

The concert starts at three in the afternoon and doesn't finish until three the next morning, with over five thousand French hippies in attendance. A giant weather balloon is suspended from the big top, and a piddling laser affair makes sporadic and halfhearted attempts at creating a science-fiction ambience. Here too are the more traditional fire-eaters, trapeze artists, and sad peripatetic clowns, who give the event more of the atmosphere of a shabby medieval fair than a convincing glimpse of the future. And then there are the bands. Splinter groups of splinter groups all loosely related to the vast amoebalike Gong phenomena, a band famous for its theatrical indulgence and hobbitlike eccentricities.

We play well and the audience applauds earnestly. The ubiquitous Phil Sutcliffe, who seems to be following me round like the recording angel, is covering the event for *Sounds*. He seems mightily impressed by the band and, in a turnaround from his response to the Police show in Newcastle, gushes enthusiastically. We stay to watch Steve Hillage, who is terrific—probably the nearest the British rock scene ever got to producing a Jerry Garcia—after which Andy, Stewart, and I escape before the grand finale. Mike, of course, is forced to stay behind.

Over dinner in a cheap but pleasant Algerian restaurant Andy, in his cups, will reveal to us that he does not share Mr. Sutcliffe's enthusiasms. He seems to want to throw his lot in with Stewart and me, although he does see himself as a direct replacement for Henry and not as his supplement. Stewart and I keep our counsel, knowing that in the short term all our options need to be kept open.

Back in London, the Police are starting to headline at clubs like the Marquee in Wardour Street, so the Cherry Vanilla Band has had to find replacements for Stewart and me. Though our set has now expanded to an hour, we still have to play some songs more than once. I keep telling Stewart that if we would only play a little slower, then the problem would disappear, but he won't have any of it.

As it turns out, all the record company promises for Strontium 90 seem to have been as ephemeral as they had been for Last Exit. Mike has tried to bring some new energy to the project by renaming the band the Elevators, but halfway through our first set at Dingwalls, when we can't seem to get the two basses in tune and the audience loses interest, we realize that this particular elevator isn't going to get off the first floor. Predictably, Andy calls up the next day to say that he is no longer going to be an Elevator or a Strontium 90 or whatever other isotope Mike might have in mind, and when are we going to sack Henry?

Though disappointed, Mike is sanguine. He is at the core a gentleman and a realist. He accepts that the balance of power has shifted, and will not stand in our way. We will remain friends. This, however, does not solve the Henry situation. Our lovable Corsican has definitely intuited that something is going on, and while his musicianship has certainly improved, his enthusiasm has dimmed, particularly onstage. But Stewart is still not convinced that Andy should replace him and wants to sustain the band as a quartet. Trusting in Stewart's diplomatic skills, I agree we should give it a try.

It's 1977 in the summer of the Queen's Silver Jubilee, and every Wednesday afternoon I walk to Lisson Grove to sign on the dole. There are flags and bunting festooning the streets in every part of the city. It will be a lavish and extravagant celebration of this second Elizabethan Age, banishing for a while the grim realities of our struggling economy and social malaise.

My usual route from Bayswater takes me past a Victorian house above a boarded-up shop. On this particular Wednesday, there is a huge black Bentley with a liveried chauffeur parked incongruously in the street below the flat, and a young man with an untidy shag of blond hair is leaning out the window on the upper floor. The young man is Paul Cook, drummer of the Sex Pistols. The rest of the band—Sid Vicious, Johnny Rotten, and Steve Jones—are falling out of the car in their expensive leather trousers and teased hair. They are all out of their trees, quaffing cans of lager and shouting up to Paul, who seems to be observing their antics with a sober, detached amusement. Sid is now halfway up a lamppost and pointing drunkenly at the window. Lisson Grove dole stands mistily in the background, and if I'd had a camera I could have captured in one snapshot a perfect portrait of Britain in this jubilee year, her wry contradictions and her wayward, hilarious sons.

I like the Pistols. The only jealousy I harbor is that they don't have to sign on today and I do. I pass by unmolested, but there is chaos at the dole. A new girl sits behind the grille at box 26. She can't cope and the queue stretches miserably all the way to the doorway like an angry snake. How much longer will I have to do this?

That night Stewart and I go to the 100 Club in Oxford Street to see Alternative TV. This is Mark P.'s band. Mark, having peaked as a critic, has decided to try his hand at performing. The band have asked to borrow my bass gear, to which I accede, if only to show that I don't bear any grudges about the lousy review he gave our record in his magazine. As Mark has only been playing the guitar for a few weeks and has never sung a note in his life, it would be unfair to offer any criticism here, but Stewart and I have scrounged enough money for a few beers and meet an old friend of his named Kim Turner.

Kim is the younger brother of Martin Turner, bassist for the Wishbone Ash. Kim had been the drummer in a band called Cat Iron that Stewart had tour-managed a number of years before. Now a jack-of-all-trades, Kim had thrown in his lot with Miles as an assistant manager. Street-smart, wily, and immensely likable, Kim would become tour manager of the Police, playing a significant role in our subsequent adventures and ultimate success. But that is light-years away from this dingy little club on a wet Wednesday night. On this occasion Kim had been drafted into Mark's band as an experienced guitarist to fill in the considerable gaps in Mark's repertoire of riffs and basic chords.

Confirming an old adage that "no act of kindness goes unpunished," my bass gear is returned the next day with the speaker blown. A few weeks later Mark will find himself even further in my debt when, one afternoon, I drive my little blue Citroën up to Miles's house in the leafy suburb of St. John's Wood to pick up Stewart's drums. Apart from my two guitars, my Citroën is my only prized possession. There is a stationary truck in the drive, so I park on the other side of the road.

Squeezing myself past the truck, I meet Mark and Harry, his tour manager, coming out of the front door looking suddenly very embarrassed to see me, Miles having just informed them that they'd wrecked my speaker cabinet. After a few mumbled apologies and an offer of some cash at an unspecified date in the future, they hurry off and climb into the waiting truck.

Moments after Miles greets me at the door, flanked by his two hideous and slobbering pet mastiffs, we hear the truck reversing down the drive and then an almighty crash. We run to the window, only to see the truck pulling away hurriedly and disappearing south toward Swiss Cottage and central London, leaving a little blue car on the other side of the road with its front end smashed like a child's toy. They have clearly fled the scene in a panic, because as I find out later, Mark has neither a driving license nor any insurance to drive such a vehicle. Miles, who owns the truck, is aghast. After my own initial shock and a flash of righteous anger, I begin to laugh.

"What's so funny?"

"There's nothing funny, Miles, except that that's my car, and Mark and Harry don't know it yet."

Miles puts his head in his hands. Mark and Harry will be staying out of my way for a while.


Andy is now officially a member of the Police, as yet a quartet, when we are booked to play the Mont de Marsan Festival in southern France with the Clash, the Damned, and the Jam. We are pretty low on the bill, but the exposure, according Miles, will be good for us. Although not entirely committed to his brother's band, Miles is taking more of an interest in us. We work hard, we don't complain, and we are flexible enough to fit in with his plans when other bands let him down. But he is still not our manager.

It takes us two exhausting days to drive there in a big yellow bus, no doubt testing Andy's resolve to slum it and be a foot soldier in this new invasion of the Continent. He proves himself to be more than equal to the task and makes an entertaining traveling companion. We arrive at the town's bullring, road-weary and starving, but we play pretty well and go down a storm. Andy is definitely an asset, although there is some friction between him and Stewart, who maintains a need to prove to the rest of the world that he's the fastest and most frenetic drummer on the bill, if not the planet.

The high spot of the evening are the Clash, who I love because they seem genuinely musical, employing simple chords and melodies played with clarity and economy. Captain Sensible of the Damned walks on in the middle of their set, drunk, uninvited, and wearing a bright-red beret. He drops a stink bomb behind Joe Strummer, who manfully continues singing, and then falls off the stage, painfully astride a scaffolding pole. He is hurriedly taken out of the bullring on a stretcher, singing "The Marseillaise."

Back in London a few days later, Andy will give Stewart and me his final ultimatum, and I am given the painful job of telling Henry that he will no longer be part of the band. When I help him load his gear into his digs, we are both very sad, although Henry says that he suspected something like this would happen when Andy joined us.

"We had some really moments, Henry."

"Yes, we did, my friend, some really moments."

Henry and I would remain friends. He will continue to improve as a guitar player, and the next time I see him he will be the new guitarist with Wayne and the Electric Chairs, after Greg had finally gone off the deep end.

I pay a visit to Stewart and Sonja, who have moved out of the palatial squat in Mayfair to a modest and tiny bedsit in Putney. We sit nursing cups of coffee in the middle of the floor, surrounded by their possessions piled into makeshift stacks of records, books, Arab artifacts, and musical equipment. My friend is not his usual self. Miles has convinced him that it was a terrible idea to sack Henry and this has sent Stewart into a terrible crisis of confidence. I remind Stewart we have a gig in two days in Birmingham and that he shouldn't slash his wrists until we hear how we sound as a trio again. Still, I can't help but be infected by this uncharacteristic mood of despondency that seems to have overtaken him after Henry's departure.

It is pouring with rain when I get home, and Joe is ill. He feels like a furnace and his little heart is beating like a time bomb. We call for a doctor, who arrives an hour later, under an umbrella. He is an elegant black man in wire-rimmed glasses and a tailored suit, with a refined English accent. Frances and I are embarrassed first by the lack of carpets and furniture in our flat and then to our horror realize that one of the neighbors has given Joe a golliwog, which sits accusingly, like a voodoo fetish, in the corner of the cot with our sick child. The rain is drumming a tattoo on the concrete of the yard outside the window. The doctor graciously ignores the ridiculous dolly and tells us our son needs medication, and that we should try to keep him cool. He writes a prescription and tells us that the nearest chemist open at this time of night is in Piccadilly.

I drive to Piccadilly in the pouring rain to find a massive queue at the chemist, a single assistant behind the counter, and half of London ill and in need of medicine. I get back home an hour later and the antibiotics seem to work and Joe settles down for a peaceful night, despite the rain drumming on the window. I don't sleep a wink as I turn our situation over and over in my head, the responsibilities of the family weighing heavily on me: how are we going to survive, how are we to keep up the payments on this flat, will Frances find a job, and what the hell is going to happen to the band?

By next morning the rain has stopped and Joe is fine. The radio tells us that last night was the wettest in fifteen years and that Elvis Presley was found dead at his home in Memphis.

Rebecca's is a small nightclub/discotheque in the center of Birmingham. Driving into town we are heartened to see many fly posters on the walls, suggesting that the promoters have done enough to pull in a crowd for what in our minds is a crucial Rubicon. We will either cross it successfully or our fragile enterprise will be swept downstream in a chaos of despondency and abandoned dreams. We know that everything is at stake tonight and we badly need a boost for our morale. Andy walks onstage knowing that should we fail, the band that he's risked his reputation for will almost certainly fold. Stewart and I peer out of the dressing room at the growing crowd in the club with the grim thousand-yard stares of the condemned.

We walk onstage, the lights come up, and out of sheer desperation, panic, and I suppose character we somehow manage to kick off the shackles of self-doubt and despondency and within the first eight bars of the first tune begin to play with the unrelenting power of a ten-ton hammer. Stewart and I are pumping eight to the bar like a churning turbine in an engine room, while Andy releases broadside after broadside of shimmering guitar riffs. And my voice is soaring over it all like a raucous, predatory bird. The crowd, at first tentative, begins to go crazy. There is total mayhem, as if the audience is complicit in our need to make this one a great gig. We walk off after three encores, destroying the drums as we wade through the audience on the way to the dressing room, and knowing at last something rare has been uncovered here, that the deeper we dig the greater the prize. I know, perhaps for the first time, that I have found a flagship for my songs. We will prevail. It will take time, but now I'm certain of it.

Galvanized by Andy's presence I start writing again like in the old days with Last Exit, prolific and joyful. It is in this period, between the end of August and Christmas of 1977, that I will write most of the songs for our first album, often salvaging fragments of songs I'd written for my old band and morphing them to new chords and melodies. The new songs are more direct, more economic than their old incarnations, but balanced with a subtlety that the band hadn't explored before. "So Lonely" shamelessly pasted old Last Exit lyrics onto the chord changes of Bob Marley's "No Woman, No Cry," the lilting rhythm of the verses separated by monolithic slabs of straight rock and roll. This kind of musical juxtaposition amused the hell out of me, and that we could achieve it effortlessly just added to the irony of a song about misery being sung so joyously.

Very few of the new bands had the finesse to be able to play reggae, with its complex rhythmic counterpoint that seems to turn traditional pop drumming on its head. This, and the predominance of the bass in the music, allowed Stewart and me to explore subtle areas of interplay that were rarely touched on by less experienced outfits. To create a hybrid using the drag-race horsepower of rock and roll and welding it seamlessly to the rolling stock of reggae music would make for an interesting journey, especially now that the post-punk landscape was beginning to look like a war zone to some people. That war zone looked like nothing less than an opportunity to us.

October finds Stewart, Andy, and me in France with Wayne County, a revamped Henry, and the band, and now they also have a new drummer. Val the bass player tells me Chris tried to get back into England. This time he jumped the ferry but was caught swimming for shore and deported again. Poor bastard. While in Paris we play the Nashville Club, a seedy velveteen music hall in St. Germain, and are staying for a few nights in a flophouse behind the Gare St. Lazare. The entrance of our hotel is in a narrow and fetid alleyway off the main boulevard. In early evening it is flanked by the garish lights of a sex shop and a dimly lit secondhand bookstore. The alley is a pitch for about twenty women leaning in doorways, chain-smoking. In their shiny open raincoats, short skirts, cheap boots, and high-heeled shoes they watch the street with hooded eyes, like spies in a B movie. Some are young and pretty, and some are older, and some of them are very old, with facial expressions ranging from sullen to wry. Most of the commerce is centered on the slightly older women, as if the majority of the clients prefer experience and world-liness. The younger, prettier girls seem to do the least business, apparent innocence being only a minority preference, much as it is for the aging crones in the alley who seem as if they've been standing there for a thousand years.

In the dingy foyer of the hotel is an old poster from La Comédie Française, sadly peeling from the wall behind the desk. *Cyrano de Bergerac,* it proclaims, a play by Edmond Rostand. I will stand for a few moments to take in its fading gaiety. It is a laughing portrait of a man with an enormous nose and a plumed hat. He is a tragic clown whose misfortune is his honor. He is a man entrusted with a secret; an eloquent and dazzling wit who, having successfully wooed a beautiful woman on behalf of a friend cannot reveal himself as the true author when his friend dies. He is a man who loves but is not loved, and the woman he loves but cannot reach is called Roxanne.

That night I will go to my room and write a song about a girl. I will call her Roxanne. I will conjure her unpaid from the street below the hotel and cloak her in the romance and the sadness of Rostand's play, and her creation will change my life.

# 13

BY THE END OF THE YEAR, HAVING MANAGED TO PAY THE RENT
on our new home, bought a carpet and some furniture, we are beginning to feel as if we are holding our own. Frances's TV work is becoming more regular and is well paid. She has worked at the BBC, in a
radio play of *The Passing Day,* ironically the play in which her father
made his name in the West End of the early fifties. She has won a big
role in a BBC production of a play with music called *Catchpenny
Twist,* set on location in Northern Ireland. It is an important job for
her as an actress and also for her spirits after this difficult year.

But I still have no regular income apart from the dole, and I've
been trying to increase our coffers by doing some modeling with
Pippa Markham's help. I will get parts in commercials for Brutus
Jeans and Triumph Bras, and I even rope Andy and Stewart in for a
Wrigley's Gum commercial directed by Tony Scott. In this way I
find myself doing something I never would have anticipated, being
paid purely on the strength of how I look. Hardly my finest moment, but all in all I am proud that we are at least keeping our heads
above water and have even managed to return the money our parents lent us for the flat. I thought my father would have been more
pleased than he was.

"We'll you haven't exactly set the world alight, have you?"

"It takes time, Dad."

"But you've been down to the bones of your arse for over a year now, and with a wife and kid and all."

"It's getting better, Dad."

"Oh aye?"

This last phrase is loaded with the sarcasm that I know provokes my mother into violent rages, but I don't rise to the bait. It's not worth arguing with him. He's largely right and he's unhappy.

Frances and I are spending Christmas with my family, and whatever warm glow the concept of "home" is supposed to engender, it is sadly missing. There is the usual background hum of quiet hysteria in the house, but percolating just below the surface of my mother's pre-Christmas frenzy of shopping, decorations, and food, the mood is more like the stockpiling that goes on before a war. A war that seems likely to erupt at any minute.

While delighted to see Frances and the baby, my father is only barely civil to me, at pains to communicate that he thinks I've lost my mind and that I'm wasting my time in London. It's almost as if any success or independence for me in the big city would be another nail in his coffin. In further spurious, niggly exchanges he tells me that London is a terrible place to bring up a kid and that it's a nest of muggers, thieves, crooked lawyers, and sharp practices. I don't point out that his arguments are ignorant, provincial folk tales, because I recognize that in his own curious way he's telling me he misses me.

My elder sister, Angela, is now married and in a home of her own, and I wonder if her leaving and my exodus to London has disturbed the delicate balance of détente in the house. My youngest sister is still at school and now the only dependent remaining. My brother, who works the milk rounds with my father and whom I've been closer to than anyone in my family and is my greatest supporter, has now adopted the air of someone getting on with the real business of life, and not "gadding" after pie-in-the-sky notions of stardom and the high life. He is the responsible heir to the family business, while I seem to have squandered my "fancy" education and my hard-won local celebrity on nothing more than a whim.

On Christmas morning, more tension. My mother has bought Joe a plastic trundle racing car and despite my dad's attempts to sit him astride the thing and push him around the room, the shiny crinkly wrapping paper is far more compelling. Frances is given a revolting synthetic green waistcoat that somehow makes her look like a Christmas tree. In a less-charged atmosphere we could have just had a good laugh, but our smiles are unnaturally rictus-like, neither of us wanting to seem ungrateful but still desperately uncomfortable.

I never wear jewelry and my mother knows this, but inside the ostentatiously wrapped box she gives me is a gold-plated identity bracelet. It is gangster-ugly, garish, heavy and uninscribed, and if there is some hidden semiotic meaning in the blankness of the ornament, it can only be unconscious. Perhaps she thinks I have yet to define myself since I have broken away from home, that I don't know who I am anymore, or perhaps that we no longer know each other. She may not be wrong, but this message will reach me when it is too late. There is a terrible sadness in a kind gift that is unappreciated, unwanted, and misunderstood.

Frances has to return to London for a TV job, and I have a gig. My mother kindly agrees to look after Joe over the New Year holiday. I will pick him up in a week because I have to return, oddly enough, for a Last Exit reunion.

Ronnie has been pestering Gerry and me for the last six months to come and do a Christmas gig for the fans at home. He has booked the bar of the University Theatre and it's a sellout. Gerry, who has been doing pretty well with gigging and the odd tour, has the same mixed feelings about the reunion as I do, running the full gamut of emotions between dread and sentimental nostalgia, but we finally agreed and now that it's a fait accompli we are both quietly pleased.

We have a rehearsal in Wallsend at the arts center, the converted Victorian school where my mother was educated. She must have sat in this very hall as a little girl in her pretty cotton dresses and her white socks, her fair hair tied in bunches, dreaming wide-eyed of her future beyond the war and of the dashing prince who would rescue her.

The old band is a little rusty, but the rehearsal goes well. We are all pleased to see each other. Ronnie and Terry haven't changed a bit since we saw them last, and I wonder if they feel the same about us. We select about fifteen numbers from the old pad, and after we blow off the cobwebs and refresh our memory of the arrangements, we soon get up to speed.

The following night the theater bar is crammed with hundreds of people, just like at our farewell concert of a year ago. It is an amazing turnout, and surprisingly touching, as everyone I've ever known seems to be there. My brother, Phil Sutcliffe, et al. Gerry and I had thought we'd be taking a huge risk, that maybe no one would turn up and we'd end up feeling foolish with egg on our faces. But this is staggering. We are way over the limit as far as the fire regulations go, but everyone is smiling, packed like sardines, and happy to see us back. *This* is the warm glow of "home."

Phil Sutcliffe introduces us, the room erupts, and we can't seem to put a foot wrong. I'd thought I might have trouble remembering some of the lyrics after a whole year, but the audience seems to be singing every last syllable with me at the top of their voices.

I imagine that surfing must feel something like this, carried effortlessly on a joyful wave of emotion and memory. We play until we can play no more, with some admittedly overly inebriated souls unwilling to leave and begging us to keep the band together.

I don't think Ronnie and Terry really expect us to give up our London dreams, but something has been resolved between us. We have closed the chapter on a high, and whatever loose ends were left after the confusion of a year ago seem to have been neatly tied.

It is an odd trio who walk into Newcastle's Central Station next morning: Gerry and I muffled in our overcoats with a suitcase each, and Joe, asleep, openmouthed in his pushchair, wearing a silver snowsuit that makes him look like an exhausted astronaut. It is depressingly cold and damp. The minute hand on the enormous station clock suspended high above the platform shudders to a halt at eight-thirty. We hurry out of the wind and into the warmth of the coffee bar to join the other frozen souls waiting to make their way south. As we sit nursing our two plastic cups of tea, some wag at the jukebox selects "We Gotta Get Out of This Place" by the Animals. Everyone seems to get the joke, as if we are all exiles from the land of disenchanted irony and bound to the uncertainty of the future. The record is well over ten years old and I can only imagine it is still there because it's played often. The same grim song, the same grim gag.

The train is full but we manage to find two empty seats opposite an elderly couple who remain silent for the entire journey. There is condensation on the windows and the smell and heat of damp woolen garments. The train seems to stop at every station and the journey is long and tedious. Joe, now awake, is terrorizing the taciturn couple who seem impervious to his normally infectious charm. He throws his plastic blocks at them. I apologize. He spins and slides like a break-dancer on the table. They must rescue their teacups. Again I apologize. Now with his gummy grin he ambushes other passengers as they pass by. More and more apologies, until he performs his coup de grâce, his new phrase. Repeatedly dropping his teddy on the floor he deliberately, clearly, and unmistakably shouts his latest mantra, "Oh fuck!"

Gerry groans and goes to sleep against the window, or at least he pretends to, as snowy fields and telegraph poles race past us and the couple glower and tut-tut at my delinquent son and his irresponsible father.

Surrey Sound Recording Studios is situated on the upper floor of an old converted dairy in Leatherhead, and while certainly no more salubrious than Pathway or any of the other studios I've worked in, it is spacious, homely, and inexpensive. Its owner is a medical doctor named Nigel Gray, and the studio, having started out as a hobby, has now become an abiding passion for him, so much so that he wants to give up the medical profession entirely and make a living solely as an engineer and producer.

By this time Miles Copeland has agreed to help us, or at least to release our first album on his burgeoning Illegal label. While still not entirely convinced—we are still the poor relations—he does need to increase the volume of product in his company to be taken seriously again in the business. Miles has always had a predatory instinct for any kind of bargain, and recognizes in Nigel Gray's ambition an opportunity to make a deal. As Nigel has no track record as a producer, Miles will offer him a coproduction credit in exchange for an extremely favorable studio rate. We will complete our first album in ten days and for less than fifteen hundred pounds, which even by the standards of the day is remarkably fast and extremely cheap. If we were to inherit a reputation for frugality, then the legend surely began with this deal, and the fact that we would use secondhand tape that we'd found lying around in Miles's garage, dubbing over the recorded efforts of one of his previous bands like unrepentant cuckoos in a borrowed nest.

Nigel is only a little older than Stewart and me but in his shy manners, neatly parted school haircut, and painfully straight clothes, he seems far more like an eccentric country doctor than someone at home among the bohemian jumble of the studio. I half-expect to see a stethoscope dangling from the pocket of his tweed jacket, but he is nonetheless a thoroughly adept engineer and can navigate the studio's complex electronic anatomy as skillfully as a surgeon slicing layers of tissue from an etherized patient.

We are all thrilled to be making an album, particularly me, as I've never gotten this far before, and as Stewart points out rather sullenly, I seem to have written almost all of the material. He had used two of his songs on the first single, and since Andy joined the band due democratic process had marginalized the rest. As the Police was Stewart's creation in the first place, he is understandably peeved. However, while I'm obviously the novice in terms of recording, I have been writing songs for over ten years, and while few if any were masterpieces I feel they have attained at least some level of craftsmanship. Songwriting for the other two is a relatively new and unfamiliar skill. I can do nothing but shrug at Stewart's uncharacteristic sullenness, not wanting to apologize for being prolific, although I can sense that this issue will be the cause of some serious problems in the future.

In calculating royalties for a record, the writer of the song gets as much as the performer. Consequently, if we are successful I would receive a far greater percentage of any royalties earned for most of the songs on the new record, dwarfing by comparison whatever would be left for my colleagues. This would admittedly render our already fragile democracy somewhat tenuous, until either they were to contribute more songs, or we could come to a mutual agreement whereby they would share in more of the spoils. The latter is what I eventually agree to, giving Andy and Stewart a percentage of my publishing royalties that will keep them sweet while not reducing too much my incentive to write hits. This agreement will resolve the issue in the short term, but the problem will fester, continuing to dog the relationships within the group and in fact be the reason for its ultimate demise.

We lay down the basic tracks for the album in the first few days.

"So Lonely": a revamped Last Exit number, reupholstered in the color and pace of the current vogue.

"Dead End Job": based on Stewart's riff and a couple of lines provided by his brother Ian, where I'd been employed in enough cul de sacs in my life to lend the song a certain authenticity, with Andy reading employment ads from the *Leatherhead Advertiser* in the background.

"Landlord": inspired by the Southgate incident and my anguished hunt to find a home for my family.

"Born in the Fifties": the first stanza, a fragment of my childhood. ("*My mother cried when President Kennedy died/ She said 'it was the communists'/But I knew better.*") I was a grassy knoll theorist even then.

"Peanuts": one of Stewart's tunes for which I penned the lyrics, inspired by a former hero, Rod Stewart, and my judgment of his extracurricular exploits in the tabloids, never thinking for a moment that I would suffer the same distorted perceptions at their hands a few years later.

"Would You Be My Girl?": a repetitive one-line riff to which Andy offered a piece of doggerel about a blow-up doll.

"Hole in My Life": another song of misery paraded and dressed up in Saturday clothes.

And "Roxanne." While originally written as a jazz-tinged bossa nova, the song will evolve into a hybrid tango through the trial-and-error of the band process. It is Stewart who suggests stressing the second beat of each bar on the bass and bass drum, giving the song its lopsided Argentinian gait. It is also Stewart who forces me to re-think the original melody, asking me to add more of the angular and unpredictable qualities that had attracted him to my voice in the first place.

After I complete the multitracked vocals of the chorus, we realize that we have stumbled onto something unique, but our confidence is somewhat restrained because of the romantic albeit tortured nature of the subject. I have already had to defend the lyrics of "Next to You" as a displaced love song in a preferred landscape of posturing anger and aggression. Miles, years in front of the parody, "Spinal Tap," already wants to call the album *Police Brutality* and envisions us dressed up as cops interrogating some scantily clad female on the cover. The others, to my horror, seem reasonably amenable to this ludicrous folly, but I am already planning sabotage and sedition. But it is in this climate that we will play the album to Miles, who is still not officially our manager.

He seems reasonably impressed by our efforts, although we hold back on playing him "Roxanne," afraid the song's defection from any style mandate will alienate him from the project. It is only after he has heard everything else that Stewart suggests we play it. I shuffle un-comfortably, and offer a few token caveats that the song is a little strange, all the while praying that my instinct about it will be confirmed and steer us away from the disaster I see looming in Miles's imagination. I wait anxiously as the song begins. An atonal piano cluster played by my backside on an upright behind the microphone, a nervous laugh, and then the chop-chop of the chords underpinned by the awkward rhythm of the tango. Miles remains unsmiling, his body rigid, his foot stubbornly still as I begin wailing in the keening, strident tenor that will provoke Elvis Costello to want to "clip" me around the ear. This isn't going well. I can barely look at anyone, so palpable is the tension in the room. It seems to take an age to reach the final coda. My eyes are fixed firmly on the floor in a silence pregnant with doubt, for if Miles sways the consensus away from this song I know my days in the band will be numbered on one hand.

I finally look up to see that the back of Miles's neck and the lobes of his ears are bright red. I brace myself for the worst of his anger and derision and prepare to make a sullen retreat. He draws a long breath, shaking his head.

"It's a goddamn classic, it's a fuckin' smash."

He moves as if to kiss me and I instinctively recoil, sinking into abashed, gratified modesty. I receive copious slaps, as if I am one of his pet mastiffs.

"Goddamn it, I just signed Squeeze to A&M. When they hear this, lemme tell ya, they're gonna flip." His reaction to this song is so powerful that it renders his previous enthusiasm lukewarm by comparison. He is fizzing with excitement, and leaves the studio clutching the tape and crooning the chorus in a faux southern twang. The other songs are left on the tape machine, like the ugly sisters after a prince's ball.

We leave the studio in high spirits, well aware that A&M is one of the most respected and successful companies on either side of the Atlantic. Whereas before we'd been perfectly happy to release the record independently on Illegal, we were now, with Miles's blessing, setting our sights higher than we'd ever thought possible, on an international record company.

Miles calls his brother next day, "drooling," as Stewart describes it. Yes, the company loved the song too, and the executives there think it can be a hit, and if that turns out to be so we'll have our album released not on the tiny Illegal label but on the mighty A&M. Our excitement and anticipation are somewhat tempered that evening at the studio when Miles tells us he is not going to negotiate a large advance for us.

"Listen, a large advance is just a bank loan. What I want to sign is a single deal on this one song. If it's a hit, then I'll be able to negotiate a much better album deal and a higher royalty. If you can manage the way you have for the last year, without an advance, you'll reap the benefit in the long run."

This, again, was a shining example of Miles's legendary shrewdness. In contrast to the feudal relationship that most bands normally fall into when seduced by large advances, this was the beginning of a genuine partnership between the Police and the record company. We would benefit from more artistic freedom, and whatever we earned would be ours. I would subsequently be able to describe the Police as "a nice little business," but it was Miles who was the architect of this and we would reap the rewards for our patience in spades. Another benefit that "Roxanne" would grant us was to divert Miles 180 degrees from his ridiculous Police Brutality idea and more toward the romantic idealism that would increasingly inform the songs. He would now officially become our manager.

It is January 26, 1978. Miles Axe Copeland III walks triumphantly into the studio with the bare outlines of a contract with A&M for our new single "Roxanne," as well as a new idea for the album title. *Outlandos D'Amour* is a strange concoction of Esperanto and gobbledegook which Miles savors luxuriously in his mouth in a parody of a French accent that owes more to his alma mater in Birmingham, Alabama, than it does to the Sorbonne. Posing as a kind of hick Tom Parker will become a recognizable Miles strategy whenever he ventures a creative suggestion and he wants to laugh us out of any serious doubts. *Outlandos D'Amour* is certainly an odd title, but it appeals to our shared sense of the absurd, and as no one else has a better idea, *Outlandos D'Amour* it is.

By March the contract with A&M is ready for signing. All the A&M executives and company accountants supposedly have copies of "Roxanne" in their tape decks, and we are told it is the first record in a long time that the promotion staff have asked to hear more than once. Stewart, Andy, and I go to the plush company offices off the Fulham Road, where the president, Derek Green, greets us like long-lost sons, and "Roxanne" is playing triumphantly on the sound system throughout the entire building.

There we are, lounging on the cane furniture and the deep pile carpets of the presidential office, initialing each page of the white contract with a Parker pen of solid silver. After this formality, as a gesture of welcome, they let us loose on their catalog downstairs in the basement where we take about two hundred pounds' worth of albums. I get the entire collection of Quincy Jones and Antonio Carlos Jobim, although my haul is modest compared to the other two because I still don't own a record player. I walk into the house feeling like a man who just successfully robbed the store, when Frances has her turn to tell me some news. She's just been offered a series for Granada TV, playing an undercover cop. "That makes two of us," I say. The series will be filmed up in Manchester, which means long periods of separation for us, but our mutual ambition as well as the need to pay the bills will see us through the difficult times. The two of us dance around the front room with Joe between us and Buttons the dog, as usual, looking on bewildered and disapproving.

My youngest sister, Anita, will tell me that her strongest memory of the day was a tobacco-brown car reversing carefully into the short driveway in front of the open garage doors of the family home in Tynemouth.

It is 10:30 on a fine Saturday morning with a clear blue sky and a southerly breeze, as my mother throws her suitcases into the back of the car. She is accompanied by Anita, who looks fretful and uncertain as she climbs into the backseat. My mother has been planning this for months, siphoning her clothes secretly into bags and cases so that her escape can be as brief and efficient as possible. My father will return from work at eleven-thirty; everything seems to have been planned with a cold military precision.

My sister is deeply unhappy and afraid, she doesn't want to leave, but crouched in the backseat and clutching the birdcage with her pet budgie on her knee, she tries to reassure the little bird and herself that everything will be okay, everything will be okay.

My mother has that wild, hunted look in her eyes while the man in the front seat, who has left his own family, is silent and anxiously checking his watch and the street as the bags are piled higher and higher. They will spend the rest of the day driving south to a little town near Manchester and the dream of a new life.

My father returns to an empty house, scrupulously clean, like a prepared corpse or a mausoleum. There is no note.

I react badly to the news of my mother's elopement. I called my dad, who was, as expected, devastated and confused. I will send an angry letter to my mother, telling her she was out of order and basically disowning her. The letter was unforgiving, ill-considered, and rash, but I was in a blind fury of righteous anger. I felt I should somehow avenge my father's humiliation, but I wasn't smart or mature enough to seek balance in any other way.

With the wisdom of hindsight, I have to question whether my own life had been any less reckless. Long periods of separation in my own little family may have been the price of ambition, but they were equally destructive in the long term. I may have wanted to escape the consequences of my parents' dysfunction by living a life on the run, as dramatically different and removed from them as was possible, but unconsciously I carried the seed of their unhappiness with me wherever I went. My mother had always looked longingly away from home for her salvation—and I had internalized this in the compulsive aspects of what would become twenty-five years "on the road."

In the same month as my mother's elopement to Manchester, Miles will bring Randy California's Spirit to the UK, and they need another support act.

The tour begins at Essex University, followed by a sold-out show at the Rainbow in Finsbury Park. Spirit, the seminal West Coast psychedelic band from the sixties, are still playing the same brand of woozy, trippy rock and roll that made them famous. The Police and Mark P.'s ATV are booked as support, Spirit being Mark's favorite band and the tour being partly his idea. We are still bottom of the bill. Despite the promising reaction to "Roxanne" at the record company, we are still regarded as poor relations at Dryden Chambers, but we don't mind. Mark's band has improved a great deal since the last time we saw them, but we don't imagine we'll have much trouble blowing them off the bandstand. And I've forgiven them for demolishing my car, aided by Miles footing the bill for repairs to the front end.

The audiences that turn up every night are almost exclusively made up of people who look as if they've stepped out of some kind of decade-long time warp, with shoulder-length hair, beads and bell bottoms, sandals and dirty toenails. I don't get the impression that they've dressed up in honor of Randy and the trio—this is how they always look. I hadn't realized that there were so many hippies left. As we are a band called the Police, with cropped platinum hair and tight trousers, the audience is initially and quite understandably hostile to our collective gestalt, but by the first number our raucous little combo has managed to win them over, and if my arrogant stage persona comes off as alienating, then it is backed up by the inarguable fact that we can play. We are fearless, unapologetic, and cocksure of ourselves, and are rewarded with a rousing ovation at the end of our half-hour spot. Miles hugs me and tells me that I'm going to be a big star. This time I don't recoil.

Mark's band does fine and will glean a polite if sparse response, while Spirit tear the place apart, Randy California giving a more plausible impression of Jimi Hendrix than I would have thought possible. I find his rendition of "Hey Joe" very moving and heavily nostalgic, especially since Hendrix had died so tragically almost eight years before.

When the letter postmarked from Manchester comes, I first assume it's from Frances and Joe, but I'm wrong.

*Dear son,*

*I can only say I'm sorry for letting you down and hope that one day you'll forgive me. I remember in one of your songs you say that breaking someone's heart is just like breaking your own, well how right you are. The thought of losing you is killing me. Give little Joe a big hug and a kiss from me.*

*Love, Mam*

301

I am seven years old again.

There is no way that my mother could have known she had less than a decade to live, but she must have heard a clock ticking. She saw a patch of blue sky and she bolted. I had followed my dream and she had to follow hers, but part of me couldn't let her go with my blessing. My response to her, while as tender as I could make it, was nonetheless unrelenting. I would have to take sides with my father, fatuously assuming that life was some kind of emotional football game that could be won or lost by force of numbers. I think I ended the letter with some kind of self-serving explanation that I had to stick by my dad, that I could no longer maintain a relationship with her, and that "even this letter seems like a small betrayal." It hurt me to write that but it must have hurt her terribly. It hurts me now, and I realize what a pompous little fool I was, because it wasn't much later that I too would fall hopelessly in love with someone else, break the wedding vows I was so sure I could keep, and be swept up in a tidal wave of emotion and longing that none of us could stop. . . .

In mid-April, while Frances and Joe are still up in Manchester, I walk to the Virgin Record Store on Bayswater Road and buy the single of "Roxanne." There is a photo of me on the back, in full flight at the Mont de Marsan Festival, and inside, underneath the title, is my name as the composer of the song. Published by Virgin Music Ltd. I am so proud. We are record of the week in *Record Mirror,* "best of the rest" in *Sounds*; *Melody Maker* says that it could be a minor hit, and *NME* pointedly ignore it.

Gerry calls to ask if I'll put him on the guest list for our gig that night at the Nashville Rooms. He's seen our good reviews. (Though

*Time Out* warn their readers we're boring and we're damned before we play a note. Such things by now only fire me up.) I know Gerry's happy for me, but I also know part of him wants to see that the gig's not too good. Though I'm still seeking his approval, he's been my sparring partner for too long. The gig turns out to be great. Even Gerry gives us a thumbs-up.

At the end I see Miles and Carol Wilson having a flaming stand-up row about my publishing. Miles feels that they haven't done enough for me—they could, for instance, have given us some financial tour support. He wants me out of my contract, but Carol is now a friend and Miles as always has his own agenda. I've written most of the material on the album, and as my publishing deal was signed long before the Police, Miles has no legal claim to whatever publishing royalties accrue. This will be a bone of contention for years to come and even at this date there is clearly trouble brewing.

Few feelings compare to the euphoria of hearing your record on the radio for the first time, a song you've worked and slaved on suddenly released onto the airwaves. It's like watching one of your children successfully ride a bike for the first time. There is the child, undeniably part of you but no longer physically connected, spreading her wings and taking to the air.

I am balanced like a surfer on a plank in the kitchen, painting the ceiling when I hear the staccato chop of the G minor chord and then my long first syllable hanging in the air and swooping down like a question mark. I almost fall off my perch, dripping white emulsion all over the floor, desperately trying to get to the phone.

"Stew, we're on Capital Radio, listen!"

"You're damn right we are." I can hear the song through the earpiece, halfway across London.

*"And that was the Police with 'Roxanne,' one of this week's Capital climbers."*

"Wow, did you hear that?"

I sit on the floor, my heart racing, a little shell-shocked. Part of me can't quite believe it, like a long-held dream that suddenly solidifies into tangible reality.

Alas, despite the encouraging start and the early confidence of the record company, "Roxanne" will not be a hit, at least this time around. The BBC don't play the song, citing the subject matter as a reason for their reticence, but they are always looking for an excuse to exclude a record from their oversubscribed playlist. The BBC are the most important station in the country, and all the others follow suit.

Despite the failure of "Roxanne" to set the charts alight, A&M are still willing to give us another try, although they don't want to release the album until we've had some kind of chart hit. And so "Can't Stand Losing You" is slated for release later in the year. It's not as unusual as "Roxanne" but may be more palatable for commercial radio. This will be our second bite of the cherry and we are still optimistic.

A day or two later, Frances and Joe have returned from Manchester for a break, but our time together will be marred by some sadness. I will take the dog for his last trip to the vet. He's been breathing with difficulty since the morning and looking very unhappy.

The vet looks at me ominously as she listens to the poor dog's heart. "I'll give him an injection, but he's old. If he doesn't respond, I don't think there's much hope."

My own heart sinks and we take a taxi back home, where I break the news to Frances. The injection doesn't seem to have any effect and his condition steadily gets worse. It is now eleven in the evening, we ring the vet, and she tells us to come round. One of the neighbors looks after the baby and we take the dog into the hated office for the last time.

He has the strangest look in his eyes as he looks unflinchingly at his mistress of fourteen years. He seems to be saying, "You can leave now. I know I'm dying. It's okay." Frances hugs him tenderly to her chest, bravely maintaining her composure, but when we leave the office to walk home she is inconsolable.

It takes a long time to get over our bereavement. I have a recurring dream of hearing a familiar scrabbling at the front door in the middle of the night, and when I get up to open the door, there he is as large as life. "Turdy, where've you been?" I say. And that's when I wake up.

By June the weather in London is balmy, the plane trees that line the Bayswater Road loom like massive green giants above the lines of traffic and the sweltering pedestrians in their shirtsleeves and thin cotton dresses. The city is buzzing with a kind of languid optimism and I'm thinking that perhaps such weather could last forever. On just such a morning, we will get a surprise call from my dad. He's phoning from Victoria bus station in the center of London.

"What are you doing there, Dad?"

"I just got back from Germany and I'm coming over for breakfast. I'll tell you all about it."

A black cab pulls up outside and a pair of rather dapper suede loafers appears at the top of the basement steps, followed by my old man carrying a shopping bag in one hand and shielding his eyes with another as he peers into the window.

He allows me to hug him, and then I hold him at arm's length to get a better look. I haven't seen him since Christmas. He is smiling, and a bit thinner, and he seems younger too although there is a wistfulness around the eyes and a slight tinge of red. Frances cooks him a hearty breakfast and he dandles Joe on his knee while forking scrambled eggs and bacon rashers into his mouth and giving an account of his adventures all at the same time.

He tells us he's been doing a favor for a friend of his. The friend owns a coach tour business in Newcastle and had asked him to check out a hotel that he was thinking of using in Rimegen, which was near to where Ernie had been stationed after the war. Reading between the lines, I suspect that the friend had seen that my dad desperately needed to get out of the house, and knowing him to be too proud to accept a free holiday, had given him the task as a cover for a much-needed break. The trip had clearly worked wonders, bringing some of the pep back into his step and the playful mischief in his grin. I wonder if he'd managed to look up some of the girlfriends he'd known back when. I don't pry, but after allowing him to regale us with his adventures, I feel that it's time to draw him back to the real issues.

"Have you heard from Mam?"

"No, son, I haven't, but I hear they're having a tough time."

He doesn't mention Alan's name, but there is no triumph in his voice. He looks suddenly grim and long-suffering and it is clear, as always, that he still loves her, despite everything that has happened.

I tell him that I haven't heard from my mother either, failing to mention the bitter correspondence we'd shared, as if even that was a further act of betrayal.

I am clearly as confused as he is.

When breakfast is over, he looks at his watch and tells us that he has to get the bus back to Newcastle because my brother has been holding the fort for a week now. I beg him to stay. "You can sleep on the couch," I say, somehow knowing that he won't, but it's worth a try.

"Oh no, I've got to get back. Poor Philip's doing two rounds while I'm away." He kisses Frances and the baby, gives me a brusque handshake, and then he's gone.

My father too will only have a decade of his life remaining. The seeds of the cancers that will kill both my parents have already been propagated from the dark strain of unhappiness and frustration that had grown between them like a malignant flower.

# 14

MILES IS SERIOUSLY CONSIDERING SENDING THE BAND TO tour the U.S. Brother Ian, who moved out to Georgia in the beginning of the year to start a new life, is now an agent with the Paragon Agency in Macon, Georgia. They book a number of southern boogie acts such as Molly Hatchett, but Ian has convinced them that the future of the business is the so-called English new wave. Squeeze are already there, playing small clubs, and by the end of the year we shall be there too. It is an unorthodox plan: the American record company has no interest in supporting us; we'll have to do it on a shoestring, surviving on whatever gig fees we can muster, and I imagine expenses will more than account for any money we do make. But to tour America, regardless of the circumstances, is a dream for me and close to the myth that had informed my life since the Beatles' triumph in the sixties. Just to go there and play would be enough. In the meantime I have to make some money.

I had never trained as an actor, or had any desire to be one. I'd never even been in a school play, but I will be cast in small parts in three movies by the late summer of 1978, and I am intrigued enough by this unexpected development to enjoy the experience.

The first would be *The Great Rock 'n' Roll Swindle,* with the Sex Pistols. Pippa Markham had convinced me to meet the director, Julian Temple, who casts me as a member of a gay rock band called the Blow Waves who attempt to kidnap Paul Cook, the Pistols' drummer. It is not a great cinematic moment, and as it happens, thankfully, the scene will be cut from the movie. I was grateful, however, for the 125 quid at the end of the day.

The second movie, *Radio On,* is more interesting. The director, *Time Out* critic Chris Petit, asks me to play a garage attendant obsessed with the tragic death of Eddie Cochran. My character works in a garage near to where the legendary American rock-and-roller was killed in a car crash on the way back to London after a gig in Bristol. I will sing "Three Steps to Heaven" in the movie while playing an old Gretsch guitar like Cochran's and improvise a scene with the leading actor, David Beam. *Radio On* was produced by Wim Wenders and was well received by the art house critics but the public stayed away in droves.

Years later I will walk past Hampstead's Everyman Theatre to see that there is a midnight screening of *Radio On.* Trudie's never seen it, so I invite her for a night at the pictures. She used to go out with Peter O'Toole, who had once taken her to the same theater when there was a late-night screening of *Lawrence of Arabia.* Indulgent of such vanities, she graciously agrees to accompany me, while I point out that it's not an Oscar-winning epic we are about to see, but a funky little road movie shot in black-and-white on a shoestring budget from the arts council. We arrive about five minutes into the movie to find the theater empty apart from two other people sitting at opposite edges of the empty rows.

"It's a cult film," I offer lamely.

"Clearly," she says as we opt for a couple of seats near the front.

We follow the film's tortured plot from a murder in London, a noir drive through England's shires with a couple of songs from me and Ian Dury thrown in as some kind of light relief from the rather central European gloom that pervades the film. This is no Ealing comedy.

At the end of the credits we turn to leave when I notice the other two members of the audience are pulling up the collars of their coats and turning their heads toward the wall as they hurry somewhat suspiciously toward the exit. From the shapes of their heads, their shifty gait, and the apparent guilt of their body language I have the distinct impression I know these characters.

"Chris?"

The man's head ducks farther into his collar. Then I fix the other quarry.

"David?"

The game is up.

"Hello, Sting," they reply in unison, resigned to the comic bathos of the situation. The only four people to turn up for the midnight screening of *Radio On* at Hampstead Everyman are the director, the leading man, and one of its cameo performers and his indulgent girlfriend.

The third movie will be *Quadrophenia*.

Some months earlier, Gerry and I meet in the Ship in Wardour Street intending to see Dire Straits at the Marquee, but it's packed and we can't get in, so we just sit and sup. Keith Moon walks into the bar looking exactly like Robert Newton in *Treasure Island*, a wild and piratical imp of a man. If he had been wearing a three-cornered hat, brandishing a cutlass, and had a parrot on his shoulder, we would have looked out of place, not him. He buys everyone within shotgun range a drink. As Gerry and I toast his health, we wonder at the sparkling wit and mischief in his eyes, but he will be dead within a month after a night of legendary excess, and it is I who will play the bellboy in *Quadrophenia,* a character in Pete Townshend's song cycle loosely based on Keith.

I will turn up at the Who's office in Wardour Street without any real expectations, or for that matter very much enthusiasm for landing a part. I'm here because Pippa asked me to be. I don't think I have a cat in hell's chance, but I'll go through the motions. In the year that I'd been dabbling in commercials, I had learned that giving an impression to prospective employers that you couldn't care less whether you got the job or not, invariably and paradoxically meant that you were more likely to be given it, than someone who seemed desperate to work. It was nothing more than a gambler's bluff and basic chancer's psychology, but perhaps it also had something to do with the type of character I was being asked to play. Whether insouciant, cool, or plain arrogant, I would present myself intrinsically as that character from the moment I walked in the door until the moment I left, and I wouldn't crack.

On one occasion, when an ad company panel auditioning me hear that I'm a musician, they ask me to sing a song and try to hand me a guitar. I tell them, "Fuck off!" and saunter out of the oak-paneled office with a look of such confident disdain and nerve that they immediately call my agent to hire me. I may not be an actor, but I can perform.

Knowing from experience that you often wait for hours at such meetings, I would always take a book to read, for as well as relieving the boredom of waiting it also created an impression of disinterested calm and was also a clear signal that you weren't into making idle conversation with the other candidates. I'm a good two-thirds of the way through *The Glass Bead Game,* by Hermann Hesse, and seemingly engrossed in its enclosed and esoteric utopian world, when the casting director ushers me into the adjacent office. I slip the book into my jacket pocket.

There are only two people in the room, the casting lady whom I'd done an ad for a few months before and the director, Franc Roddam.

Franc is in his early thirties but looks younger. He has the air of a man exhilarated by his success, and the confidence to have replaced the plebian K in the usual diminutive of his name with the patrician and more European C. His award-winning docudrama, *Dummy*, about a mentally challenged young girl, has recently catapulted him from the staid corridors of the BBC into the heady world of the movies.

I take a seat, and the usual game begins. They size you up: the way you're dressed, the way you hold yourself, the angles of your face in the light. I know all of this, so I remain still and tolerate their scrutiny, staring back with the faintest irony in the slight upward turn at the edge of my mouth, but it's only the suggestion of a smile and my eyes will give nothing away.

He sees the book sticking out of my pocket.

"What are you reading?"

He speaks in the clipped and carefully modulated tones of the middle class, but I immediately recognize a subtle shade within the precise enunciation of his question. It's only a trace of a regional accent, faint but unmistakable, an accent not identical to my own, but very close. I now know more about him than he knows about me. The game continues.

"Hesse, Hermann Hesse," I reply, handing him the dog-eared paperback as if it were a passport. He looks at it cursorily.

"He was a great traveler," he says, turning the book in his hand. "Walked for years in the Himalayas. Did you ever read *Siddhartha*?"

"No, I haven't. What's it about?"

I allow the slightest hint of Newcastle to color the conversational tone in my question. He recognizes it and immediately we know each other. We are like two spies in a foreign land, with altered names and false papers, at first circumspect and wary, but speaking in the subtly coded language of our mutual exile. Now he can reciprocate.

"Oh it's about two wanderers on a spiritual quest for the meaning of life. Very mystical," he answers with just enough irony to get a smile out of me. "You're from Newcastle?"

"I'm from Wallsend," I say, knowing that this will have a deeper, more specific resonance to someone in the know. Wallsend is a tough place, where there are no genteel enclaves. I've wandered far from the expectations and mores of my upbringing, and so, I suspect, has he.

He tells me about his travels through Nepal and India. We talk books and music. We pointedly do not discuss the movie, and finally shake hands without the slightest acknowledgment that there is a job at stake or a significant career decision for both of us. We have observed the rules of engagement.

I know that they're seeing half of London for this role, but somehow I know it's mine. Pippa calls the next day to confirm this, but I even feign disinterest with her. I'm also not sure that Frances won't feel that I'm beginning to invade her turf. I am cautious when I give her the news. Her support of me as a musician has been unstinting, but I don't know how she'll feel about any more-serious attempts at acting. Pippa is her friend, her agent. The ads were one thing, but this is a major movie. When I do tell her I've landed the role, she is of course delighted, and so am I in my quiet way.

My only worry now is that the dates of the filming run pretty close to the beginning of our forthcoming U.S. tour. Ian Copeland has by now cobbled together a string of East Coast dates by calling in favors and appealing to promoters with a taste for adventure and sharing in the curious risk of an English band touring without a record company to support them. The club fees will cover our expenses, but no more. So, while being denied a ticker tape welcome or the keys to New York City, we will nonetheless be more than satisfied with the modest platform we've been given, and the rest will be up to us. But before that I have a movie to make, and the timing is going to be very tight.

The inertia of the summer will now give way to the frenzied activity of autumn and the following year, where so many of my dreams will materialize. I have been circling the periphery of this life for many months, but now I feel the whirlpool drawing me closer and closer, like an event horizon at the edge of a mysterious black hole. I am neither terrified nor repulsed by it. This is what I have been waiting for. Like a volunteer on the eve of a war, I want to be annihilated and yet somehow survive. This is a dangerous wish.

We will leave for our tour of America at the end of October, but in the month before that, *Quadrophenia* will be filmed on location in Brighton. My character will be called Ace, and will have only a few lines in the screenplay. He is little more than a visual and, hopefully, iconic presence and has virtually no interplay with the other characters. It is a perfect role for a nonactor. I will be on the screen just long enough to make an impression, and not long enough to blow it.

My particular shooting schedule will have to be jimmied into a hectic calendar of radio and TV spots for the upcoming release of our next single, "I Can't Stand Losing You," and at last our album, *Outlandos D'Amour*. My birthday, in October of that year, will be particularly eventful.

I am woken at six-thirty in my hotel room in Brighton. It is still dark outside and there isn't enough hot water for a bird bath. I stagger along the seafront to the location, kick-started awake by a swill of acrid black coffee from a polystyrene cup. I climb into my character's shark-skin suit, Italian loafers, and gray leather coat. After a bit of pampering in hair and makeup—my hair is now dyed platinum blond and sprayed with metallic paint to give it an otherworldly sheen—I report for duty on the set promptly at 8 o'clock. I confess to a slight anxiety about the time, as I have to be three hundred miles away in Manchester by this evening. The Police have a vitally important slot on *The Old Grey Whistle Test,* the most influential music show on television.

Today we are staging a riot between two rival gangs of "mods" and "rockers," with the hapless Hampshire Constabulary caught between the two. (As historical background to the film's parable of teenage alienation and disillusionment, we are reenacting a pitched battle that had taken place in the same location during the sixties.) I am sent onto the beach to practice throwing a beer crate around, so that I can use said crate to smash a shop window. As I'd been throwing metal crates around my father's dairy for most of my childhood, I feel as if I was born to play this role.

In an hour's time, the riot is in full swing. Police on horses are chasing us down one of the narrow side streets off the Brighton sea front, while another group of coppers on foot with police dogs and brandishing truncheons trap us from the other direction. The dogs have real teeth and some of the less professional extras are getting carried away with the action. There are real bottles and bricks flying around our heads. A hundred or so of us are now wedged in the narrow street against the prearranged shop window, where a convenient beer crate has been left for me to do my handiwork.

There is much pushing and jostling and an increasing sense of genuine panic, as the assistant directors, shouting into electronic bullhorns, try to bring some order to the mounting chaos but only succeed in making matters worse. The whole situation seems to be dangerously out of control. Nonetheless, the cameras keep turning. Franc is watching from above, perched on a scaffold like the Duke of Wellington at Waterloo, calm and inscrutable.

I know I'm now in the center of the frame. I manage to make enough space to swing the crate in a wide arc toward the window, and bingo, it smashes spectacularly into a million pieces. Girls are screaming, horses are rearing, the Alsatians are barking, and we make our escape in the ensuing mayhem, and all in one perfect take. The director shouts "Cut" and while most of us stop fighting there are still a few skirmishes continuing between the police and the non-professional extras.

By the time order has been restored they have found "a hair in the gate"—a piece of loose emulsion from the film—has ruined the take, so the whole scene has to be shot again. Resetting the window will take another hour, and more than a few extras have to seek treatment in the first-aid tent. In the meantime we shoot another scene where I drag a policeman from a charging horse and feign kicking him senseless in the middle of the street. I'm really enjoying this acting caper. There's really nothing to it. In fact it's not unlike a normal Saturday night in the Bigg Market in Newcastle. I give yet another smashing performance in front of the shop window, after which I'm hopelessly overpowered by three burly cops and thrown unceremoniously into the back of a waiting Black Maria.

It is already ten to four and here I am stuck between two genuinely blooded rockers and Phil Daniels, the brilliant, scrawny actor playing the lead in the film. Franc knows I have to get away but I wonder darkly if there isn't a plot to keep me on the set. I pray that there are no more holdups, or retakes, because I don't have time. A record company car is waiting and ready to whisk me off to Gatwick Airport, but we have two more scenes to complete from the day's schedule. I'll never make it, except that the light is beginning to fail and Franc will be forced to reschedule the battle tomorrow morning.

I change out of my costume in the car as we race to the airport. The TV show is really an enormous break for us and I can't afford to miss the plane. It starts to rain and we hit some traffic and the driver tells me anxiously that he's not sure if we have enough petrol. I sink into the backseat, seething under my own personal black cloud, the rain drumming on the windscreen as we inch forward. We eventually get there with only seconds to spare. After pelting through the crowds in the airport I am the last person on the plane and we take off in the rain.

It is still raining when we land in Manchester. Yet another car and driver are waiting to take me to the studio, where we have a sound check. The performance tonight is live. We have to play well. We have one hour before the show, and as I'm now rather into the otherworldly look, I go into makeup and ask if they have any silver metallic spray. The makeup girl digs a can out from one of the cupboards.

"Would you like me to do it?" she says.

"No," I say, "I can do it myself."

I take the can and direct it, from about six inches, at the top of my head. Nothing comes out. I try a second time. Nothing. I shake the canister, and it is clearly full. I press once more. Again nothing. I inspect the nozzle at close quarters, only an inch or two from my eyes, and like the fool I would claim my mother had never bred I press the button on the aerosol and spray the metallic paint straight into my open eyes. It feels like two razor blades are turning in my sockets and I begin screaming like some kind of platinum Gloucester, straight out of *King Lear.*

By some fortunate miracle the eye hospital is next door to the BBC studios. They spray me with anesthetic and cheerfully tell me that I have chemical burns. Stewart lends me his sunglasses, which are enormously wide, but I can't go on television looking as if I'm hemorrhaging from my eyeballs. From what I can see in the mirror, I look like a zombie.

We will be on the air for ten minutes, the longest ten minutes of my life so far. The outsize sunglasses keep slipping from the end of my nose, and as I have to keep both hands on the bass and sing at the same time, in order to keep the glasses from slipping to the floor I am forced to keep twitching my nose and flicking my head back as if I have an involuntary tic. I have been told subsequently that people assumed it was a stage affectation, like Elvis's lip curl or the Beatles shaking their hair between choruses, and that the next day impressionable kids up and down the country were to be seen in oversize sunglasses, twitching and nodding their heads like mental patients with facial dementia.

After the show I catch the sleeper to Victoria and then drive to Brighton to be on the set at 7 A.M. Luckily all of the scenes that day are in long shot, so my Nosferatu eyeballs have a day to recover. A lot of the extras keep twitching at me. I'm not sure I like being famous, but I also recognize that our appearance on television has telescoped the band into the new and undiscovered land of other people's awareness. There is a not-so-subtle change in the way strangers react around you, a distinct temperature change in any room that you walk into, which is neither friendly or necessarily hostile, just different. After a while I will come to regard this altered perception to be as much a part of me as my eyes and ears. I will view the world, and the world will view me, through this distorting gauze, and nothing will remove it.

My mother has now returned home with my much relieved sister, unable to make ends meet with the meager earnings she and Alan were able to scrape together. They have returned home to their respective families, unable to sustain the dream of their escape. I can only imagine the humiliation my mother must have felt, but true to form and according to my sister's account, she does not appear at the front door as a humbled and pathetic supplicant. She is far too proud to present herself that way, regardless of how she may feel inside. Her reappearance must be grandly theatrical and will be performed with such devastating and indeed admirable chutzpah that my dad and my brother merely stand aside openmouthed and disbelieving, too dumbfounded to either celebrate or complain. She storms into the house, dressed in her best coat, as if for a wedding. She throws open the kitchen door and lets out a shriek of outrage at the dust and grime that has settled like a pall over the house in the six months she has been gone—then proceeds to scrub the place from top to bottom, refusing to take off her hat and coat until she is satisfied that it is fit again for human habitation. She is magnificent and epic in her rage, and when I hear this story I can only fall in love with her all over again. My mother, in the immortal words of Eddie Cochran, is "something else."

✦

The moon hangs like a big ripe cheese over Manhattan, and I'm sitting in the back of an enormous stretch limousine that Miles and Andy and Stewart have sent to pick me up from the airport. It is the biggest car I've ever seen, and at first I think that it's a camp joke, but crossing the East River as it shimmers in the moonlight beneath the massive ferrous skeleton of the 59th Street Bridge, the fabled cityscape looming behind, I'm now not so sure. My first trip to New York will be the beginning of a lifelong love affair with a city that intoxicates me like no other, a city of the unbridled imagination, of giddy, vertiginous dreams, legendary rudeness, and the vertical drama of social mobility. I'm in love. The limo navigates rain-filled cavities in the road and manhole covers spew columns of white steam from some dangerous Promethean underworld just below the surface of the streets. Even the seediness of the Bowery thrills me.

From the outside, CBGB's, the famed New York club that spawned the Velvet Underground, Television, and the Talking Heads, looks like a cheap sideshow at a carnival. It's Friday night and the bums lounging in adjacent doorways seem unconcerned, preening themselves absently as the limo pulls up outside. I announce myself at the door, guitar case in hand, and am ushered into the gloom by an unsmiling girl wearing too much mascara and the weight of the world on her shoulders. The club is long and narrow and about a third full. A handful of people from the record company have turned up, although Miles was warned by one of the VPs in the promotion department that we would be wasting our time and not to bring us at all, as we wouldn't get any support. Miles coolly informed them that we wouldn't need any. So the audience is made up entirely by the indigenous population of the club and a few company stalwarts intrigued by our nerve and unusual independence. We had paid our own way on Sir Freddy Laker's airline offering a transatlantic crossing at sixty pounds a head.

The others have been in the city a day or two, and they're buzzing with excitement. But if they're buzzing, I must be levitating, exhausted, delirious with jet lag and the swooning novelty of the city.

Tonight I will give an out-of-body performance, yelling like a banshee, suspended above the stage like my own ghost, and the band playing with such ferocity that no one will be left in any doubt that we aren't here for good reason. We will play two hour-long sets that night, and between shows I will seek out some food to sustain my energy. Just along side from the club is Phoebe's, an all-night diner, virtually empty but for a few nightbirds. Glancing through the menu I calculate I have enough dollars to buy a salad and a coffee. When the salad arrives, I can hardly believe how enormous it is. I check that I haven't ordered for a family, as I don't want to be embarrassed, but no, this is a normal American portion, a "chef's" salad. The coffee is hot and nourishing, and I watch the street with the rapt attention of someone watching a musical in Cinemascope. Every yellow cab is as mythic as a Cole Porter song, the skyline seems to have been written high like a clarinet above the architecture of Gershwin's "Rhapsody in Blue," and Duke Ellington's subway rattles below the city all the way to Brooklyn and Coney Island.

The waitress returns and attempts to fill my coffee cup. Red-faced and slightly ashamed, I tell her I can't afford another. She looks at me curiously.

"Honey, I don't know where you're from, but here in America the second cup is always free."

"God bless America," I murmur under my breath as the fresh coffee warms my innards and fills me with an immigrant's gratitude and a thousand songs. "It's a helluva town."

Monday night will find us upstate in Poughkeepsie, the gig in a beautiful old vaudeville theater. We walk onstage to face only six people in the audience. They are all clearly as embarrassed as we are by their scarcity, sitting separately, in different parts of the cavernous room. Not wishing to pursue the charade of our fame any longer than necessary, I invite everyone down to the front of the stage and they dutifully troop down from the gods to occupy the six seats in front of the footlights. I ask everyone's name and formally introduce them to each other and then to the band. Having broken down the fourth wall, we then proceed to give one of the most blistering sets we will ever manage. Galvanized by the absurdity of our situation, and driven on by an audience bonded in equal absurdity, we will play encore after encore, with delirious if ironic abandon. The entire audience will come backstage after the show. As it turns out, three of them are DJs, and tomorrow "Roxanne" will make her sassy debut on the local airwaves.

In the months that follow we will play every fleapit club between Montreal and Miami, and on the West Coast from Vancouver to San Diego. We will play with equal passion to six people or six hundred, driving ourselves thousands of sleepless miles, loading and unloading our gear. We will mark out our territory, gig by gig, city by city, market by market, and while many promoters and club owners will lose money on their initial investment, every one of them will invite us back and be rewarded for their faith in spades.

The lasting legacy of the band will be the songs, but as well as that, the backbone of our legend will be that we would play anywhere, travel any distance, sleep anywhere there was a bed, give 100 percent and never complain. We were the poor relations who became the dogs of war, and then nothing could stop us.

Within a few years the Police, with Miles's guidance, would become one of the biggest bands in the world. The songs I had written in the obscurity of our basement flat would become some of the most celebrated songs of the decade, and all of our albums became platinum selling records in every country. This success was confirmed and reinforced by endless concert tours in massive sports stadiums, and all the attendant hoopla and hype of a traveling circus. That the band would break up at the pinnacle of its career when our position seemed virtually unassailable, surprised everyone but me. I saw my own future very clearly outside of the band, because I wanted more freedom. I couldn't have played with two better musicians than Stewart and Andy but I wanted to make music that wasn't tied to the limitations of a three piece band, where I didn't have to compromise my own standards as a songwriter to maintain what was in truth only the semblance of democracy within the band. One commentator would say that the Police would have stayed together if the other two had needed me less and I had needed them more. And while this is a massive oversimplification I recognize that there was some truth in it. I sought escape yet again and in the face of all conventional logic or even common sense I would follow my instincts into yet another uncharted chapter of my life.

The band wasn't the only casualty of this frenetic period because my marriage to Frances would not survive either and the demise of the Police would coincide with the break up of my family.

# 15

NINE YEARS WILL PASS. FRANCES WILL GIVE BIRTH TO OUR daughter, Kate, but we will be divorced soon afterward. There would follow a season in hell for everyone involved. Trudie and I, desperately in love from the beginning, will have a daughter, Mickey, and a son, Jake. In the interim I will have become famous and ridiculously wealthy. The Police will have broken up by the end of 1983. That I have managed to maintain even a modicum of my sanity through this period is owed more to Trudie's love, and patient faith in my deeper self, than in any Damascene revelation I might have had. She had thankfully seen enough of a remaining spark in me that she thought worth salvaging. As a consequence, I have been allowed to glean more wisdom from my failures in life than from the giantism of my worldly success, and for that I am eternally grateful.

My mother too is divorced, and now lives in a house less than a mile from my father with Alan, the man she has loved for thirty years. My father lives alone.

Audrey has been working as an auxiliary nurse in a local hospital, but has grown used to living with secrets, so the lump in her chest has gone unremarked, growing in silence, the malformed child of her sadness. By the time she admits to herself or anyone else that there is something wrong, her condition will have spread to the lymphatic system and be medically inoperable.

Trudie and I and my four children have traveled up from London on the train to say goodbye to her. We sit with Alan at the small table in the dining room of a modest house. This will be the first time and last time I will visit her in her home.

There she is, sitting in a corner of the room by the window, coupled to an oxygen machine that whirs malevolently at the side of the armchair, her face and body cruelly bloated by the drugs and steroids that sustain what is left of her life. She is fifty-three years old. She knows she is dying yet maintains a sardonic humor, joking that they ought to send her to Chernobyl to help with the cleanup, as she is by now immune to the effects of radiation and has nothing else to do at the moment. She laughs weakly at her own joke, but this exhausts her and she tries to catch her breath, inhaling deep into her chest in short desperate gasps.

The children begin to look concerned, but she regains her equilibrium. She still manages a brave smile behind the clear plastic mask secured by a band of elastic that forms a ridge in the graying hair at the back of her head. Her eyes are shining, wet, and still beautiful. Is she resigned to her fate, or is hers just an extraordinary, courageous performance so as not to frighten us with the enormity of what is happening to her? She is drowning far out at sea and none of us can reach her, but she is trying to reassure us. Her instincts as a mother are intact. The children, three of them under five years old, resume playing contentedly at their grandmother's feet.

I have not seen Alan in thirty years. He has existed in all that time, not as flesh and blood but as a shadow, never alluded to, never acknowledged, never given the oxygen to be more than a ghost haunting the family. He is frail and somewhat diminished by the weight of my mother's illness, but still handsome, and for the first time I am shocked to see the similarity between him and my maternal grandfather. There are so many ghosts here, shadows of shadows of shadows. There is so much of the past that has been unvoiced, and now that we are together there is neither time nor a suitable language to even begin to deal with it. The ritual of the meal will have to suffice. Food will be passed silently and cordially between us, like a secular mass, a last supper.

When we are finished, Alan will wash the dishes and I will dry, placing the clean crockery in neat piles on the draining board. My mother, still surrounded by the children, watches us from the corner. Little is said between us, relying on the shared task of passing the cleaned plates from hand to hand. I suppose there is an unconscious symbolism here, belated notions of reconciliation and forgiveness, mundane domestic gestures of normalcy and acceptance. I reassure myself that these are probably more eloquent than any words that could now be mustered. I understand my mother now; I know what she has sacrificed and I am no longer her judge, no longer my father's grim deputy, and this is the last time I shall see her.

"I love you, Mum, I've always loved you." She is crying and smiling at the same time; we all are. The children kiss her and we say good-bye.

A few months after the funeral, my father, at the age of fifty-nine, will be facing his own mortality. I have no doubt that he loved my mother to the end. Her death had foreshadowed and signaled his own.

He has been in and out of hospital all year. The cancer, which had begun in his prostate, has spread upward to his kidneys. Specialists, surgery, radiation, and chemotherapy have all proved fruitless. He has now been committed to a hospice for the days that remain to him.

I'm led into a room there with a single cot against the wall where a crucifix hangs. I haven't seen him in a number of months and in the bed is a man I do not recognize. I imagine for a moment that they have put me in the wrong room, but the skeleton below me is my father, watching me with the bleak staring eyes of a starving child. The kind nurse who brought me in quietly pulls up a chair.

"Here's your famous son come to see you, Ernie," she says.

"Oh aye?"

I try to compose myself; part of me wants to run out of that room like a frightened boy.

"Hello, Dad."

"I'm going to leave you two alone now. I'm sure you have a lot to talk about," says the nurse. Then she leaves us.

I have no idea what to say, so I take his hand in mine and gently massage the soft triangle of flesh between his thumb and his first finger. I haven't held his hand since I was small. They are big square hands, massively knuckled with strong muscular fingers, deeply lined and grooved. My father's hands are not the delicate, expressive hands of an artist, but they have a kind of elegance, and so close to death they possess an honest and translucent beauty. They are the hands of a working man.

"Where did you come from, son?"

"I came in from America last night, Dad."

He chuckles. "It's a long way to come to see your dad like this."

"You were feeling better a month ago."

He shakes his head. "I haven't been the same since your mother died."

I remain silent, knowing how much that small confession has cost him. I reach for his other hand and begin to massage it, but he winces. I wonder how much pain he is in. Perhaps he needs another shot of morphine. He seems a hundred years old now.

I look from his eyes to the cross on the wall and then down at his two hands cradled in mine. It is then that I receive something like the jolt of an electric shock, because apart from the color, his hands and mine are identical. The square width of the palms, the same carved scars in the folds of the skin, the big wide knuckles wrinkled like the knees of an elephant, and the musculature fanning out from the wrists to the thick and still powerful fingers. I stare at them for a long time, turning them over and over. Why had I never noticed this before when it was so obvious?

"We have the same hands, Dad, look." I am a child again, desperately trying to get his attention.

He looks down at the four separate slabs of flesh and bone. "Aye, son, but you used yours better than I used mine."

There is absolute quiet in the room. There is something like a small bird fighting to get out of my throat and I can hardly breathe. My mind is racing, trying in vain to remember when he'd ever paid me such a compliment, when he'd ever acknowledged who I was, or what I did, or what I'd achieved, or what it had cost me. He had waited until now, when his words would be devastating.

His eyes are closed now as if the last few minutes have exhausted him. It is dark outside. I kiss him softly in the center of his forehead, and whisper that he's a good man, and that I love him.

I would attend neither of my parents' funerals. I would tell myself and my close friends that I was afraid that the tabloid press would turn the events into a degrading circus, that my grief was a private matter and not a photo opportunity, that I'd said good-bye to my parents while they were still breathing, and what possible difference would throwing a handful of soil onto a coffin make to them or me? Part of me still believes this to be true, and part of me knows I was simply afraid. I escaped the ritual in the same way I had escaped my family when they were living, by pleading the pressure of work, where out in the world ambition had been replaced by responsibility, responsibility to honor contracts and concert engagements, to keep a crew of over sixty people working. But would it have been so difficult to have canceled a few shows, sent everyone home for a week or so? Probably not, but the simple fact is that I didn't want to, because escape and the need to keep moving had by now become endemic in me. I was addicted to work and endless travel and could no more keep still in one place than I could stop breathing for any length of time. Even the idea of attending a funeral had the effect of strangulation; I couldn't get enough air into my lungs, and so I would shut it out of my mind, brace myself for the next gig, and keep moving.

But there was a psychological price. I couldn't mourn properly, so I carried the grief with me. I couldn't cry or reveal my feelings even to myself, fearful I would be overwhelmed, my carefully constructed self-image destroyed to reveal absolutely nothing beneath. It was in this troubled state in November of 1987 that I made my way to the biggest concert of my life, in Rio de Janiero, outwardly impregnable but inwardly broken. And the rebuilding would take the rest of my life.

# Epilogue

THREE YEARS AFTER THE DEATHS OF MY PARENTS, TRUDIE AND I will move into Lake House in the Wiltshire countryside. Not more than a mile from the abbey where Queen Guinevere is said to have been banished by her jealous husband, it is a sixteenth-century manor house set in sixty acres of parkland and deciduous forest. The mullioned windows of the house look out onto the green banks of the river Avon, which forms a meandering eastern border to the property, running south to the sea through the ancient, wooded valley. An enormous copper beech, three hundred and fifty years old, from its massive girth to its giddying uppermost branches, towers above the house like a majestic sylvan god.

The house was built in the reign of James II by a powerful wool merchant named George Duke, Esq. The Duke family, having fought on the side of the royalists in the English Civil War, found themselves not only defeated but also dispossessed of their property by the victorious parliamentary forces. After Cromwell's accession they were transported to the West Indies as indentured slaves, and would live there in exile until the Restoration, when Charles II would restore them to their former stature and their ancestral home. They continued to live at Lake House until the end of the nineteenth century.

The facade of the house is grand and rather eccentric with its checkerboard face of stone and flint, five gables, and two-story bay windows on either side of the entrance, and topped with discrete faux battlements. The inside of the house is dark, gloomy, and drafty, a rambling series of dingy rooms, murky passages, and creaking staircases. There is a kind of architectural schizophrenia between the house's confident exterior and the labyrinthine and puzzling folly inside. That I feel at home here shouldn't surprise anyone.

The river is brimming with gilded trout hiding in the swaying reed grasses that billow beneath the surface like a pre-Raphaelite dream of a drowned Ophelia. Following the riverbank and around a stand of horse chestnut is a large empty meadow, which is overlooked by a steeply wooded escarpment of primary uncut forest. There is a strangely neglected and melancholy atmosphere that pervades this stretch of land where a few isolated cows graze, and whenever Trudie and I "beat the bounds" of the property, like all first-time landowners, we rarely linger there.

It is on one of our early morning peregrinations that my partner has one of her regular brain waves. She wants us to dig a lake. A lake, she says, would bring some much-needed light to this gloomy meadow, and we can stock it with trout at the same time. She points out that there is some irony in living in a "Lake House" without a lake and even though, as I pedantically remind her, the word *lake* is Anglo-Saxon for "running stream," which we do have, and not a standing body of water, which we don't, her logic does not escape me.

My real objection to the endeavor is the mess that such a project would cause. Excavating tons of earth, relandscaping, finding somewhere to deposit the displaced soil. This in addition to the legal permits needed in an area as archeologically sensitive as this one, which includes hundreds of Neolithic burial mounds and sacred earthworks. The prospect of dealing with such bureaucracy fills me with a paralyzing dread. But my partner is not one to be easily deterred, and I have learned from experience that it is usually to my benefit to trust her instincts and for some reason she is adamant about this.

The legal and archeological protocols are indeed complex. A public tribunal opens us up to many objections, some fair, others downright potty. One national broadsheet reports a claim that we are chopping down an entire forest to accommodate the lake, when in fact there have been no trees on the site for hundreds of years. The story is indignantly reported as if it were the hubris of a guitar-shaped swimming pool we were building in a cathedral close and not a discrete lake in a neglected field.

Finally, there are no substantive objections, and the tribunal grants permission for a one-and-a-half-acre lake to be excavated during the summer of 1995. The only proviso is that we have an archeologist on the site at all times, just in case anything is turned up, which we happily agree to.

That night I sit bolt upright in bed after being woken by a macabre dream. Trudie and I are pulling a bloated white body from the lake and laying it out among the bulrushes. It is a startling image, and a frightening one. Despite a passing interest in Jungian psychology a number of years before, I am not given to the exhaustive interpretation of dreams. I accept their presence and recognize they may have some significance, but more often than not will have forgotten them by the following morning. This one seems no different, plucked at random from the subconscious and most likely prompted by the turbulent events of the day. I will think no more about it.

Months pass. I am in Los Angeles in the middle of a long U.S. tour, when I receive a phone call from Katie Knight, our assistant at Lake House.

"I have some bad news about the lake."

"What?"

"They've had to stop the digging."

I have an uncomfortable foreboding. "Why?"

There is a slight pause on the line. "They've found a body!"

"A what?"

"A body."

I am now reduced to a monosyllabic stutter. "Wh— Wh— Who is it?"

"It's a woman, and she's been ritually murdered." Katie is now beginning to sound like a coroner.

"What do you mean, ritually murdered?"

I have to admit I'm panicked and inexplicably searching for alibis, as if I'm about to become the prime suspect in an appalling murder.

"She's had her hands tied behind her back, and whoever it was that murdered her has thrown her facedown in the mud, placed a heavy piece of wood on her back, and stood there until she drowned."

I now feel like a character in some Hercule Poirot mystery.

"Do they have any idea when this might have happened?" I ask, silently counting the days since I arrived in America.

"About four hundred A.D.," she replies, without missing a beat. "The archeologists have taken her away to do some tests but they estimate it was sometime after the Romans left."

I breathe an audible sigh of relief and then I remember the

damned dream. I don't have prescient dreams, and I'm thankful not to be gifted in that way, but the connection between the dream and the fact that our meadow is a murder site, albeit a sixteen-hundred-year-old murder site, has an irresistible logic.

Upon my return, the archeologist tells me that the skeleton, though discolored brown by the mud, has been perfectly preserved. That the female victim was probably nineteen years old, had all of her teeth, and that she now officially belongs to me.

I am somewhat taken aback by this new and unexpected responsibility. When I ask him why she may have been murdered, he shrugs and tells me that the Dark Ages were so called because that's exactly what they were, "dark." No one knows what was going on between the withdrawal of Pax Romana and the Middle Ages apart from the countless invasions by the Saxons, Jutes, and Danes and a few Arthurian legends. The girl could have been killed by a raiding party, or have been punished as a suspected witch or even an unfaithful wife. The circumstances do not indicate a normal burial, fully prone on a north–south alignment on the riverbank. The ritual significance of water to Celtic peoples is well documented, pools, springs, and rivers being regarded as entrances to and from the afterworld. Individuals selected for such treatment were viewed as being special cases. She may have been sacrificed willingly or unwillingly, perhaps to treat with the spirit world on behalf of those still living. We shall never know, but the reality of her death was particularly gruesome, and it would be impossible to imagine any crime that could have warranted such punishment. But perhaps the dark energy of this event has somehow lingered, and this feeling of melancholy that pervades the narrow strip of land between the river and the woods is her only memorial.

The archeologist asks what we are going to do with the body

when she returns, and I tell him we are going to bury her with due ceremony.

We stand on the little island we left at the center of the lake, Trudie and myself, our neighbors from the valley, and Vicar John Reynolds, who married us. Our lady of the lake is lying in an open coffin with her face up to the sky for the first time in two millennia, her perfect bones like those of a child, with some bright yellow flowers on her chest. Across the mists on the far shore stands a lone piper, and the skirl of his mournful dirge floats across the still water. The coffin lid is secured and as she is lowered into the ground again, the priest prays that her soul will be granted its final reward.

My two sons, Joe and Jake, shuttle everyone back to the shore in a wooden rowing boat. It takes some time and I am the last to leave the island. Tonight we shall throw a party in the house with a traditional Irish band providing the music. There will be dancing, feasting and celebration, but for now I want to be alone for a few moments with the lady of the lake.

I have to wonder if it is significant that it was our particular family that uncovered her. The field has been worked for centuries, a water meadow since the Middle Ages, with waterways and sluices excavated in order to flood and drain the land following the rhythm of the seasons. But our lady has lain here century after century, undisturbed. Perhaps others would have found the bones and ignored their significance, carried on with their work, thrown away the remains, and never given them a second thought. There is a romance in me that she may have been waiting to be discovered, to be honored, and for things to be put right somehow. But along with this idea, I can't help thinking about my parents, how I hadn't attended either of their funerals, that ritual hadn't been served, and asking myself if I wasn't trying to put something right here, in this symbolic way.

Around the fresh soil of the grave are a profusion of wild irises, speedwell, and a cluster of tiny blue flowers whose name escapes me although I have seen them before. Kneeling down in the grass for a closer look, I see that at the center of the five blue petals is a five-pointed yellow star, and I am reminded of the tiny flower I witnessed in the Brazilian jungle so many years ago, yearning for light in the darkness between some stones on the steps of the church.

I pluck a stem from the group with three flowers that now sit delicately in the palm of my hand and I make my way across the lake and walk back to the house.

Preparations for the party are well under way. The band are tuning up in the hall, there is the smell of delicious food from the kitchen, the house is decked with flowers, and candles are being lit as the evening draws in. I find Trudie in the library.

"You're a country girl, tell me what these are. I can't remember," I say while offering her the posy of tiny blue flowers in my hand.

She looks at them thoughtfully, turning the stem between her fingers, as the tiny blue-and-yellow flowers dance in the light from the garden window.

"You're funny," she says.

"Why am I funny?" I ask puzzled.

"Because they're forget-me-nots, aren't they?" she says, laughing. "That's what they are, forget-me-nots."

She hands them back to me. "Why do you want to know?"

"Oh, it's a long story," I say, smiling, unable to articulate a host of memories that swirl around the room like ghosts.

The meadow is a happier place now, and the new lake is a haven for waterfowl, and ducks and Canada geese and the swan nest on its banks in the springtime. From the shore you can see the mound in the grass where our lady lies beneath the hanging willow among the wild irises and the speedwell and the blue-and-yellow forget-me-nots. I like to think she is at peace at last and that whatever was broken was somehow mended.

# Dedication

*This book is dedicated to the memory of my parents,*
*Ernie and Audrey, and my grandparents, Tom and Agnes,*
*Ernest and Margaret; to Auntie Amy, Tommy Thompson,*
*Barbara Adamson, Mr. McGough, Bill Mastaglio,*
*Bob Taylor; Don Eddie (Phoenix Jazzmen), Nigel Stanger*
*and John Pierce (Newcastle Big Band); Kenny Kirkland,*
*Tim White and Kim Turner. I shan't forget you.*